S0-AYD-125

Praise for *'That Bear Ate My Pants!'*
by Tony James Slater

"I laughed all through the book until the end, where I became sad to have to say goodbye. I enjoyed myself that much." — *Night Owl Reviews*

"...not only well-written and entertaining but downright hilarious. I have not laughed so hard while reading in quite a while. And when I mean laugh, I mean I laughed so hard I was screaming. Warning, do not read this book while on the toilet." — *Indie Eclective*

"Tony Slater is very gifted at writing comically, and laughter accompanied every page I read at the account of his daily routine looking after animals, birds and reptiles of all shapes and sizes and degrees of ferocity. Despite the tomfoolery of the writing, Tony never forgets the seriousness of the work carried out by the rescue centre, he never forgets to inform us of the beauty and uniqueness of Ecuador, and more importantly, never forgets to reveal not only how much the animals came to mean to him in the short time he was there, but also how much the whole experience touched him. This is one I will read again if I ever need cheering up. It's a guaranteed tonic." — *Kath 'n' Kindle Book Reviews*

"Absolutely brilliant book! I loved every bit of it. Tony has such a fun, absorbing way of writing and you can't help but be swept along on his adventure with him. He might be a self-confessed idiot abroad, but he comes across as an extremely likeable idiot. Definitely the sort of person you would want to go for a beer with, or at least share a bit of fried, cheesy Ecuadorian street-food with.
Buy this book! You won't regret it." – George Mahood, author of *Free Country*

"I bought it on the spot just for the title. It is truly the most hilarious book I have ever read, and I've read some good ones. It was a "In-Starbucks-laughing-so-hard-the-tears-came-and-I was concerned I was going to pee myself" kind of reading experience."   – *TravelingCrone.com*

"I can completely imagine Tony standing and enthusiastically delivering each chapter to a wide-eyed audience whilst they think inside their heads *'This guy is a little bit mental'*."   – *BookC*nt*

"[The] writing captures your imagination immediately and paints a picture of a world I'm unlikely to see that is so vivid, that I feel I have been there with him, every step of the way. I sweated up and down the mountains, I avoided being eaten by the Jaguar, I too chased an unruly teenage bear around an enclosure; I loved every minute of it."
    – *WomanOnTheEdgeOfReality.com*

Fun. Fun fun fun. Did I say fun? It's been so long since I've been able to read a story that I could describe that way. You can pick this up and set it down at will. Read a chapter or two, have a laugh or a gape at the page, then go back to it in a couple of days. An easy read, and an enjoyable one at that.
    Intranuovo.com

...it's pee-your-pants funny. It's like a travelogue gone horribly amuck. Brilliant.   – Shéa MacLeod,
    author of *Kissed by Darkness*

THAT BEAR ATE MY PANTS!

By
Tony James Slater

HOOKSETT PUBLIC LIBRARY
HOOKSETT, NH 03106
603.485.6092
http://hooksettlibrary.org

Various THINGS
@*t*Different *Times*

ISBN-13: 978-1481155373
ISBN-10: 1481155377

Copyright © Tony James Slater 2012

All rights reserved. No part of this publication may be reproduced, stored in a retrieval system or transmitted, in any form or by any other means without the prior written permission of the author, nor be otherwise circulated in any form of binding or cover other than that in which it is published and without a similar condition being imposed on the purchaser.

Although this is a work of non-fiction, some names have been changed by the author.

An e-book edition of this title is also available.

This first paperback edition was printed by CreateSpace.

Cover Design by **Various Things At Different Times**
Formatted for paperback by **Heather Adkins**

Please visit the author's website for a selection of photographs that accompany this book:

www.TonyJamesSlater.com

Books by the same author:

Dear readers of
Hooksett,

Hope this gives
you all a
chuckle,

Best wishes,

Yeah, I know what you're thinking – not a lot!
What can I say? I'm working on it. Watch this space…

THAT BEAR ATE MY PANTS!

Contents

(Brace yourself – there's a few of 'em)

(See? I told you so!)

Author's Note

It's true. A bear did eat my pants. Luckily I wasn't wearing them at the time, or this book would be called 'That Bear Ate My Balls And My Ass' (not to mention my legs and my feet) and I'd probably be writing it from hospital. In fact all of these stories are true; only the occasional name has been changed because some of them know where I live...

This book is dedicated to the hard work, bravery and sacrifice of my fellow volunteers all over the world. What you do makes a difference every day. And to those poor souls who worked with me – especially those who grace these pages – thank-you so much! Without your constant help and protection... well, let's face it, I'd have been eaten. Enjoy the book. Please don't sue me.

Prologue

"MONKEY!" I shouted, as a brown blur swung out of the cage and onto the path.

The chase was on.

He skipped away with incredible speed, dodging around the corner and heading for freedom as though he'd thought of nothing but this moment for years. I bolted after him, grabbing the edge of a cage to swing me round in hot pursuit. The monkey was a good way ahead of me, and far more manoeuvrable. But I was faster on the straight. I accelerated down the narrow corridor between enclosures, and was closing the distance between us when he reached the steps down to the main road through the farm. This was my chance – if he paused, if he found the stairs confusing, I'd be on him. But no. Being a monkey, he didn't have much use for stairs. He just jumped.

He made the ten foot leap to the ground with ease, landed on all fours, and scurried off down the road. Pounding along behind him I had less than a second to make the choice. If I slowed to negotiate the stairs even part of the way down, it would all be over. Once he reached the trees by the first bend in the road he'd be gone for good.

Time was up. I reached the top of the steps at a dead run and launched myself over the edge.

In the seconds I was airborne my entire life flashed before my eyes. I seemed to have spent a disproportionate amount of it chasing monkeys.

Somehow I landed on my feet, with bone-jarring force. I was only a step behind the monkey – my leap had taken me considerably further than his – but my body was moving too fast for my legs. I managed to push off with my feet at the same moment as I started to fall headlong on the ground. The result: I bounced forwards another metre, sailing high above the form of the fleeing monkey, then crashed to earth and flattened the fucker.

The impact knocked the stuffing out of me. It temporarily turned the monkey two-dimensional. Pain shot through me. I felt like I'd fallen ten feet onto a small primate. For the monkey it must have been like being beaten around the head with a banana tree. For a split second neither of us could move.

He recovered quicker than I did. Amazingly he wriggled out from under me and leapt towards freedom, just as I, still lying prone, reached out with both arms and caught him.

Unfortunately I could only catch him around the middle. Which meant that while he wasn't going anywhere, he wasn't particularly happy about it.

In far less time than it takes to tell, the monkey writhed around in my grasp and sank his fangs into my hand.

"ARGH!"

The monkey switched his attention to my other hand and bit down hard.

"Arrr!" I shrieked. I let go with the recently bitten hand, but I had no other options – I had to grab him again or lose him. As I tried to grab his neck he bit me again, puncturing the thick leather glove easily and scoring my vulnerable flesh. Again and again he bit down, faster than I could even register the damage.

I lay on my belly, flat out on the floor, both arms

outstretched in front of me and both hands wrapped around a frantically flailing ball of teeth and rage. There was sod all I could do – without my hands free I couldn't get to my feet, and without standing up I had no way of controlling the beast. It was not the first time I had the thought; what the hell was I doing in Ecuador?

Seeking Refuge

All I'd asked for was a little more adventure in my life. Now, I appreciate that in hindsight this was obviously a huge mistake. There's even a proverb designed specifically to warn against it. It goes something like 'Be careful what you wish for – you could end up with your fingers in a monkey'.

The thing is, I'd spent several years trying (and failing) to be an actor. I'd been forced to give up when, after a lot of soul-searching, I realised I wasn't getting anywhere because I was crap. It was not my happiest hour. But to console myself I bought a book called 'Work Your Way Around The World'.

It seemed like the answer. All the dead-end jobs I'd done whilst pursuing my theatrical dream suddenly revealed a glimmer of potential; translate any one of them to a different country and they became a lot more exciting. Why work in my local pub when I could do the same job in a bar in Bondi Beach or Miami?

And so I set out on my grand tour, aiming to do a different job on every continent. I would visit the far-flung corners of the world, explore their secrets and discover all there was to know about life in the process.

I got as far as France. After three months of picking prunes on a baking hot plantation south of Bordeaux, having lost the ability to walk normally due to spending sixty hours a week on my knees, I decided to give up.

It wasn't that the place broke my spirit, though it came perilously close; it was when the boss got drunk with us one night and confessed to drugging a gypsy who worked for him, and feeding him into the prune-drying furnace. That made up my mind. By daybreak his entire workforce had evaporated. By midnight the next day I limped through the door to my parents' house, exhausted, malnourished and penniless.

All in all it had been a bit of a shitter.

So on my list of preferred career choices (the one they get you to make in school) I'd already crossed off 'Actor' and 'Explorer'. Number three was 'Astronaut' and to be honest, I didn't fancy my chances. So I did what I usually do when I get depressed; I bought a book. This one was about volunteering abroad. And that is how I found Santa Martha Animal Rescue Centre in Ecuador, South America.

Santa Martha's website described it as a volunteer-run wildlife refuge perched high in the mountains of the Avenue of Volcanoes. At any given time it was home to monkeys, parrots – even big cats – plus dozens of other creatures I'd never even heard of. All of them had been rescued from cruelty; chained up in market places, kept illegally as pets or destined for the black market. The job of the volunteers was to accompany the police on raids, rescue the animals, look after them and eventually release them into the Amazon rainforest! It was the most amazing job description I'd ever read.

I signed up instantly and Toby, the English co-ordinator of the refuge, approved my application despite me having absolutely no relevant experience. I convinced myself that this was the shadowy hand of Fate, rather than a blanket policy of employing every idiot that sent them an email.

Surely there would be some kind of training programme before they sent me in to feed the lions...

And before you could say 'eighteen hour flight', there I was in Ecuador. Heavily in debt to my credit card company and strapped into a rucksack the size and weight of a chest freezer full of dead rhino. I wish I could say I was happy about it.

Nestled into a hollow in the Andes mountains, Quito is the highest capital city in the world. Even the airport is over nine thousand feet. Planes that land there don't need to make a descent, they just go straight on. It's a banana of a place, curving halfway around the side of a gigantic active volcano. And nestled into the centre of Quito is the ugliest bus station in the world. *Terminal Terrestre* it's called, which has a disturbing ring of finality about it. This is where I found myself on Day One of my adventure.

Through clouds of exhaust fumes I could just about make out... well, nothing actually. Visibility was about three and a half feet. Petrol was clearly not too expensive in Ecuador, as the drivers seemed keen to leave the buses revving the whole time they sat in the station. Or maybe they were just afraid that if they ever turned them off they'd never start again. A squint through the haze told me this was the more likely of the two reasons. Thick black smoke was coming out of the back of every bus. In fact thick black smoke was coming out of the front of quite a few of them.

Their destinations were displayed on little signs in the windscreens, ranging from a 'proper' plastic thing to bits torn off a cardboard crisp box and scrawled on with a felt-tip pen. I was looking for somewhere spelled 'Tambillo' – though how it was pronounced could be anyone's guess.

The central island of the station was filled with dingy little shops and stalls. It must have been fairly obvious to any casual observer that the added weight of a carpet on my burden would have snapped my spine like a twig, yet that didn't deter the carpet stall owners from bawling the benefits of their carpets at me as I passed. I was alone, downcast and dangerously overburdened. Even if a colourful woolly carpet had been just what I needed to brighten my day, what the hell was I supposed to do with it, shove it up my arse?

A little way ahead of me I spied a whole gang of young guys hanging out, doing nothing. They had the look of people who did that a lot. Their clothes had started to take on the colour of the atmosphere. Maybe I should ask them, I thought. What's the worst that could happen?

"Um… Tam-bee-low?" I ventured.

"*Tambeejo?*"

"Yes! Yes, *Tambeejo!*" I'd studied Spanish intensely for almost an hour on the flight over and it was already starting to pay off.

Suddenly the youths were racing around me in all directions, shouting constantly to each other as though it was some form of echolocation. A couple of them dodged right into the traffic and flagged down a pair of shuddering buses. A quick glance in the windscreens and they started shouting and gesturing wildly at me. This could only be good news! The guys were standing in front of one of the buses and not letting it move. I took my life in my hands and sprinted between the cars. Arms reached down through the doors and I was simultaneously dragged and pushed on board. My helpers banged on the side of the bus as though to reassure the driver that no more walking rucksacks needed crow-barring through the door. Then they generously stepped out of the way and the bus lurched off.

It had worked! No matter the difficulty, I had overcome. I felt elated. Or possibly I was going into toxic shock from the smog. But I was on my way!

It was a lovely journey. It would have been lovelier if I

hadn't been wedged between several kneecaps and an armpit, but with about two hundred people on a bus built to hold forty you really have to appreciate the small things. I had a turn at breathing every so often, and the involuntary motion of my nose against the filthy window cleaned a spot through which I could see a tiny part of the scenery I was travelling through. The foothills of the Andes mountains were thick with vegetation. Their sharply sculpted flanks were tamed into fields despite ridiculous, near vertical slopes.

I saw a land so wild, so incalculably vast; I saw tin-roofed concrete shacks, sprinkled liberally throughout it; and occasionally I saw a piece of tinsel hanging from the roof of the bus. It draped itself across my face every time the driver flung us around a hairpin bend. I never did figure out the Ecuadorian urge to decorate the inside of a bus like a Christmas tree. I even saw one with a mirror ball in it once, which begged the question: just what part of my anatomy had room to dance?

After forty minutes of the most intimate bodily contact I've ever had with half a dozen strangers simultaneously, my journey neared its end. I caught a glimpse of a sign saying 'Tambillo' and the bus skidded to an almost stop. The door flew open, and I was helpfully rolled out of it by the driver's assistant. Further up the bus another door had opened and people were leaping courageously out, as more people from the bus 'stop' matched their jogging speed to the bus's and grabbed for outstretched hands which hauled them on board. "They don't waste much time around here," I said to myself as I picked myself up out of the dust. Only I said it with a few more four letter words. I'd landed on my stomach, which was lucky, as if I'd ended up on my back I'd quite likely have died of starvation before managing to turn over. I dusted myself down and gazed across the road at my new home town.

And was very nearly cut in half by the next bus. It thundered along hot on the heels of the one that had so casually dispensed me. A few passengers fell out of the door in my general direction and the bus accelerated onwards towards the horizon.

I'd never seen so many buses. And never a single bus so crowded. Where the hell were all these people going? Not to Tambillo for the most part, which was fine by me. The place seemed small and deserted, quite a relief after the Mad Max intensity of Quito.

I was standing at the base of a mountain which rose majestically behind me. A road in fairly poor repair veered off upwards at a crazy angle, past a few half-finished buildings that clung precariously to the slope. They gave me the impression that someone had started to build one, then realised he'd never be arsed to walk all that way up to his house every day. When he'd abandoned the project halfway through, most of his neighbours thought 'bloody hell, he's right!' and they all buggered off to the pub.

Tambillo town proper began on the other side of the Quito road (which is actually part of the Pan American Highway, and is probably the main reason that road is described as 'of variable condition'). Marking the turn-off for Tambillo was a shop full of payphones. Which struck me as a bad idea. I mean, twenty people on the phone in one room? How hard can you push your finger into your ear before you hit brain? And what the hell do you do if you need to make a call after closing time? Obviously someone was making money out of the racket though – parked outside the *'Telecabin'* was the biggest 4x4 truck I'd ever seen. It gleamed white and chrome, like a poster child for the Size Does Matter campaign. 4x4s were popular over here I'd noticed – by my calculations they were the third most popular vehicles on the road in Quito, after knackered buses and the boxy little yellow taxis made by some company too embarrassed to put a badge on them.

I needed a taxi for the next leg of my journey. It wasn't long before one of the battered yellow things rattled into view. I flagged it down and half expected to see the driver's feet shoot out the bottom of the car and skid along the road to brake it. Instead it coughed to a halt in front of me and stalled.

In the driver's seat was a tiny, weather-beaten man. In the passenger seat was an equally tiny, equally weather-beaten woman. They looked two weather-beaten kids short of a family outing. I almost mistook her for a paying passenger until she began to bark at me in Spanish.

Hell, I thought, here goes.

"Um, *Santa Martha, centro por animales?*" I enquired.

The couple exchanged astonished looks.

"Um, *hacienda Don Johnny?*" I tried. It was what I'd been told to say.

The man squinted at me, as though checking I was not a mirage. Then he waved me towards the back seat. Finally! I opened the door and manhandled my rucksack inside. Both of them regarded it sourly. There was a creak of protest from the car's rear suspension. And I hadn't gotten in yet.

The driver craned his neck to look at me as I sat in and closed the door. He looked at me for quite some time. I started to feel a little self-conscious, and his head looked like it was going to fall off at any minute. Then he spoke, which must have been difficult with his windpipe twisted at such an angle. I was thrilled that I understood his question, though a little concerned about the need to answer it.

"Where you want to go?" he'd asked.

"Um," I tried again, "*la hacienda de Johnny Cordoba. Refugio des animales?*"

I got a blank look.

God damn it! I knew this would happen! Ask for 'la hacienda Don Johnny', Toby had told me – they all know it.

What a load of bollocks! As soon as I'd read that phrase my blood had run cold, just at the potential for complete disaster inherent in relying on such a dubious piece of advice. Now I was stuck in a taxi with no way of explaining my desired destination beyond repeating the same useless statement and shrugging my shoulders.

"*Hacienda de Don Johnny,*" I said, and shrugged at him.

Inside I was starting to cry.

"*Cerca de aquí?*" the driver asked. (Near here?)

"Yes," I said, for want of the ability to say "I haven't got a bloody clue mate."

So he fired up the engine and we sped off in the same direction as the endless stream of buses. As we charged down the highway the driver occasionally twisted round in his seat to ask me "Here?" I could only shrug.

Then he spied a little track branching off to the left, and with a cry of triumph he headed down it at top speed. Neither track nor car were particularly well suited to this, as the top of my head discovered immediately. It was a painful way to travel, but I had a feeling that the roof of the car would give out long before my skull. Thankfully after a couple of minutes we came to a group of tumble-down buildings surrounding an open expanse of concrete. We pulled up in the middle and the car shuddered into silence.

We had arrived at a farm of some kind, and one that didn't get many visitors from the looks of things. The car had barely stopped shaking when an enormous bearded man emerged from a corrugated iron barn and approached us at what must have been his top speed. For which I was grateful, since I was on the meter. I glanced at the dashboard. No meter. This crappy car didn't even seem to have a speedometer. I guess I was paying whatever the driver thought his time was worth. Oh-oh...

By the time I'd had this uneasy revelation the fat farmer and the driver were conversing at volume. Every so often one of them would glance at me as though expecting something. There was something in the farmer's gaze that made my buttocks clench involuntarily. It was time for my broken record bit.

"*Hacienda de Johnny Cordoba?*" I pleaded.

They both just stared.

"*Santa Martha!*" I begged.

They exchanged puzzled looks, then returned to staring at me. Not making much headway, I thought. This clearly wasn't the place, and even if it was there was no way I was staying here. To gain a gut that size, the farmer must have eaten his whole family. I was not going to be next on the menu.

They'd started to jabber at one another again, punctuating each rapid burst of dialogue with a gesture in my direction. I felt a cold trickle of sweat run between my shoulder blades, and prayed they weren't negotiating a price for my anal virginity. I waited for a natural pause, and interrupted them.

"Look, this is the wrong place, let's go," I told the driver.

No response.

"Do you speak English?" I asked the farmer.

Nothing.

"Okay," I addressed the driver in my mother tongue, "we're not going to find the place like this, because you don't have a clue where we are. I want to leave before this fat bastard tries to rape me and eat me. Please take me back to Tambillo, and if your car doesn't disintegrate or explode before we get there I'll give you five dollars just for being brave enough to drive the fucking thing."

"*¿Qué?*" he asked.

"*Tambillo,*" I said, making 'let's go' motions with both hands. He got the picture. He started the car, a minor miracle in my opinion, and with a few parting words he screeched away, leaving the farmer still standing there with his mouth hanging open. What a sight. Thank God it was receding.

As we bounced back up the dirt track at top speed I could tell my driver was in a bad mood. This was pretty much confirmed when we shot out onto the main road again. The car skidded to a halt and died.

"*Tambillo?*" I asked tentatively.

He helpfully pointed back up the main road.

I took the hint. I shoved my bag out the back door, then climbed after it. I dug in my back pocket for some dollars, and was grateful indeed that I had several single notes. I didn't like my chances of getting any change if I'd had to offer this guy a twenty.

He scowled at me as he took the cash, then turned his attention to reviving his vehicle. This left his tiny wrinkled wife to scowl at me while he coaxed some life into the engine. What a tag-team. He favoured me with one more black look before his trademark top speed exit left me choking on a cloud of dust.

The walk back to town was an epic one. Stumbling along a rough gravel bank beside the highway, wearing what felt remarkably like a grand piano on my back, I was for the first time at the full mercy of the sun. As each bus thundered past its slipstream would drag me slightly further from my goal. It was a long, long time before I recognised a café on the other side of the road, signalling my return to civilisation. Soaked through with sweat, bent practically double and breathing in gasps, I staggered over to the payphone shop and collapsed. For a while I just lay in the shadow of the monstrous white truck, inventing choice phrases to throw at Toby when I finally got to meet him.

I mean! Ask for hacienda de Johnny Cordoba? What an arsehole! For all I knew I was asking for a mythical character. I felt like I was standing in London asking for Mr and Mrs Smith – or worse, at Loch Ness looking for the home of A. Monster…

My air of quiet desperation must have intrigued the locals. A couple of guys approached me wearing concerned expressions. They asked me something, and I fell back on the only piece of information I had.

"Please," I begged, "where is *hacienda de Johnny Cordoba?*"

"Johnny Cordoba?" one asked, looking alert. "You want taxi?"

"Yes, yes!" I told him.

"*Ah, hacienda Don Johnny. Sí, sí.*"

He walked back to the gleaming white truck and pulled open the door.

No! Was I about to get a lift? Then I noticed. Numbers on the side. Identical truck parked behind it. And another a bit further down the road. Well bugger me backwards with a greased vegetable… this thing was a taxi! The mother of all taxis. This corner was a taxi rank.

And I'd been dropped off right opposite.

About two hours ago.

And so I set off on a journey which would astound me every time I made it. Pretty much every day for the next three months I would marvel at the tenacity of people determined to live on the side of this mountain. The single track road was more pothole than surface in some places, it twisted and turned across the face of the mountain in a series of hairpin bends and switchbacks, and the gradient was insane. We passed people (and donkeys!) walking up and down, and at one point another massive four-wheel drive taxi swung past us with inches to spare and at least three of its wheels hanging over the precipice. My driver didn't even bat an eyelid, which was just as well because I was concerned that if he blinked too often we'd end up nose first in one of the half-finished concrete block houses scattered along the route.

Amazingly he knew every crumbling chunk of road, every gaping chasm (of which there were several), every protruding boulder and lethal bend. We raced past the lot, making decent speed despite the angle of the truck. Yet about ten minutes into the journey we'd still not arrived. We were so high I was starting to feel faint. Back home this journey would already have cost me £20 – and done at least £250 worth of damage to the car!

If anything could handle this punishment, the truck could. No wonder the taxis here were bigger than most of the houses. All of a sudden it hit me – the insanity of trying to coax a crappy yellow city cab up here! I felt quite glad my previous driver hadn't known of my destination and tried to attempt it. It'd have been easier to carry his car up there than to drive it!

We crested a long, straight section of road and arrived at a huge pair of rusty wrought iron gates. The driver winked at me as we turned in down my boss's driveway, and another few minutes of twisting and bouncing brought us to a small cluster of buildings perched tenuously on the hillside, surrounded by fields.

This was Santa Martha.

And it was gorgeous.

Baptism of Fruit Juice

The view that was to greet me every morning in this country never lost a smidgen of its impact. This first sight of its rugged beauty took my breath away. Before me the land fell away dramatically, lush green pasture plunging out of sight down the mountainside. Beyond rose the far side of the valley, at once seeming impossibly distant yet almost touchable; scruffy white wisps of cloud decorated the space between us. A tangle of trees straggled here and there across the land, dividing rough fields so steep that it would defy all laws of gravity to work on them.

I hardly paid any attention as the taxi executed a smart three-point turn behind me, and totally unfazed by the incline of the driveway, sped off in a cloud of dust. I only had eyes for this storybook panorama. It beat the snot out of London.

Unlike most of the houses I'd noticed thus far in Ecuador, the building in front of me looked finished. Deliciously so in fact. Three stories with real stucco on them gleamed white in the afternoon sunlight, topped by a wide flat sun deck. There was no doubt that this was an expensive dwelling. Next door sat a cheery yellow cottage with a certain homemade quality to it – and a sheet of what looked disturbingly like asbestos for the roof. A path connected the two, and the most pointless fence I'd ever seen separated them. It was three strands of wire running on a series of posts around the entire cottage, an obstacle only mildly more forbidding than the long grass beneath it. I struggled for a few seconds trying to think of any animal on earth to which this would form a barrier. A really big penguin was the only thing that sprang to mind.

Plonked seemingly at random into the surrounding grass were a couple of more typical buildings – a tiny breeze block shed with a washing machine outside it, and behind me a rusting sheet of corrugated metal on stilts, which seemed to serve as a carport.

A skinny white guy in a stained t-shirt was just coming out of the cottage. I could tell it was Toby as soon as he opened his mouth. He was one of the few people I've ever met that types an email exactly the same way he talks.

"Alright mate!" he called, and threw me a casual wave as he closed the gate behind him. I looked him over as he walked towards me. Average height. Relaxed. A bit dirty. But better looking than me, damn it. He was wearing a pale red baseball cap, so faded that it verged on the pink.

"Hi!" I greeted him enthusiastically. "Nice place you got here."

"Yeah. Sweet, innit? Did you have a good trip?"

"I, err…" Suddenly it didn't seem right to launch into a massive rant about the shocking inadequacy of his instructions.

"Yeah, not bad," I told him instead. I shook his hand vigorously and grinned back at him. It was infectious. I could afford to wait a few days before explaining just how close I'd come to being shagged up the bum by a Sasquatch.

"Good to meet you mate. Right, well I'll show you around shall I?"

As Toby was leading me back towards the pointless fence, a middle-aged Ecuadorian man emerged from the back door of the main house. He was tall, nearly my height, and powerfully built – practically a giant compared to the locals I'd seen so far. His black hair was thinning and closely cropped, and he wore a watch that looked big enough to control the national nuclear defence.

This had to be the legendary Don Johnny Cordoba, who had founded Santa Martha on his own land, and with his own money, after realising just how widespread the problem of illegal animal possession and maltreatment was in Ecuador. The website made him sound like one part humble animal lover, three parts crusading superhero. The man himself looked calm and confident – indisputably in charge, yet approachable. A sly smile and a gleam in his eye told me he was finding something amusing. It was a fair bet that that something was me.

"*Johnny, esto es* Tony," Toby explained. Then "Tony, this is Johnny," he added helpfully.

"*Mucho gusto,*" Johnny greeted me with a manly handshake.

Words danced in my head. My chance to make a first impression!

"*Me gusta mucho!*" I responded enthusiastically.

Johnny's arm froze mid handshake. Just for a second. A slight confusion quirked his bushy brow, and then was gone. He smiled widely and surrendered my hand. He glanced over at Toby, and some unspoken jest passed between them. Then he cleared his throat, looked back at me and rattled off a few comments in rapid Spanish.

"He said, good to have you here, and he's off to do something with the cows," Toby explained. "He'll be back later."

Johnny waited for the end of Toby's translation, gave me one last measuring glance, and strode off down the path.

"That went well," said Toby.

"What did I do? Did I say something?"

"Nah, mate. It's all good."

"He said *mucho gusto*... that's 'Nice to meet you', right?" I asked.

"Yup."

"And I said...?"

"*Me gusta mucho.* Slightly different."

I could tell he was trying not to laugh. It was the first phrase I'd learned from my one-hour audio course. Actually it was the only phrase I'd learned. But something wasn't quite right. "Toby..."

"Ha!" He couldn't resist any longer. "It means, 'I like you – a lot!' I think you surprised him."

"Oh shit!"

"Yeah, that's probably what he's thinking! Maybe he'll put it down to bad grammar."

"So he said hello, and I..."

"You came on to him, yeah. Well you're the first new volunteer to do that!"

"Oh. Shit. I should probably go home right now..."

"Don't worry mate. He thought it was pretty funny, I'd say. Or else... maybe he likes you too!"

Toby I did like, and straight away. He was a very smart guy, with a ready wit and a readier smile. His attitude was very laid back, as was his manner of speaking. He rarely seemed worried or annoyed – and even when he did it was amusing. From the beginning I never felt like I had to impress him, or that he was judging me in any way. He seemed genuinely honest, though remorselessly sarcastic, and he became one of my best friends.

But he couldn't cook for shit.

Especially not an omelette.

That first afternoon he took me with him as he fed the whole menagerie of animals. I was amazed. Surrounding a small garden next to Johnny's house were a series of smaller cages containing monkeys of every possible description. Black, red, brown, ranging in size from tiny little balls of fluff to something that looked like it could pull your arms off and beat you to death with the wet ends. There were bendy-nosed beasties so daft-looking they could have been glove puppets sewn by glue sniffing school kids. I swear they had an E.T. in there somewhere, and at least one of The Wombles.

Toby deposited a heaped ladleful of bright orange slop into each animal's food dish while I guarded the cage doors against escape attempts. The creatures loved the stuff, although to me it looked like the contents of the toilet bowl the morning after ten pints and a dodgy curry had fought their way back out of my stomach. Toby kept up a running commentary on the feeding process, listing off the names of the animals in English and Spanish and explaining a bit about where each was from. I heard none of it. Somewhere behind me about a million parrots were screeching. Monkeys howled. Things I couldn't even name turned back flips or poked sticky fingers through the bars at me. More than once I was hit in the back of the head by a monkey flinging something which I hoped and prayed was part of its breakfast.

With the slop bowl finally empty and every animal totally focused on rooting through their food to find the best bits, Toby told me a little about Santa Martha's larger denizens. The centre was home to big cats that looked like scaled-down leopards, eagles with shotgun holes in them, a puma with a weight problem, a deer and one chubby bear cub.

And a horse.

"Maybe you can ride him," Toby offered in an offhand manner. The horse didn't look up to much. It probably would have been easier for me to carry him. He eyed me nervously as though he'd just had exactly the same thought himself, and edged a little further away. I didn't feel inclined to intimidate the poor beast, so I filed the possibility of riding under 'things to consider later' and followed Toby on down the path.

The path, referred to by Toby as 'The Road' (which I still maintain was entirely unjustified) ran from the end of the driveway, past Johnny's house, then twisted back on itself as it ploughed downhill past a large cow-milking shed. Santa Martha was primarily a working dairy farm; that was where the money came from to feed the growing refuge. It was a financial balancing act which, I would come to discover, constantly teetered on the brink of disaster. Johnny used every ounce of his formidable presence to bully favourable deals from local producers. Somehow, it worked.

The 'road' was lined with cobblestones and heavily textured in shit. If this was the mess the cows made every morning on their way to being milked, well, I could only be glad they weren't led past the puma cage first…

After another switchback the road cut a rather meandering line across the hillside, past a series of massive enclosures for the bigger beasties. Sooner or later I'd be getting to know them all, but for now Toby wanted to give me a special treat. Tall trees lined the path for most of its length, draping their leafy tendrils across our shoulders as we wound our way deeper into the landscape. He was taking me to meet his favourite animal of all.

I could hardly believe my eyes. Enormous, ancient, placid… the Giant Galapagos Tortoise was all of these things. And a cheeky bugger to boot. I knelt in awe beside him as he sprayed me with chunks of his breakfast.

Toby would offer him a peeled banana, and he would slowly, ponderously, stretch out his neck and yawn for it. Toby stuffed as much inside as he could, then pulled his fingers out quick before the beak-like jaws ground shut. The excess – assuming it was banana – would slide down the tortoise's chin and add to the soggy mash of remnants on the floor. After the first time Toby fed him an apple I learned to kneel slightly further away. When he bit into one with crushing force it had a tendency to explode in my direction. I could almost see the old git smirking slightly as I wiped the pulp off my forehead.

But what a magnificent animal! He was almost waist high at the top of his shell, and if I'd had to lug that thing around I wouldn't be moving too fast either. The mottled green and brown dome of solid bone looked like it could withstand a direct hit from a cruise missile. And a series of shallow indentations scattered across the surface of the shell stood testament that at the very least it was bulletproof.

Toby had helped rescue the tortoise, whom he had christened 'Meldrew'. A six-strong crew of volunteers had brought him back from Quito in Johnny's truck, knackering the suspension in the process. The tortoise had been poached as a youngster, and could never be returned to his natural home in the Galapagos Islands because of their extremely stringent quarantine regulations. Meldrew had been discovered by the Quito police in the back garden of a very bored, very wealthy man, who had evidently been using him for shotgun target practice.

As disturbing as his life had been previously, he seemed happy now. Every other morning, Toby explained, he was fed an enormous bucket of fruit. He'd been fed yesterday, so this was really just a get-to-know-you (and-cover-you-in-apple-juice) visit. I would get the chance to see that beak in action plenty more over the next few weeks.

"He's got a great enclosure," I mentioned to Toby as we hiked back up the steeply inclined field. We crossed a small stream and climbed a flight of stone steps to reach the main road back to the houses.

"Yeah," came the reply. "Doesn't stop him trying to escape though."

"What? Really? When? I mean, how?"

"Oh, a few months back. We came to feed him and he was gone. He'd walked right through the fence and taken a section of it with him."

"No way! But you got him back then? How long was he gone?"

"Oh, about a week."

"Wow! I bet that was a scary time."

"Ha! Yeah… well, not really."

"You spent a whole week out looking for him?"

"Nope."

"How come?"

"Well, we could see him the whole time. He'd only gotten to the bottom of the field."

"Ah."

"We thought we'd give him a decent head start before we came after him. He wasn't very hard to catch."

"Oh."

"Trying to roll him back up the hill – that was the difficult part."

As we passed back through the circle of cages near the house I spotted one of Santa Martha's weirdest inmates taking a casual stroll across the garden. The raccoon-like thing was snuffling his way around a very low log fence, probing every nook and cranny with his ridiculously long bendy nose. A few feet away his mate was giving the same attention to a big rock in the middle of the grass.

"Ah, look!" I pointed at the fuzzy interloper. "It's one of them… um, whatdyamacallitz!"

Toby glanced round. "Oh shit! It's the coatamundis! They've escaped again!" He took a long stride over the fence and deftly swept up the first animal mid snuffle.

Not to be outdone, I lunged for one of the furry critters myself. And I caught it! The beast was either too trusting or too stupid to run away from me. I grabbed it two-handed, by the scruff of the neck and the tail. The fox red fur was thick and coarse. It was my first official handling of an animal! It bode well for the rest of my stay. This little guy was as cute and cuddly as a stuffed toy – and seemed about as intelligent. Definitely my kinda critter. I longed to sit him on my knee and stroke him.

"Careful!" Toby warned.

"Oh? Why?"

"Cause it hurts like hell when they bite."

Suddenly I was aware of just how precarious my grip on the creature was. And that he was struggling ever so slightly. His nose was bending up at me as though seeking a target for some unnecessarily long, lethally sharp incisors.

"Let's put them back then," Toby suggested. I was only too happy to comply. He led the way back around to their enclosure and stopped before the fastened door. "Here mate, take this for a sec," he said, and thrust the second coatamundi into my arms.

"Woah!" I had to let one hand go on my beastie to take Toby's off him. I instinctively reached out with my left hand for the new critter, leaving the original dangling by its tail from my right. Toby handed it across by the scruff and I took it the same way. Then I stood there as he worked the troublesome door catch. With a wriggling coatamundi in each hand – one upside down, one right-side up. They clearly weren't comfortable any more. I could tell because both of them decided to put a lot more effort into their squirming. I was already holding them both out at arm's length in front of me, but it was suddenly not far enough. How bendy were these creatures? Could they still get me? I had a brainwave, and moved my arms so I was holding them out on either side of me. Better. More balanced. But now I couldn't see them both at once. I flicked my gaze from one to the other and willed Toby to make the door work.

Don't show fear, I thought. They'll smell it, and fight harder. Damn these things were heavy! Suddenly I had a desperate urge to scratch my nose. I tried to twitch it violently instead.

"You alright there mate?"

Toby had mastered the catch, opened the door and turned around to see me – stretched out like a weightlifter, eyes wide in fear, glancing from side to side and wiggling my nose. In each hand I held a small bushy mammal, and all three of us were twitching frantically.

I could see him suppressing a laugh as he calmly removed one of the creatures from my grasp. And just like that everything became easy again. We deposited the coatamundis in their cage and retreated back through the troublesome door. Toby got the thing shut again and turned to lean on it, a grin on his face.

"So how'd you like that?"

"It was cool!" I was enthused by my victory, and emboldened by my continued survival.

"So, you don't mind handling them?"

"Nah, they were no problem at all."

"Great!" Toby exclaimed. He glanced back at the cage behind him and sighed. "Then catch that one again will you?"

I looked where he was pointing. A small red furball was in the process of making another bid for freedom. Behind it was a small hole scraped in the dirt under the edge of the cage.

"I'd better fill that in," he added.

"Oh shit! They'll both get out again!" I really didn't fancy my chances of recapturing them both single-handed.

"Nah, don't worry," said Toby. "The other one's blind – it takes him ages to find the hole again!"

True enough, the poor beast was stumbling randomly around the enclosure, testing the air and the soil with swift bends of its nose.

"Do you have anything here that isn't shot, blind, fat or crippled?" I asked.

Toby adjusted his cap and put a mock serious face on before answering. "Well, there's you and there's me. At least until one of the above happens to us."

"That's not terribly likely is it?"

"Wait and see, mate. Wait and see."

Cold Comfort

That night it began to get cold.

Then it got colder. And colder. Just before my testicles froze solid and snapped off I felt inclined to mention it to Toby. We were sitting in the dining room of the volunteer house (which was really the only room if you didn't count the bedrooms). His reply was not encouraging.

"Ah, it's not that bad really, tonight. It was well cold last weekend. You'll get used to it though. You only notice it more because there isn't any heating in the house."

"What? No heating at all?"

"Nah mate. We're in Ecuador!"

"So it doesn't get that cold here? Because we're near the equator?"

"It doesn't get cold in the rest of the country. Here in the mountains it's frigging freezing at night. This is actually quite mild."

"So how come they don't have heating then? Does everyone just freeze at night?"

"No mate. They have blankets." He proved it by walking into the bedroom and returning with an enormous woolly pair of them.

"Thanks man," I told him.

"Nah, these are for me," he said, "they're on a shelf on

the back wall if you want some."

"Oh! Right." I stood to go.

"Nah, I'm only messing with you! Here!" He thrust a massive bundle of material at me. "You know what? It does get too cold in here. It's the only real problem. Can't do much in the evenings, unless you're wasted or you do it wrapped in five blankets."

"Have you got any booze?" I asked.

"Nah. We'll go down to Tambillo and get some beers, this weekend maybe. I need a haircut anyway."

We sat in comfortable silence for a moment. My gaze wandered around the sparsely furnished room, from the narrow kitchen at one end to a pair of uninviting wooden chairs at the other. We were also blessed with a bookcase (which was empty), and a TV – which had to be older than me – was perched atop it.

It wasn't hard to figure out how the cold outside made its presence felt inside. The walls were of concrete block – one block thick and painted a cheery yellow on both sides. The roof was also one sheet thick. Whatever that corrugated stuff was, we were staring right at the underside of it from our dinner table. Even the worn floor tiles seemed to absorb the icy temperature and radiate it back into the room. I was suddenly glad there were only two of us to split the stash of blankets between.

"You play chess?" Toby was studying me as intently as I'd been studying the room.

"Yeah man! I love chess. Almost no-one I know plays, so I hardly ever get the chance."

"You want a quick game?"

I thought about this for a few seconds. "I'm not very good though," I admitted. This is a cunning double bluff used by many males of the species, giving rise to two possible scenarios; either losing badly, and therefore being proved both right and honest, or winning handily and being proved both skilful and modest about it.

"Nah, me neither," he lied.

Three rapid and humiliating defeats later I made my escape, pleading extreme coldness. It wasn't a lie – I was shivering so hard it took quite a lot of effort to place a piece on the right square. How had he won so effortlessly? I had no idea. Clearly Toby was some kind of mutant-genius chess prodigy. Or else he'd been sitting here alone with the chess set for more nights than I dared ask about. In which case he was probably insane to boot.

"We can play again tomorrow," he pointed out as I backed apologetically towards the bedroom.

"Yes, yes, of course. Goodnight now!" I walked into the bedroom, set out like a dormitory with bunk beds lining the walls and a set of shelves at the far end bearing the promised stack of neatly folded blankets. Toby had his own room opposite.

"Oh crap weasels," I moaned softly to myself after the door had swung shut behind me. "I'm gonna get my ass handed to me at chess three times a night, every night for the next three months." There was no denying the gleam in Toby's eye. I suspected that he'd been waiting for a worthy opponent for some time. And he was still waiting. But that wouldn't stop him from taking advantage of me in the meantime. Declaring my undying love of the game had not been my cleverest move of the night. I'd backed myself into a corner – I couldn't refuse to play, or I'd look like a sore loser. I'd just have to smile sweetly and play, and be beaten constantly. At least then I'd just be a garden-variety loser.

I made a pile of blankets on the top bunk bed nearest to the door and surveyed my new domain. Behind me was a tiny bathroom cubicle, with walls that rose for about six feet then abruptly stopped two feet short of the ceiling. There was a fanlight window above the door with no glass in it, so light from the lounge, and the sound of Toby clearing away the chess set, spilled into the dorm room. There were a couple of windows looking out into the darkness surrounding the house. No street lights. This high into the mountains and with the property bordered by immense trees there was no light pollution of any kind. I could have poked my head out and seen a sky full of stars, if the windows hadn't been sealed shut and heavily barred on the outside. Rough neighbourhood? I wondered. Whatever the case, it was my neighbourhood now.

My rucksack was propped against the wall and the bed – I felt that neither one could support its weight alone – so I was as unpacked as I was likely to get. The blankets were already looking inviting. I set the alarm on my phone, which being English was good for sod all else in Ecuador, and hauled myself up into the super-tall top bunk. Why the top? I like heights. Or maybe since I never had bunk beds as a child I still get excited by the prospect of sleeping so far off the ground. My choice was also based on preventing any future volunteers from sleeping above me and it allowed me to pile the bed below with everything I owned, in the hope that no-one would sleep there either. It did require an investment of energy though; there were no ladders and the top bunk was roughly level with the top of my head. If I fell out I'd be in a world of pain, but that didn't seem too likely. I sank into the mattress with a squeal of ageing springs, then sank some more, finally ending up suspended hammock-like through the frame of the bed. The mattress conformed perfectly to my body shape – rather like the foam lining in an assassin's rifle case. Where do they get those? I wondered briefly about a hired killer all in black, standing in a marketplace buying foam. Holding it up against his gun to check it was thick enough...

At last, I was alone again, safe and comfortable. Although I'd probably have to cut my way out in the morning.

I awoke to the screeching of a rooster. Actually I was awakened *by* the screeching of a rooster. A quick glance at my ex-patriot phone told me I didn't need to get up for another hour, for which I was very grateful. The only part of me protruding from the mountain of blankets was my nose, and even that could tell that it was very, very cold out. The temperature in the room was so low it made me shiver just thinking about it. Luckily I could still go back to sleep – if only the bloody rooster would shut up.

It never did.

Nor did the temperature increase significantly by the time my alarm went off. The vibrations sent the phone skittering out from under my pillow and straight over the edge of the bed, where it plunged to a violent death on the icy tiles six feet below. Verdict: suicide. It obviously didn't want to work today either.

The first item on my morning agenda was to meet Jimmy. Since Johnny was the rich and powerful landowner he had rather more to do with his day than boss volunteers around. Instead, to give us our jobs each day (and hopefully to show me how to do them), there was Jimmy, who lived with his wife Nancy and their two children in the breeze block shack I'd taken to be Johnny's outhouse. The couple had clearly named one child apiece; their daughter was called Myra, while their son, who was of course under no pressure to follow in his father's footsteps, was called Jimmytwo.

Jimmy the First looked to me like the very essence of an Ecuadorian, distilled into a compact, muscular frame. He was wiry and small; his skin was the colour of strong tea, and well-weathered; his age was impossible to guess. Jimmy could have been born with a machete in his hand, already wearing his fraying jeans and sporting a ridiculous tuft of facial hair on his upper lip.

I liked him. Whether or not he liked me was a moot point. He was to be my boss so it wasn't really required of him. But for my part I desperately wanted to impress him. Of all the hundreds of volunteers that must have come and gone through Jimmy's work gang, I wanted to be the one he would remember. He cracked a sarcastic smirk as he looked me up and down a couple of times. 'This is what you've brought me?' his eyes seemed to say. Nothing malicious, but not overly impressed either. Well, that was something I would have to change.

Jimmy aimed a question sideways at Toby, without taking his eyes off me.

"Ha!" Toby replied. "He wants to know if you're a man," he informed me.

"I'm not wearing a skirt," I pointed out.

"No, no. He wants to know if you're a MAN. They have this whole macho thing going on here."

"Um…" This didn't seem like a good time to be hesitant. I locked eyes with Jimmy and smiled. "*Si*," I told him.

At this Jimmy roared with laughter. Was he mocking me? Probably. But I felt like I'd passed muster. Now all I had to do was live up to what I'd said.

Unfortunately I have a mouth so big I'm sometimes in danger of swallowing my own head. When I put my foot in it, it goes in up to the knee. I've gotten quite used to looking spectacularly stupid as a result (and being the envy of yoga teachers worldwide). Why stop now?

"*Yo soy el hombre,*" I told Toby and Jimmy. Literally: I am THE Man!

Jimmy laughed so hard I thought he was going to fall over. Toby joined him.

"Oh, mate," he managed when he could breathe again, "you really know how to make an impression!"

There were two other Ecuadorian guys on the full-time staff at Santa Martha. Jimmy's number two was Danielo, a younger, scrawnier farmhand with several missing teeth. He probably thought it made him look tougher – I thought it made him look like he'd been beaten up lots. He was more arrogant than Jimmy, though with less reason to be; he never seemed to wash, yet was convinced that women everywhere were drawn to his charms. Oh, and he lived in a shed.

The last guy I christened 'Tractor Driving Dude', since I never met him; I only ever saw him from a distance driving Johnny's enormous tractor. I had a theory that he was actually just a torso, permanently mounted on a giant spring in the cab. In three months at the centre I never once saw any evidence that he had legs. But his top half seemed quite friendly. He would wave occasionally, which made me feel better about the guy. At least he had arms.

And so, with the most daunting chore of the morning over it was finally time for breakfast. Not for us though. For every parrot, monkey, aardvark and armadillo in the entire refuge.

Then for us.

Feeding Time At The Zoo

In the beginning there was The Bowl.

And yea! We did fill it with yummy things. Overripe fruits and vegetables for which I knew no name in any language, and oats from an enormous bin in Johnny's kitchen. Toby gave me a running commentary as he went about his carefully practised routine.

"The softer stuff we cut up, the tougher bits we blend, and some of them need peeling first. Be careful with this one," he held aloft a fine specimen of a pineapple. "It's pronounced 'pin-ya'."

"Pin-ya," I echoed.

"Right. See, they spell it P-I-N-A, only with a little accent over the 'N' that turns it into a "NY" sound."

"I see," I said. I didn't see at all.

"When I'd been here about a week, I asked Johnny's wife Brenda if I should put a pineapple in the blender, only I forgot to pronounce it with the accent. She totally cracked up, laughed at me for about twenty minutes, then went and told everyone in the house, and then they all laughed at me too. It turns out I'd just asked her if I should blend my penis."

There wasn't much I could say to that.

Next into the bowl we sprinkled vitamin powder and

added more fruit to cover it. By the time we were finished we had a vast vat of goo, thick and brightly coloured. With chunks in it. It did look disturbingly like it had been eaten once already.

It smelled heavenly. All the potent fruity fragrances mingled indistinguishably, making the very air around the bowl tremble with mouth-watering vapour. If I closed my eyes, I could almost eat the stuff. If I opened them, and caught myself in the process, I'd most likely be adding last night's supper to the mix.

"We do it the same every morning," Toby was explaining, "and again every afternoon at four. Sometimes Johnny's wife Brenda likes to do it, if she wants to try adding new stuff or if she thinks we're late getting up. It's the most important part of the job, getting the food right and getting plenty of it out to the animals."

"I can guess at the next most important part," I told him.

"Yeah?"

"Well, we're pretty much feeding all these guys their body weight in mashed fruit and oatmeal twice a day. That's gonna make for a big pile of shit."

Toby's eyes gleamed. "You're not wrong mate," he said. "Shovel it in one end, and away from the other. For everything else, we have Jimmy."

Today was also the day to feed our resident big cat. Since the fat puma's enclosure was quite a distance, Toby ordered me into the passenger seat of a white truck, similar in style to the monster four-by-four taxi that had brought me up the mountain. This truck gleamed rather less however, and appeared to be composed largely of rust. My door didn't shut all the way and the windscreen was cracked. Death Trap, I'd have named it given the chance. But this was Ecuador. I'd already noticed that the local health and safety standards were a little behind the UK. Perhaps it was better not to ask too many questions in case I didn't like the answers.

I instinctively reached for my seat belt, and froze halfway through the gesture when I caught Toby staring at me.

"Sorry! Force of habit," I explained.

"S'alright mate. We don't normally bother round here." He gave me what I had already come to think of as his trademark grin. "I'll try not to kill you."

He then spent the next ten minutes trying to do just that. To say that Toby drove like a maniac was an understatement on a par with saying that he liked chillies. Toby's love for chillies was unhealthy right up to the point of severely endangering his digestive tract. His driving was fucking scary.

As we bounced along the road from pothole to pothole the repeated hammering of my head on the roof began to leave a dent in both. My knees were wedged under the dash and even my toes were straining for purchase on the inside of my trainers. When he finally skidded to a stop in a clearing beside the puma cage I collapsed back in my seat in sheer relief.

Breathing. I'd somehow forgotten it, and now seemed like a suitable juncture to start up again.

Gasp.

Sigh.

Unclench.

"Nice driving," I hissed.

"Yeah, sweet innit! Can you drive?" He seemed totally immune to my sarcasm.

I was a little shocked for resuming normal conversation. "Ah… no. Well yes, but no. That is, I can but I haven't got a licence. Yet." I could feel bruises developing on my knees, elbow and forehead. My neck had gone stiff. I think I had whiplash.

"No licence?" Toby eyed me thoughtfully. "Ah, don't worry about that mate. Me neither." And he climbed out of the car.

"His story is a bit of a tragedy actually," Toby explained. Totally unfazed by the drive, he had already switched back into helpful tour guide mode. I climbed out of the truck and stared through the chain-link fence, looking for any sign of the tubby puma.

"He was being kept as a pet by some guy up in Quito. Like, kept in the back garden! The guy didn't want to get hurt accidentally, so he had his claws pulled out, his teeth pulled out... fucking sick, man. And to stop him being aggressive, he had him castrated. So when Johnny rescued him he was in a really bad state, living in a tiny garden in his own filth. So they brought him here. He was one of the first animals to arrive, after Johnny saw what was happening to the local animals and decided to do something about it. This was one of the first enclosures they built."

"Was he always fat?"

"Yeah. It comes with having your bollocks chopped off. Of course now he gets plenty to eat, and still doesn't move much, so he's just getting fatter! His belly drags along the ground. It's pretty bad – he'll never be able to leave. Can't release him into the wild without teeth or claws, so he'll be here 'til the end."

Following Toby's outstretched arm I could just make out the massive tawny head, surrounded by scraggly bushes in front of what seemed to be a natural cave. Fat Puma was asleep.

"I guess he sleeps a lot...?"

"Yeah. I call him Garfield. You'll get to see him a lot better when we go inside."

"Wow! When do we go inside?"

"Every week. We get to pick up what's left of all the

chickens he's eaten, and pull 'em out."

"All the chickens he's gummed you mean?"

Toby gave me an exasperated look.

"What? I was only wondering how he could eat chickens. I mean, does he suck them like a fruit pastel?"

"You're not supposed to make fun of him, you tight git! It's sad!"

"I know, I know. Ha! He'd probably kill himself, but he hasn't got the balls…"

"Just feed him the chickens."

The back of the truck had a hideously stained tarpaulin covering a small pile of chicken carcasses. Toby directed me as I chose a couple in slightly better condition and lobbed them over the fence into Garfield's enclosure. The great golden head didn't move at all.

"Have you ever seen him move?" I asked.

"Oh, he can move," Toby told me, "and it's pretty freaky when he does. He's not little. When he comes towards you when you're in the cage, it's like… shit!"

"But he's got no teeth or claws," I pointed out. "What's he going to do, sit on you?"

By way of punishment Toby drove back extra fast.

Man's Work

For my first proper day's work I was led into a rather dilapidated-looking garage beyond the monkey cages. The floor was presumably poured concrete, though it was impossible to tell. Like a boulder sitting in the jungle, this floor had attained its own ecosystem. An inch of dirt gave the impression of bare earth underfoot. Scrawny weeds fought for growing-room with mechanical debris of every possible description. I remember thinking it would make a perfect TV set for a post-apocalypse style bombed-out factory. Or a torture chamber. I placed my feet very carefully. It wouldn't do to trip over some ancient pipe and impale myself on a decomposing scarecrow. Not on my first day. Gigantic cog wheels leaned against the stone walls at random intervals. Why? Who could say. Perhaps Jimmy was the crazed inventor type? It didn't seem likely. Within seconds of meeting him I had figured that Jimmy was as hard as nails – and about as bright as one. I'd nicknamed him Mighty Mouse.

He was sorting tools out from several piles behind one of the barn-like doors. Toby took a narrow shovel and a pickaxe. I was handed something unchristenable – two gigantic spoons, hinged together where the long wooden handles protruded from the business end. Beyond delivering a mean ass-pinch from six feet away I couldn't begin to imagine what they were for. Luckily I had Jimmy to enlighten me.

Next door to the coatamundi cage was an overgrown garden, the back of which butted up against the side wall of Johnny's house. We followed Jimmy there and dropped our tools alongside the brace of lethal-looking machetes he'd been carrying. It was time for my first lesson.

"*Excava-dora*," Jimmy named my peculiar burden. He picked it up and, with a practised arm, drove the spoon ends deep into the soil of the garden. With a swift wrench of the handles he pulled the tool free and deposited a double spoonful of earth next to the hole he'd made. It was a digger!

Jimmy grunted and passed over the handles of the '*excavadora*'. Copying him, I took up a wide-legged stance and threw the thing at the ground, with the predictable result that it bounced off the iron-hard dirt and smacked me in the mouth.

The bastard.

It took several tries before I achieved the right balance of control versus letting go. I hauled on the handles and grudgingly the ground gave up a pathetic amount of soil, which I proudly added to the pile.

"That's right mate!" Toby said. He'd been watching the procedure with a smirk. "Keep doing that in the same spot and you'll end up with a post hole."

I eyed the spoons doubtfully. "How long does it take?"

"Quite a while at first."

This was true.

The hole grew deeper and wider at the same speed as if I'd actually been using a spoon. A teaspoon. By the time it was done my palms sported a couple of nasty blisters from the dry wood of the handles, but Jimmy made a careful examination of the hole and gave me a little round of applause. I basked.

Then he indicated with one foot the spot where he wanted the next hole digging. It was alarmingly close to the first one. And covered by the pile of dirt I'd just extracted. As I shovelled this off to a more convenient location behind me I muttered a few expletives, and sneaked a peek at the rest of the garden. "What are we doing anyway?" I asked Toby.

"We're building a new enclosure," he explained. "We're gonna put posts in all round, then fasten wire mesh to it."

"And the posts go in these holes…"

"Yeah."

With two sides of the garden already bordered by the house and the coati's cage, that left two sides in obvious need of post holes. Neither side was more than ten metres. And it looked like the holes were going to be spaced about a metre apart…

My first day was shaping up to be a long one.

"Keep at it mate!" Toby encouraged me. And left.

So I dug. And dug. By the fourth or fifth hole my blisters had burst, and new ones had formed in the less trafficked areas of my hands, and burst as well. The loose flaps of skin were clogged with dust. Two holes later they even stopped hurting. Instead my hands throbbed in time to my digging. Or was it my heartbeat? The two had married their rhythms – beat, thrust, release, beat, grasp, twist, beat, remove.

That's when it occurred to me that I was getting good. Instead of a constant inner diatribe on the unjustness of my situation and the dubious birth circumstances of Jimmy and Toby, I'd attained a kind of mental calm. My mind had drifted to other things – cheese sandwiches featuring strongly – and without even realising, I'd dug hole number eight nearly twice as deep as necessary. I smiled to myself as I moved one long pace to my left and raised the *excavadora* again. 'When those lazy bastards get back I'll show them,' I thought.

I didn't have long to wait. Both men returned carrying a whole tree trunk each – the daddy of all fence posts! They must have hacked the trees down with machetes. I started to wonder if I hadn't gotten the easier job after all. For every hole I dug, one of these guys had to cut down a tree! A skinny tree for sure, but both machetes had very thin, fragile-looking blades and cheap plastic handles. I could imagine them standing up quite well to clearing jungle vines, but deforestation was really pushing it.

With a bit of gentle persuasion from a shovel the first fence post soon occupied its hole. Soil was filled back in and we all got to do our best Riverdance impersonations to compact it. We now had the beginning of our new enclosure. It was going to be very tall.

"What the hell are we keeping in here?" I had to ask. "A T-Rex?"

Toby wasn't sure himself, so he quizzed Jimmy. It didn't seem to do much good though.

"I think he wants to put a deer in here?" He sounded confused. I could understand why. Whilst evidently tall enough to prevent a deer from escaping, the enclosure would be nowhere near wide enough to house such a creature. Not if it was fond of exercise anyway.

Toby shrugged the mystery off. "You get used to it," he explained. "I never understand what's going on around here. Getting info out of these guys is kind of like using the *excavadora*. You dig, and dig, and get a little bit out here and there." Then he grinned at me. "Welcome to Ecuador!"

My turn at the machete work was more to my liking. True, by that point I'd already lost most of the skin on my palms, but I do love sharp things. My first attempt, with a white-knuckled death grip on the handle, resulted in score one for the tree. I deployed all my strength in one brutal swing, only to find that contact with the solid wooden trunk simply redirected most of the force back up my arm. As I staggered back clutching my shoulder the machete didn't even have the good grace to remain lodged in the tree. It clattered to the ground, a steely ring of defiance from my adversary. "Take *that!*" the tree said. After a bout of extreme eye-rolling Jimmy demonstrated the proper technique again. With much exaggerated looseness and a precise swing he smoothly embedded the blade three inches deep. It looked effortless, as though he knew which parts of the tree were secretly made of painted foam. To me the problem was insurmountable – the tree was clearly harder than I was. But it was a sitting target! Could I really lose a fight with an inanimate object? Even if it was bigger than me?

I swung loose and was rewarded with a bite. Not quite a Jimmy, but a start – the narrow edge of the blade had chopped clear through the bark and on into virgin wood!

And it took nearly five minutes for me to get it back out.

Score two to the tree.

By the time I chopped down my first tree, Toby and Jimmy had cut enough posts between them for the rest of the enclosure. I consoled myself with the thought that there had to be a knack to it and it had to be learnable. Jimmy might actually have been a machete in a former life, but Toby was a Londoner. He had to have picked up his skills since he got here – I couldn't see him hacking his way through rush hour on the tube train.

Felling a mighty giant of the forest made me feel a bit guilty. A proud living entity had been callously cut down in its prime, hacked to pieces by an arrogant youth with a knife fetish. But it was for the greater good, I told myself. And anyway, it served it right for being so cocky.

I reclaimed the machete and wiped my blood off the handle as the others eyed my handiwork. Jimmy's critique was a simple, two-stage process; first he pointed at the log he had just finished with. its end was a neat point, as was the corresponding end still rooted to the ground. Slivers of wood were scattered in a rough circle around the scene. Then he gestured towards the fruits of my labour. My tree had been severed by sheer violence. The length that lay on the ground was badly wounded by cuts ranging up all sides. The rooted portion showed evidence of the same treatment. It looked like Edward Scissorhands had had an epileptic fit in front of it. Everywhere lay chunks, shards, splinters of wood. I was ankle deep in the stuff. Between the bit that was cut and the bit that was left, there had once existed a clear foot of tree trunk that I had reduced entirely to sawdust.

By the end of the day our new enclosure was finished. We'd hauled logs, raised logs, and jumped around the bases of them like wasted druids. Finally Jimmy had shown us to an area opposite the garage where several huge rolls of wire mesh lay slowly disintegrating. With much cursing in a mixture of languages we'd dragged the mesh over to the new enclosure, unrolled it, and nailed it firmly around the posts. It was, of course, a lot more work than that, but describing it is not even as much fun as doing it was. Suffice to say the cage was built. Apart from the door; that would be tomorrow's job.

The day had been one hell of a learning curve. In addition to turning half a tree into kindling I'd begun to understand the true meaning of the word 'manpower'. I'd learnt that Jimmy, though tiny, was clearly made of the same stuff they built The Terminator out of. And that when people back home talked about making something with blood, sweat and tears they really had no idea. None.

I wasn't going to let it defeat me though. Today had been a triumph! I had taken all the punishment thrown my way and asked for more. I'd dug, chopped and nailed harder than I'd thought possible. Work here was obviously going to be painful, but I could handle that. I was going to prove it. I would become a MAN!

The upwelling of pride carried me all the way back to the volunteer house and lasted right up until I put my hands into a bowl of hot, soapy water.

Wet Dreams

It was some time before I dared consider whole body immersion. There was nothing wrong with my body – other than intense pain in every major muscle group. Bruising to the arms, legs and mouth. A few chunky splinters, the occasional laceration and a stink like something that's been dead for three weeks. But it was my hands. They burned with a fiery agony I had never known before. Toby charitably called it 'hard work'. How was I supposed to hold soap? To rub it against my body? To sweep the suds off myself, when my hands could hardly bear to be opened?

But then, there was the stink.

The shower, when I dared brave it, was awesome. For about three and a half minutes. Then for no immediately apparent reason it decided to hate me. The water instantly turned icy cold causing me to shriek at high pitch and high volume. I leapt out backwards with a speed I never knew I possessed, and swore violently.

Toby was obviously passing by outside. Actually he could have been anywhere – I reckon they heard my scream in Tambillo.

"Alright mate?" he enquired. "Water gone off?"

"Fucking cold, is what it's gone!"

"Oh, yeah, no problem. The boiler's gone out. Hang on."

I heard the back door open and close, then Toby's voice bellowed through the window.

"Try now!"

My big toe ventured back into the water stream.

"No!"

"Right." I heard the crack of a match being struck. He was obviously standing right under the bathroom window trying to relight the gas boiler.

"Okay. Try now!"

Straight away I felt the heat returning to the water. "Cheers mate!" Thank God for Toby, I thought. And for showers. I stood under and let the piping hot water flow over my aching body. Sheer luxury. I could have stayed under there all night. Except that two minutes later like the flick of a switch the water turned to ice again. "BOLLOCKS!" I shouted as I repeated my earlier feat of bathroom agility.

"TOOOBEEEE!!!"

There was no chess that night.

The next couple of days passed in a blur. Having proved what real men got up to in an average day, both Toby and Jimmy had decided to take it a bit easier on me. The almost-finished cage, fruit of our ground-and-back breaking labours, was largely ignored in favour of cleaning the entire refuge from top to bottom. As I may have mentioned, there was a long way between those two points.

I got to visit the miniature leopards, which I'd been eager to do ever since seeing photos of them on the Santa Martha website. Ocelots, they were called, and we had a six-strong pack of them. We fed them over the fence with the last of the dead chickens and spent much of the next day inside their enclosure, clearing away the scraps. One ocelot emerged straight away, purring like a house cat on steroids, and proceeded to wind her way around and between my legs as though begging to be petted. Which was pretty surreal, since she was the size of a German shepherd. My entire hand would fit comfortably in her mouth, so I resisted the urge to give her a stroke.

We had one more ocelot in solitary confinement, reigning supreme over a maze of an enclosure with ramps, walkways, tree trunks and kennels. She was a regal-looking creature, the black swirls standing out like fresh ink blots on her gleaming golden hide. Toby (very daringly, I thought) led the way inside as she growled a deep, throaty warning. He stopped just out of arm's reach and levelled a finger. "Stop that," he told her. She ignored him. But she seemed content to grumble, threatening our backs as we stooped to collect her leftovers. The other cats were beautiful sure enough, but this lady was nothing short of magnificent. I paused for a last look as Toby searched for the door chain in the long grass. My body thrummed with the danger inherent in being this close to something so powerful.

"She's incredible," I told him. Within earshot, in case she was listening.

"Yeah…" Toby's voice had a melancholy edge to it. "She's got HIV. The feline version of course – caught it from a street cat before we got her. We have to keep her separate, but… Johnny wants to kill her. Put her down, like."

"No? That's… harsh." I had nothing better to say.

"What else can you do though? He suggests it every time the vet comes around, and I argue with him every time. Sooner or later I'll lose."

He was right about one thing. There was nothing I could do.

Next there was a trip to Garfield's enclosure and, as promised, inside it. We each took a homemade tool called an *azadón* with us from the garage. They were rough lengths of steel pipe, with flat trowel blades welded onto the bottom at right angles. A kind of rake/hoe/pickaxe, they would also crush the skull of a woolly rhinoceros with a single blow, were we ever in such need. Relatively few of Jimmy's tools were not weaponized.

We worked our way across Garfield's enclosure, collecting chicken corpses from the undergrowth as we went. Garfield himself was asleep. The shredded remnants of one bird lay mere inches from those gigantic forepaws and the head nestled comfortably on them.

"Go on – get it," Toby said.

"Fuck off! You get it!"

"Oh, so now you *are* scared, eh? I thought so."

"I'm not scared."

The puma stirred slightly, grunted in his sleep. We both recoiled instinctively.

"Go on!" Toby urged. He was loving every minute.

"You gotta be kidding me," I muttered.

"Come on. Be a man." It was a phrase I already dreaded. Jimmy used it to convince me to dig deeper, chop harder and carry things that weighed more than I did. It had resulted in the distinct lack of skin on my palms.

"That shit's not going to work on me forever you know."

Toby wisely kept his opinions about that to himself.

I edged forward, almost close enough to touch the beast. Then I knelt and slowly extended the pole of my *azadón*. I winced as the flat blade glanced off a rock in its path. I hooked the carcass and dragged it backwards – whereupon it split into several smaller chunks. I swore and Toby giggled. One by one I retrieved the chunks, gathered them in my hands and sprung back to a safe distance.

The puma slept on.

"There," I told Toby. "Now I'm a man."

He wisely kept quiet about that, too.

The eagles were also due a visit. We had a pair of them –

black-chested buzzard eagles to be precise. Both displayed large, ragged shotgun holes in their wings. Shot by farmers fearing for their chickens, a tragic yet understandable act. We'd been doing the same in England a little over fifty years ago. The birds shared a vast enclosure, stretching many metres up into the cloudless sky. Which seemed a little cruel, since neither of them could get more than waist height off the ground. There were perches of course, but they couldn't be placed too high up. There was the ever-present danger of the birdbrains forgetting the reason for their incarceration, jumping from a height, flapping pitifully, then hitting the ground with a thump – and possibly a broken leg or two. They couldn't understand that they now had the same lift generating potential as a sack of house bricks.

But Toby had left the best 'til last. *Osita* is a contraction of the Spanish *'oso'* (for bear) and the diminutive *'~ita'* (meaning something small and cute). Osita lived up to her name in all ways but one; for a small, cute thing, she was about the size of wheelie bin. She was the bear equivalent of · a teenager and almost fully grown, but she lolloped around her enclosure with such enthusiasm that it was easy to think of her as a boisterous child. Just not the kind you want sitting on your knee. Toby passed her a few chunks of fruit through the bars, which she gobbled up instantly. Then he scratched her nose. "We'll have to come and fill her pond up pretty soon." He pointed out a deep depression, lined with concrete, some way down the hill. "No matter what I do, she always manages to drain it. I've tried everything to plug the outflow pipe, but whatever I stuff in there she removes and eats. It's like a game she plays, but to be honest I'm getting a bit sick of it. It takes hours to fill the damn thing."

Osita knew that. You could just tell. But it was a game that she was not even close to being tired of. She might have radiated innocence and cute, fuzzy lovability, but I could see through all that. She was crafty, that bear...

Shopping

When Toby had first described the living arrangements to me via email he'd explained that shopping for groceries was a weekly affair, with all the volunteers coughing up ten bucks or so to buy supplies from a local market. I'd been looking forward to this trip more and more with each passing evening. I didn't know how long it had been since Toby's last shopping trip but all he seemed to have left was vegetables and rice. Toby couldn't cook rice, which was a bit of a shame since he was living almost exclusively on it. His cooking of vegetables was also questionable. Not that I was much help – beans on toast was really pushing the limit of my culinary abilities, so it hardly seemed fair to complain. I couldn't have cooked a thick, juicy steak even if we'd had one.

Toby could have. But he wouldn't have. Because Toby was a vegetarian. Discovering that not only was I living with such a deviant, but that I was also largely reliant on him for my food, was possibly the scariest thing that had happened to me so far. At times, as I lay beneath Mount Blanket fighting back the sleep-inhibiting cold, I fantasised about meat. Good, grain-fed animal flesh. Fat, crispy-skinned sausages and the heavenly smell of frying bacon. In those times, with the memory of crunchy carrot and even crunchier rice laying heavily on my tongue, I tried not to think that as a herbivore Toby was technically lower on the food chain than me. Sure he was skinny... but he had nice firm buttocks. I think it's fair to say that I was considering eating him.

I wondered if vegetarians were like Pringles – once you pop, you can't stop? Was it a valid lifestyle choice to be a vegetarian-ian? The madness had to end. And so as Friday night rolled around, marking the end of my first week at the centre, I got to celebrate in the best way possible. I went shopping.

Johnny's truck rolled into town and dispensed a pair of hungry volunteers. I had no idea where we were in relation to Tambillo or Quito, and to be honest I didn't really care. We left the truck parked in a gas station and threaded our way through the colourful crowd to a row of battered-looking shops. Night had fallen on the drive into town, so it surprised me that the street was so busy. There wasn't another foreigner anywhere in sight as we ducked into a room lined with shelves and stacks of products on all sides.

Every square inch of space was crammed full, either with the goods for sale or with Ecuadorians trying to buy them. It was like trying to stand waist-deep in white water rapids. The tide of shoppers surged around us, frequently crashing against one of us like a wave breaking on the shore. Toby struggled to stay upright whilst balancing an armful of smaller groceries and digging in a tight jeans pocket for his shopping list. Sacks and bags hung from every square inch of ceiling. Every time I turned my head, one bounced off my skull. I swear they were filled with lead ingots. The air was thick and warm. The shopkeeper had fixed me with a black look as I entered, and continued to stare at me in spite of the torrent of sound hurled at him by his other customers. I was starting to feel a little nervous. I wasn't prepared for such an invasive shopping experience. Back home the supermarkets have aisles so wide you have to go out of your way to accidentally ram raid the trolley of someone reaching for the last packet of marked-down bread rolls. This was like being at the epicentre of a hot, sweaty tornado. Every time some hairy midget jostled me I had to stifle the urge to seize an overgrown cucumber and beat my way out of the crowd.

From across the mob Toby was calling me.

He was telling me we needed sugar.

This at least was progress. I turned to the shopkeeper and met his glare full on. Then realised he wouldn't understand 'sugar' no matter how sweetly I said it. My mind groped for an answer. I knew the words for 'small', or 'white'...

I glanced back at Toby and made a shrug with my eyebrows.

"*Sucre!*" He supplied the word.

I rotated back to that thundercloud face. "*Sucre...?*" I asked hesitantly.

BANG! A sack of what must surely be sugar hit the counter like a... sack of sugar. With force. I turned again to Toby.

"Rice," he explained.

"Urr...?"

"Oh. *Arroz.*"

"Thanks. *Arroz!*" I grinned nervously at the shopkeeper.

A sack of rice slammed down next to the sugar. I raised an eyebrow in Toby's direction.

"Hang on a sec," he told me, reading with eyes and fingertips, "Umm... chickpeas...?"

It was at this point that I realised this wasn't going to work. I mean, what the fuck? I didn't even know what chickpeas were in English. I wouldn't recognise them if I was drowning in a vat full of the bleeding things. I shot what I hoped was an apologetic look at the shopkeeper and retreated back past Toby, relieving him of some of the sundries.

"Sorry mate, I'm about as much help as a poo sandwich. Plus I think this guy wants something really bad to happen to me. If I mispronounce something and end up asking for his hand in marriage… I think you better take over."

Beyond the shop the whirling melee of the market assailed my senses. I could hardly take it in as I had to devote all my attention to not standing on any of my fellow shoppers. Toby waded through the crowd with minimum difficulty, stopping here and there for a lightening-fast acquisition of some basic necessity. It was here that I first began to appreciate just how well Toby had integrated himself into the local environment.

"*Cuanto bal-e?*" he asked, sounding casual. It wasn't a phrase I knew. I recognised his shrug of feigned disinterest at the quoted price though. With a shrewd '*Uno mas*' (one more!) and on occasion by actually walking away from a stall mid-negotiation, he managed to skilfully shave a dollar here and there, and build up the bags and piles of supplies we were carrying until neither of us could walk easily. Then he led the way again and cut through the swarm of brightly-clothed bodies back to the gas station where Johnny's truck sat alone, squat and powerful. The tray back was already overflowing with a dizzying array of bags, loose fruits, cloth, boxes and bric-a-brac. I thought we'd been moving pretty fast – Johnny must have shopped like greased lightening on roller skates.

Smells filtered past as we stashed our cargo wherever we could find room. Meat… Barbecue. Strange spices gave a sharp edge to the smoke. My mouth watered so much I was standing in a puddle of drool. A quick glance around showed that Johnny was still deep in conversation with what I assume must be the owner of the gas station – I briefly entertained the thought that Johnny could be a Mafia boss, visiting his 'family' and laying down the law. There was a certain intensity to him, a presence, that made me believe he could be anything. He was certainly a big man in local circles.

The smell of charring meat washed over me again, and it was more than I could stand. I mumbled an excuse to Toby, waved a hand in Johnny's general direction and bolted for the nearest food stall.

A tiny old woman and her daughter, both heavily wrapped in scarves of wool and silk, were serving oddments of unrecognisable meat from an enormous wok balancing awkwardly on a gas burner. It smelled like heaven.

"*Cuanto bal-e?*" I tried, and was rewarded with an exchange of eyebrow raises between the two. The daughter was quite pretty, I thought, with smooth skin and wide, dark eyes.

"*Uno dollar,*" came the predictable response. Most things were one dollar, I'd noticed. I had the cash ready and greedily exchanged it for a wooden skewer laden with dripping flesh. I bit straight into it, causing red hot fat to spray all over my chin. The old woman laughed as I winced and handed me a paper napkin.

My cool irretrievably blown, I slunk back to the car. It was worth every second of humiliation for the rich juicy meat. I never did find out what it was. Knowing my luck it was bound to be something's penis. At least I'd resisted a side serving of the meatballs. Toby showed up a few seconds later with a bag of hot chips from a stall a little further away, and we munched happily until Johnny strode over to usher us back into the car.

From start to finish the experience had taken about twenty five minutes. I was left in a state of shock. It had been the shopping equivalent of a drive-by mugging.

"*Cuanto bal-e?*" I asked Toby, between mouthfuls of cock

and chips.

"Gotta speak the lingo," he explained. "Don't wanna sound like a tourist! Instead of asking *'Cuanto es?'*, like 'How much is it?', I go with *'Cuanto bal-e?'* – 'What's it worth?'"

Toby, bless him, was still a Londoner at heart.

Flying Solo

The next morning, just like that, Toby was gone. Officially he was trying to drum up volunteers for Santa Martha by visiting hostels around Quito and talking to backpackers. I happened to know that he had a somewhat different agenda. His plan was to visit one of Johnny's friends who lived on an estate nearby – and had an extremely hot daughter. After that he was off to Quito, with Hot Daughter in tow if all went according to plan. Either way I wasn't invited, as someone had to stick around to feed the animals over the weekend. I guess he'd been fretting away, alone at the refuge, itching to blow off steam on a night out in the capital but unable to leave until some brave soul arrived to take up the slack in his absence. It goes without saying that I was nervous. The whole place seemed on the brink of collapsing into chaos at any moment. Toby took it all in his stride, calmly solving problem after problem with infallible common sense. On the feed he always knew when an animal was about to bolt, and always had a spare limb ready to hook them back inside. It was a hard act to follow – the man was some kind of psychic octopus.

On the upside I was really looking forward to making friends with all the animals, and bribing them with an extra large dollop of food seemed like a good way to start. I sneaked an extra fifteen minutes in bed. It felt decadent simply because it was illicit. Toby wasn't a slave driver, but rather one of those depressingly well-motivated people whose obvious dedication either inspired others to leap out of bed full of enthusiasm for the day ahead, or made them feel lazy and guilty for not being so inspired. I tended to alternate between the two positions depending on how sore I was from the previous day's exertions.

By the time I left the volunteer house the mixing bowl of thick fruity mush was already sitting on the doorstep of Johnny's house. Oops! Evidently Johnny's wife Brenda was also the dedicated sort.

The round started with a circuit of the animals nearest the house. I tucked the bowl under one arm and made my way down the path towards the cages. In the first cage on the right (after passing the sleek black truck parked in Johnny's drive) lived a creature called a kinkajou. It was adorable. It was a big ball of fur with eyes. I was in love with it from the beginning. How could anyone not be? The thing was almost entirely eyes! Such enormous, soulful eyes. its natural defence against predators was to be so cute that they couldn't bear to eat it.

As I leant down to reach through the low door for his food bowl, the open cave of my fleece must have looked very inviting. With no warning he scrabbled straight over to me and climbed inside!

I nearly crapped myself.

Panic! How could I contain him? If he dropped through the bottom of my fleece he'd be on the ground and away. And how sharp were his claws anyway, separated from the delicate skin of my stomach by only a thin t-shirt?

I dropped the food bowl and clapped both hands round my waist to hold the bottom of the fleece tightly closed. Then I risked a look down the neck hole.

A huge pair of eyes stared calmly back at me from the

shadows. He'd curled up in the pouch created by me leaning forwards, and was peering out through the neck hole. I think he liked it there.

"Hey little fella, you scared me for a minute!"

The kinkajou said nothing.

"Wait till I tell Toby about this, eh? What do you think he'll say?"

No reply. He just blinked at me.

"Well, I think you should go back in your cage, you know? Much as I like having you in there."

He reproved me with those enormous eyes.

"Sorry! I've got to feed you though. And pretty soon it'll start to smell in there…"

Nestled comfortably in his warm, dark den, the kinkajou had no intention of going anywhere.

I gradually bent lower, tipping the neck of my fleece back towards the open cage door. At the same time I moved my hands up, pushing the little beastie up and out. His head emerged under my chin. I could feel him looking around by the tickling of his fur on my neck. He must have taken stock of the options and realised there were none. Obviously sulking, he clambered slowly out past my collar and back down into his house. All of a sudden I felt a bit guilty. Surely this poor creature just wanted to be loved? Keeping my eyes firmly on him I scooped a big spoonful of food into his dish.

"I've given you a bit extra, okay?" I told him. He looked back at me forlornly.

"I'll come and see you again at four. I promise."

As if to show what he thought of promises from humans he turned his back on me and started rooting through his breakfast. What a loveable little critter. He was first on my list to kidnap when I had to go home.

Twenty minutes later, and only halfway through the feed, I spotted a wayward coatamundi making yet another bid for freedom. It had reached the patch of grass that lay in between all the cages. Rather stupidly they always chose to flee the same way. It certainly made my job easier, though God knows how they survived in the wild. At the grass it had paused, nose bending frantically, to analyse its new surroundings.

I picked the truculent fella up by the scruff of the neck and returned him to his enclosure. His blind mate was still stumbling about looking for the hole. I filled it with earth from the cage floor and stomped it down with my boots, but it was a temporary measure at best. If these guys kept digging eventually they were going to get away.

"Please," I implored them, "not until Toby gets back!"

At least food would keep them occupied for now. I knelt down and dropped a ladleful of chunky goodness on their feeding shelf, expecting them to mob the bowl as usual. But the blind coati approached me cautiously, and began to snuffle around my face. This close I could see how the opaque disc in both little eyes nearly filled them. Poor critter! He twitched his long, bendy nose at me. Was there ever a valid evolutionary reason for such a bendy nose? Unless a comedy appearance ranked high on the list of reasons not to be eaten by big beasties. His nose was soft and wet, and tickled. I stayed perfectly still as he came closer. It was a moment of beautiful intimacy, being delicately probed by that long, slightly furry proboscis.

Then it was over and the nose retreated.

Leaving a great big glob of snot on my forehead.

Ahhh…!

Staring into the parrot cage was the closest thing I can imagine to being on an acid trip. It was a kaleidoscope of colours – huge red birds, bright blue and yellow ones, and darting around at high speed were flocks of smaller parrots of such a brilliant green it looked like they would glow in the dark. Everything was in constant motion, to the point where it was impossible to count them. Toby, when pressed, had put the number between twenty and thirty – give or take five or ten. Possibly not including all the small ones. Trees and planks and perches were everywhere. There were dozens of plastic bowls scattered around, some filled with filthy water, others filled with wet parrots. And if it was difficult to make sense of the view from the outside, inside was… well, it was an experience.

I hadn't ventured more than a couple of steps into the cage when I felt something land on my head. I could feel tiny pinpricks as the talons sought purchase in my scalp, but it didn't *hurt* as such. It tingled. By the time I reached the first empty dish I was already wearing at least half a dozen parrots.

The squawking was deafening.

"A lot of them were being kept as pets when they were rescued, so they're quite affectionate," Toby had told me. "Of course, some of them aren't so friendly…"

Two of the fluoro-green birds were bickering over the best perch on my shoulder. I suddenly wanted very much to regain control over my head. With a parrot of indeterminate emotional state firmly attached I didn't feel like I could move much. I really didn't want to give him cause to hold on any tighter. Both my hands had parrots on them. As did my feet. In fact a red and green chap was trying to climb up my jeans using claws and his beak. I didn't dare shake him off, but I also didn't like the idea of him climbing my groin in the same fashion, particularly after he dug into my knee for better footing. "Oww!" The scarlet macaw on my other shoulder was pecking at my ear. Time to go.

I slopped food into every dish within sight and bent down for the huge water bottle I'd been hauling around. Tried to keep my body mostly upright as I did so. Bend from the knees! There was no longer a parrot on my knee anyway.

He was playing with the zipper on my flies. By hooking the tip of his beak into the little hole on the end, he could jerk it up and down with a flick of his head. I had a horrible feeling he'd done that before. And been rewarded with a fat pink worm...

Run away! The dishes were clean, filled with cool fresh water. That encouraged a few birds to leave me, to fight for the right to bathe in their water dishes. Almost instantly there was a handful of clean parrots and all-new filthy water, which I grudgingly replaced. Claws were tightening in my scalp. About now I started to notice patches of wetness on myself – warmish liquid was trickling down my ear, my neck and my forehead. Realistically it was one of two bodily fluids; one of theirs, or one of mine. Neither was a comforting thought. So I made for the exit. I had to offer the parrot-laden parts of myself up to various areas of mesh surrounding the door, and most of my passengers reluctantly got off. They seemed to know the drill. But the big guy on my head wouldn't budge until I walked out, running the top of my head along the low wooden door frame. He took the hint and clamped onto the wire above the door with his beak. A fairly angry screech followed me as I ducked out and dragged the door shut behind me. I patted my head and shoulders and twisted around to check the back of my legs for stowaways. All clear! What a relief. Nothing on my ass. And I wasn't bleeding from a series of shallow head wounds. I had mixed feelings about that one.

Feeding the parrots had been one of my biggest worries. Just getting in and out without losing anyone was traumatic enough. But the cage itself looked as though two ten-year-old girls had put it together for a school project, and then run out of time and had to rush the ending. To put it another way, it was crap. I'd kept this observation to myself so far and was half expecting to pay for my lack of conviction by haemorrhaging parrots the entire weekend. Those beaks were so powerful and the cage mesh… tinfoil? If they didn't get out sooner, they'd surely be gone later. But hopefully on Toby's shift.

The rest of the feed went without incident. I don't think I could have handled anything else! Every time I opened a cage there was a chance that its occupant would make a break for it. I had to open all of them in turn, a task which demanded the use of both hands. The only way to manage it was to place the enormous bowl of food on the floor between my feet, freeing my hands to work whatever bizarre system had been chosen to fasten any given door. Bolts, twists of wire, elaborate constructions involving wooden toggles, chains, hoops and latches – the complexity of the lock generally reflected the cleverness of the creature within. So with cage successfully opened, and my vulnerable body plugging the gap between occupant and freedom, I was then faced with the inevitable dilemma – the food bowl was still on the floor. I couldn't pick it up without revealing that square window of opportunity for a few perilous seconds. And bugger me if the animals didn't all know it! Whether they merited a clothes peg for a lock or something more suited to a bank vault.

All things considered, it was a fairly eventful morning.

It was going to be an eventful day as well.

Lesson from a Bright Spark

Work didn't simply stop in Toby's absence. It just became less comprehensible. With the feed finally over I presented myself at Johnny's door, and was duly handed over to the gentle ministrations of Jimmy.

Jimmy, with an impressive though utterly unintelligible monologue, and much exaggerated gesturing with appropriate tools, informed me that today he was going to teach me to weld. Actually I think he was expecting me to weld spontaneously, as though I'd always known how to but had never really had the opportunity to prove it. I fervently wished for Toby to reappear before I managed to set myself alight.

I followed Jimmy into the garage, which he called the '*galpón*', and watched as he switched the welding machine on. It was the size and shape of a battered fridge, and looked like it had existed in this space since before humankind crawled out of the swamps, coughed up green slime and breathed air for the first time. Jimmy didn't seem to comprehend the phrase 'health and safety violation'.

He pulled on a thick steel mask, knelt over one of the bars which were to become a door for our newly-constructed deer cage, and welded it. The machine buzzed, there was a massive shower of sparks and an intensely bright light for about half a second.

Jimmy raised his visor and grinned at me. Then he shifted over to another section of bar, lowered his visor and aimed his welding iron at the next target. Another deadly explosion of sparks and he seemed satisfied. "Good?" he asked, in Spanish.

"*Sí, sí*," I replied.

So he dropped the welder, took off his mask and handed it to me. "Like that!" he said, pointing to his handiwork. "Careful!" he added. "Very hot!" And then he left.

I eyed the welding machine squatting lethally in the corner. I was supposed to just start using this thing? I edged to the doorway and glanced out. Jimmy was nowhere in sight. I had a nasty feeling he wasn't coming back. The newly-welded metal bar was still glowing dangerously. An evil hum came from the ancient machine. I could tell it was taunting me. Death stood in the corner sharpening his scythe.

I've never been particularly good with electricity. I wonder sometimes if it's got it in for me. I was eight when I had my first direct contact with electricity. We had our first computer – a Sinclair ZX Spectrum, the last word in home computing in the 80s. It was grey, it was sleek, and it had more processing power than a sandwich toaster, though not by much. All I wanted to use it for was annihilating triangular green aliens with my triangular green spaceship. Pretty much everything was triangular and green back then. My sister was more keen on an excessively dull spelling game, so when she finally offered to try her hand at saving green world from the triangular menace I leapt to her assistance. To start a new game we had to turn the computer off and on again. I gave the wall socket a damn good booting but the switch had long since succumbed to such violent treatment (so far we'd managed to conceal this act of destruction from our parents). It didn't normally present a problem – all we had to do was pull the plug out. But man that was a tough plug! Like a gay man in the Iraqi army it had absolutely no intention of coming out. I pulled, heaved, hauled… no way. There was a very slight chance it had been accidentally-on-purpose glued in the last time I was on the computer. So I went to the kitchen and grabbed a fork.

In my defence, I was very young.

I stuck the fork in behind the plug and began to pry it out. I was doing quite well – it was about halfway out when the fork connected the live and earth pins and a massive jolt threw me across the room. I think I hit the far wall, stuck there for a moment, and then slid slowly down it like a cartoon character. Mum was less than happy when my sister's screams brought her to the scene. How she got the fork out of the socket I don't know, but she kept it as a memento of the very first time I nearly killed myself. It looks quite normal except for the middle, which is a melted, twisted black scar.

As I said, in my defence, I was very young. Of course I was a couple of years older the next time I did it. In my defence, I'm also pretty stupid.

There wasn't anything else for it. I carefully picked up the welding torch by the slightly less red-hot end. I considered how completely unprepared I was for my imminent death. Then I pulled the mask over my face and looked at the metal in front of me. I couldn't see a thing. The little window in the mask was completely opaque. How the hell was I supposed to weld? I opened the window and peered out. Aha! Now I could see what I was doing. I had to bring the tip of the welding iron in my left hand into contact with the precise spot on the metal framework in front of me. At the same time I had to resist the urge to brace myself for the fireworks by leaning on the metal – the welder worked by shooting a shitload of electricity through it and I had no guarantee that it wouldn't fry me in the process if I was touching it at the time. I took a deep, calming breath, and carefully lowered the iron. There was a massive burst of sparks as the two metals met and annihilated each other. I cringed back and blinked frantically. The image of white-hot metal was burned into my retinas. It was a few seconds before I could see properly again, and even then there were purplish blurs dancing round the edge of my vision. So that was why the window in the mask was so dark! Bugger. Shaking my head in a vain attempt to scatter the sunspots, I resolved to be more careful. I closed my tiny window this time and lowered the torch again. I missed. Braced for an explosion, or a violent death by electrocution, I felt nothing at all. I tried again, waving the torch around in what I was sure was the right area. It was no good. Frustrated, I opened the mask window again to see what had gone wrong. Nothing much it seemed – I'd just missed the target by a couple of centimetres. No problem. I corrected my mistake and was rewarded with a blinding flash of light. My eyeballs cooked in their sockets as I squeezed them shut in reflex. The afterimage glowed before my eyelids like a miniature sun. "Arrrghh!" I gave voice to my pain and annoyance. "Mother FUCKER!"

Calm. Be calm, I thought. I have to master this.

Closing my eyes and breathing rapidly through my nose I swung the torch at its next intended target. By pure chance it connected squarely, and I felt rather than saw the resulting pyrotechnics. YES! Success. I had welded! Perhaps now I was a man. I risked a quick look at my handiwork. A big hole was all that greeted my streaming eyes. The same chance that had guided my torch into contact with the metal had convinced it to separate instead of uniting – where I had hoped to see two neatly combined steel bars I saw only a gaping hole in one bar.

The other remained untouched.

Triple bugger with a big chunk of bugger on top. And a side order of shit arse bollocks.

I was not happy. How could this possibly be so difficult? Squatting malevolently in the corner, the welding machine just hummed to itself in smug satisfaction.

It was the better part of an hour before I emerged from the *galpón*, admitting as much defeat as victory. I'd managed to create a half-assed framework, badly welded in almost the right number of places, and scarred, pitted and with holes burnt in all the others. It looked like it had picked a fight with a pissed off dragon. But it didn't matter, as I could hardly see the thing anyway.

Amazingly I'd resisted the urge to kick the stuffing out of the welding machine. I'd only have broken my foot. That thing was tougher and far more dangerous than me. Probably older. And possibly smarter. I collapsed in a stripy hammock on the front porch. I hoped Toby was having fun. Because next weekend that son of a bitch could learn a special skill while I seduced hot chicks in Quito.

An hour later I awakened to darkness.

Confusion was my first reaction. It was dark already? But no, this was something else, this darkness – the total absence of light; solar, electric, starlight – nothing. Aha! Because my eyes were still shut. Cautiously I tried to open them. Nothing happened. My eyes stayed tightly shut. Not a chink of light streamed in, though I could feel the sun warm on my face. I tried again with the same result. I couldn't open my eyes at all.

My second reaction was panic. I groped around me for some clue to what was wrong. All I discovered was that I was still sitting in the hammock, and that getting out with my eyes shut was going to be bloody difficult. I eased a leg out and put my foot on the floor. Contact with the ground helped to restore my sense of normality. Okay, so I couldn't see. I could still move all my other bits – just my eyelids seemed to be broken. I explored them with my fingertips and confirmed that they were still there. A small relief, that. It meant that there was a chance I could open them and restore my sight. I tried gingerly to push my eyelids upwards.

Pain was the third reaction.

Searing bolts of white heat lanced through my skull. I jerked my fingers away and squeezed my eyes shut tighter against the pain. Slowly it subsided, and the accompanying strobes of colour faded from my vision. Blackness reached up to me, cooling, soothing, and I decided not to fight it.

When next I woke the sun on my face felt less intense. I was probably burnt to hell, but I was far more concerned for my eyes. Experimentally I tried to open them. A tiny chink of light seeped in under one eyelid, but it was enough. My eyelids felt huge. It felt as though I had a thin layer of crushed glass trapped beneath them. Even the tiniest of movements was like scouring my eyeballs with sandpaper. Closing them more tightly seemed to offer a temporary relief, but I couldn't keep it up. A million tiny pins pricked my eyeballs as I opened them to the crack of light again.

I could see. Not much, and only for a fraction of a second, followed by several minutes of intense, pulsing headache. But I could see. I lurched out of the hammock, determined to die in my bed if necessary. It was only when I reached the dorm room that I realised I either had to climb six feet into my top bunk or shift everything I owned from the bottom one. Neither appealed. What I still couldn't cope with, was what the fuck had happened to me? I was terrified.

I sat heavily on the edge of the bed. Something square lodged its corner between my buttocks. My dictionary. And my salvation! With it I could communicate my pain to the only people around. And so for the next hour, after staggering back to the haven of my hammock, I studied. Each time I opened my left eye a crack it felt like someone was pushing a knitting needle into it. Yet I could see with it, just enough between my shielding eyelashes (for which I have never before, or since, been so grateful) to make out a word from the book held point blank against my face. Slowly a sentence took form in my mind which exactly expressed the difficulty I was experiencing. *"No puedo* (I cannot, a classic from my audio course) *abrir* (to open, infinitive verb) *mi ojos* (my eyes, plural)." I had it! With this one phrase I could solve all my problems. I only had to find someone to tell.

I made it out of the hammock, out of the gate, down the drive and up to Johnny's front door. I knocked, and after a short while Brenda answered. *"Hola?"* she greeted me, surprised.

"Hola," I responded, then rolled out my hard-won phrase. *"No puedo abrir mi ojos!"* It was the make-or-break moment.

"Ojos?" she asked. I imagined her tapping her own eyes.

"Sí, SÍ! Ojos!" I was excited, and desperate.

"Tienes una problema con sus ojos?"

"SÍ!"

"Ah..." She seemed to have some understanding of my problem. Maybe because my eyes were screwed up so tightly my cheeks ached. She can't have believed that was normal behaviour, even for someone from England. I heard her bustling around the kitchen for a few seconds, then she pressed a cloth soaked in icy-cold water to my face. Though I understood nothing of the accompanying commentary of presumably helpful advice, her tone and demeanour was the first indication that I was going to get better. If she'd had a volunteer permanently blinded within a week of arriving I

figured she'd have been a little more frantic. That kind of stuff almost never looks good when you're in the middle of a volunteer recruitment drive.

The light was starting to fade as I made my way slowly back to the volunteer house. It was a total walking distance of about twenty five metres. I shuffled it in less than five minutes, which was a feat unto itself. I made it as far as the hammock, and rested there for a while. But the temperature was rapidly cooling, and soon I would have to be inside, or face freezing to death. Not that it was any warmer inside, but at least there were blankets.

I was sitting in a chair in the lounge wearing three jumpers when Johnny knocked on the door. He looked concerned. I almost felt guilty. I mean, I'd been freaked out to start with – blindness was a totally new experience for me, and not one I was anxious to continue. But it was hardly his fault. The last thing I wanted was for him to think he'd picked the wrong guy, and to regret letting me come here. I had to convince him that I was cool. The only thing I could think of was to underplay how scared I was. My eyes? So what! It happened all the time... well maybe not, but there was no reason to let him think that I was pathetic.

"*Tienes una problema?*" he asked straight away. "*Con sus ojos?*"

I was thrilled that I understood what he was saying. "*Sí,*" I replied, then laid out my phrase for him. It was certainly earning its mileage. Johnny nodded and held up a little bottle. Just the shape of it screamed eye drops. I could have kissed him. Better not though – given the slight misunderstanding when we first met. I might really scare the poor bloke.

Sunday was also spent in the hammock. My eyes were still filled with glass, but it was soft glass with all the rough edges ground off. Probably ground off on my eyeballs, judging by the amount of juice and gunk that had seeped out of them during the night. My pillow was a hideous sticky mess. I'd had to peel my face off the unpleasantness before even daring to try opening my eyes. It was several minutes before I managed it. They were sealed with a crust of something so unspeakable that I won't even try to describe it. Eventually I steeled myself against the hideous ripping sensation and prised them open. It made me want to vomit, but it worked. Well, kind of. My vision was like something out of a poorly-animated computer game. I could see out of the very bottom of my eyes, and light of any kind hurt like a head-butt from a filing cabinet. I took my music out to the veranda, wincing at the metallic scream as I dragged the front door open. Was it louder because the empty house was so much quieter? Or had the loss of my vision honed my other senses to an almost superhuman sensitivity?

Or maybe the door was just fucked.

I lounged, eyes blissfully closed, listening to soothing music. Had someone complained that I was sleeping in the middle of the day, for the first time in my life I could respond honestly that I was 'just resting my eyes'.

The firm step of booted feet nearby brought me back to wakefulness. Jimmy stood over me, looking down at my tranquil form in the hammock. For a guy less than five feet tall it must have been a novel experience to look down at anyone.

"*Qué pasa?*" he asked with his usual sly smile.

"*No puedo abrir mi ojos,*" I told him, ignoring the fact that it was by now a blatant lie – I was looking at him as I spoke, albeit through the smallest of squints.

"*Ah,*" he responded knowingly, then launched into a rapid explanation in Spanish, of what I presume was his innocence and lack of responsibility for the accident. Then he studied my face pityingly. "Not look," he suggested with a gesture of his hand towards an imaginary welding scene between us. They were the first words of English I'd ever heard from him, and from the effort he'd put into pronouncing them, probably carefully learned and rehearsed over breakfast.

"Yes," I wanted to say in a burst of sarcastic bitchery, "no look at fire! Now tell me not to try and eat the fucking thing!" But he didn't speak English, so there was no point. Or was there?

"Fucking idiot!" I grinned back at him. "Teach me to weld in ten minutes? You fucking blinded me you arsehole! I'd gouge your eyes out to see how you liked it, but it'd only make you prettier, mutherfucker!" I said it all with a smile.

Jimmy smiled back, seeming to share the joke. "Fuck!" he agreed.

"If only I could grin like a fucking idiot when I didn't understand something, I'd be happier too!" I pointed out. Then "Fuck!" I added, waving my hand in front of my eyes for emphasis.

"Ha!" Jimmy laughed. 'Fuck.' The universal gift of the English language to foreign nationals.

And with that everything was okay again. Jimmy wandered off, shaking his head and chuckling under his breath, no doubt at the ineptitude of foreigners and his easy mastery of their language.

I chalked up a rather childish victory to myself on equally flimsy grounds, and sank back into my hammock. I closed my eyes leisurely, then partially opened them again just to be sure. Never take anything like this for granted again, I told myself. It could be taken from me so easily. There was a deep philosophical point to be explored here, about my life, youth and fitness, and how to make the most of it before it was gone. But I really couldn't be arsed with that right now. Instead I yawned and dozed off with the heat of the sun on my face.

And bless their hearts, my employers didn't forget me – Johnny sent Brenda over with an enormous plate of fried chicken and rice for my lunch.

It was much later when Toby arrived back from his sojourn in Quito. "Alright mate!" he greeted me jovially as he strode in the door. I was sitting in the lounge in the last of the light, testing my eyes on my Spanish dictionary. The weekend's events had strongly encouraged me to learn more. If I had to explain in court that I'd accidentally inserted a welding iron into Jimmy's rectal passage I wanted the judge to know that it wasn't due to a lack of cultural sensitivity.

"I see the deer's arrived for our new enclosure. All makes sense now doesn't it!" Toby was relentless in his upbeat attitude. Obviously he'd had a good time in the capital.

"Erm... it does? I didn't know."

"Haven't you seen it? It's a mouse deer! About the size of a big rabbit! I've never seen one before, it's cute as hell." He gave me a second to digest the news. "So, how's it going?"

"Not too bad," I told him, "but not great. You know, a few problems."

"Oh!" It stopped him in his tracks, the cheerful wind stilled in his sails. "What, um, what went wrong, like?"

"Well..." I couldn't decide whether to be dramatic, and seek sympathy, or be subtle, understated, and earn admiration for my quiet strength in the face of adversity. Sympathy won. All I'd wished for throughout the ordeal was for my mum to be there. I guess I still had a lot of growing up to do.

"I blinded myself welding."

"What?"

"I blinded myself. Jimmy showed me how to weld, for

about ten minutes, then made me do it. I burnt my eyeballs 'cause I couldn't close the mask and still see what I was doing, so I looked right at the light. I lay in the hammock to chill out, and when I woke up I couldn't see at all. Shit, it was like my eyelids were completely glued shut! I was really fucking scared, you know, but after a few hours I could just open my eyes a crack. So I looked in my dictionary for how to say "I can't open my eyes" in Spanish, then I crawled over to Johnny's house and told Brenda. She sent Johnny round with some eye drops. I can just about open them now, but it still hurts like hell. It's like my eyes are full of glass." That seemed to cover it. "Man it hurts!" I added for emphasis.

Toby was silent for a few moments, digesting this information before commenting. His answer, when it came, was fairly concise.

"Shit mate, that sucks. Anything else?"

"Oh! Well... the coatis escaped again, but I caught them."

"Nice! Good job mate."

I had childishly hoped to elicit a bit more sympathy, but it didn't seem to be forthcoming. I clearly wasn't impressing the desperate nature of the accident on him. I tried a new tack. "It's really fucking scary, not being able to see. I didn't know if it was temporary, or if I'd be blind forever. You know what I mean?" I prompted.

"Yeah," came the reply, "I did the same thing myself the first time I welded. Hurts like shit don't it?"

I was lost for words. Well, almost. "Er... yeah, it does!"

"Nothing else though?"

"Um... no, that's it. Did I mention I couldn't see for two days?"

Toby considered me with a slight smile.

"Did you use the mask?"

"No, I wanted to see the pretty colours," I retorted.

"Ha! You know the thing to do?"

I had a nasty feeling that I did. "What's that?" I humoured him.

He did a fair approximation of Jimmy's mock sincerity. Gesturing at the ground between us, he fixed me with a gaze full of feigned concern.

"Is Very Bright... No Look!"

A Close Shave...

To me, a trip to Tambillo town meant food. There was a tiny bakery which sold bread rolls and an equally minute dairy shop which sold a kind of weak-tasting, soggy white cheese. I was living almost exclusively on these two products. Shopping with Toby had been such a sensory overload that I hadn't really spared much attention for what he was buying. A day later I'd awoken to the realisation that we still didn't own any meat – in a country where the staple diet was chicken and rice, living with a vegetarian would be a singularly bland experience. We had an infinite variety of fruit of course and plenty of oatmeal. Hell, we might as well be eating straight from the animals' feed bowl. It suited the monkeys. But alas, Toby's shopping list had been utterly devoid of anything I consider food.

He'd bought a carrier bag full of chillies though. Seriously, the man was obsessed. He put them in his cheese and bread rolls. He put them in his rice. He put them in my rice. At times he put so many in that they outnumbered the rice. I could tell from his face when he was eating his cornflakes that he was wondering whether or not a dash of chilli would spice them up.

So when Toby decided he needed a haircut (and insinuated that I might be similarly in need), I jumped at the chance. A hike down and, later, back up again was adventure enough by itself, since it involved leaping crevasses in the road, climbing several fences and trying to walk for almost an hour at a forty five degree angle to the slope. It was murder on the thighs. At the bottom was the short road into Tambillo town – and on that road sat the Empanada Woman.

What is an *empanada*? Now that's a tough one to describe. It's… some kind of substance, not unlike Play-Dough, deep-fried, covered with sugar and filled with cheese. Sounds disgusting eh? But they tasted like heaven. Especially since there was no burning sensation associated with eating them. I'd tried them twice and was already considering offering the woman who sold them hard cash for the recipe. She was so friendly, sitting on the step behind her pavement stall. She had merry eyes and deeply etched laughter lines, and skin-tight blue jeans. Probably a stunner twenty years ago – or maybe five? Ages were almost impossible for me to guess as I had no basis for comparison. The Empanada Woman was weathered in body, but young in heart. She always smiled and asked simple questions like 'How are you?' and 'How are the animals?' This meant I could actually formulate answers, and feel good about myself in the process. I guessed that Toby had taken other volunteers to sample her delights (by which I mean her empanadas!).

With the late afternoon sun on my face I strolled casually along the street next to Toby. Stallholders and the odd passer-by threw us an occasional "*Buenos días!*" Across from us stone steps led down to a series of formal gardens arranged around a central monument. Together they formed a square, bordered on all sides by the road, and the whole lot sloped sharply away from us. The buildings that lined the square formed Tambillo town – apart from the gas station on the Quito road and the payphone shop on the street leading back up to it, there really wasn't much else. It was peaceful, especially at this hour, and quaint. Every wall needed paint, every shutter repairing, but the people seemed relaxed and friendly. I was starting to like Tambillo for more than just its sodden cheese.

We ducked into the hairdresser's minuscule shop, and a slim, middle-aged woman with smiling eyes wasn't there. She was in the shop next door, chatting happily to its owner with no fear at all of what was happening in her own little place. Which was strange, because there was a young lad with half-cut hair still sitting in the padded armchair and picking his nose in front of the mirror. Our presence was clearly the reminder she needed though, and she quickly scooted in through the door making the place feel quite crowded. She seemed scaled to fit the room at about four foot nine, and as he stood up, apparently satisfied with what I still maintain was an incomplete haircut, the boy proved to be equally small. I watched him leave, fascinated by his sense of style. Or maybe he could only afford the first stage and was having his hair done in instalments.

Toby took his turn first, chatting amiably to the young woman. She seemed very friendly. It didn't take long, largely because he emerged from the chair unchanged to the naked eye. Apparently he'd had something cut off somewhere, and I decided to pursue the matter no further than that. I was starting to believe his faded red baseball cap was actually grafted to his skull anyway, so it seemed unlikely that his life would be changed overly much by the absence of such a microscopic amount of hair.

He nipped next door to buy us a couple of beers, leaving me alone and within clear speaking distance of the hairdresser. I gave her a wide smile, then carefully studied the lino floor.

"*Something something something?*" she asked. I recognised by the rise in her voice at the end that it was a question. I glanced at the door. Toby was still very inconsiderately buying me a beer. I groped for an appropriate response, and came up with a technique I'd been falling back on more and more recently.

"*Sí,*" I replied.

She seemed satisfied.

Then as if by magic Toby was back, handing me a nearly-cold beer, joking with the hairdresser, and beckoning me forward for my turn under the scissors. I was feeling a little nervous as I parked my ass in the chair. I really hoped she wasn't fond of small talk. I was liking silence.

Toby asked me what I wanted.

"Just a bit shorter, really – short back and sides, nice and tidy. Not too short though," I warned him.

I still don't know the exact Spanish words he used, and I'm sure he doesn't remember them either, so I'm probably paraphrasing here. He turned to the hairdresser with the barest trace of a grin. "Shave it all off," he said.

And she did.

"Yeah, I stitched up a few of my mates like that back home," he elaborated, as we sat on the kerb outside the hairdresser's with our beers. "They always say 'Don't stitch me up, right?', so I persuade them it'll look great."

I couldn't stop running my hand over the back of my head. At least in a couple of weeks, I thought, I would be able to clean my nails this way.

"They must think you're an asshole," I diplomatically remarked, careful to keep myself out of the equation.

"Yeah," he agreed.

"Well, I don't care," I lied.

"It's easier in the mornings! And easier to wash shit out of!" he reminded me.

"Yeah. True." I wasn't actually planning on rubbing my head in much shit regardless of the length of my hair. Toby himself seemed to have managed to avoid the problem of a head covered in crusty shit despite having hair infinitely longer than mine was now.

The hair on my arse also never seemed to suffer from this particular problem, despite it too now being considerably longer than that on my head. I was clearly thinking way too much about this situation. But at least it was taking my mind off the shape of my skull.

We returned our empty beer bottles and set off back through the town. His hair stirring gracefully in the wind, me staggering jerkily along behind him in a state of shock. Letting out an occasional anguished moan. Two feet taller than anyone else around, with a pallid bald head the shape of a dented light bulb. I wondered if any of the locals had ever seen *Frankenstein*.

Arrival of Ashley

It was a typically beautiful afternoon when the monstrous 4x4 taxi rolled down the driveway (though as usual it had rained briefly and intensely in the morning – this seemed to be the standard weather pattern for the area). The sky smelled of growing things, and vaguely of poo since Danielo had recently driven the cattle back up the drive to pasture. It was the perfect day to welcome our first new volunteer to the centre.

Ashley had a cheeky face and a cheeky manner to go with it. She was *very* Canadian. She looked Canadian – funky short hair framed twinkling eyes and a mischievous smile. She was small, but lively and energetic, a barely-contained bundle of enthusiasm and fun. Don't try to sleep with her, I told myself, at least not yet. It'll only complicate things...

I did try to befriend her however, and it wasn't too hard. She was talkative and likeable, and her accent made her sound like she was on TV. And perhaps due to the continent she was from, where in my opinion people give themselves a lot more credit just for being themselves, she didn't have quite the same sense of awe that I had. I wasn't afraid of Johnny as such, and certainly not of Toby, but I held them both on a kind of mental pedestal. They were creatures of a higher order than me, bosses and bearers of responsibility. They were to be appeased, joked with perhaps, but never taken for granted, never challenged.

Ashley was rather more sensible about things.

"Jeez it's kinda boring here," she pointed out on her first night in the house. "Whadda you guys do for fun?"

I leapt to Toby's defence. "We play chess!"

"Right." Ashley wasn't impressed.

"There's a TV," Toby said, "and I've got Johnny's old DVD player in my room."

"Oh! You get any TV up here?"

"Uh… not really. It's mostly just good for DVDs."

"Y'got any DVDs?"

"Well… no."

"Great. So you play a lot of chess then."

"We learn Spanish too," I interjected. Which was almost the truth. I'd redoubled my efforts after my near-blinding – but only for about two hours.

Toby had a better answer though. "You can get DVDs real cheap at the Sunday market in Machachi," he explained.

This was totally new information to me. "WHAT?" I demanded. "There's a market? In 'Machachi'? What's it like?"

"Oh, massive mate. Fucking huge! You should go."

He was only telling me this now? Then another thought occurred. "Is there food?"

"Oh yeah mate, everything. Meat, weird barbecue shit, cheese fritters. Definitely worth a look. You just take the bus from the bottom of the mountain, opposite direction to Quito. Takes about fifteen minutes."

Sudden excitement gripped me. No more cabin fever weekends. No more boredom. I could escape to the market, see things and buy things and eat things. Eat meat!

"Wanna go?" Ashley asked me.

I could have kissed her.

Not now! I reminded myself. Bad Tony! Maybe on Sunday.

Room Service

There comes a time in every man's life when he says to himself "Jesus Christ! I'm about to get eaten by a bear!" For me it came only moments after I sallied nervously into Osita's enclosure for the first time. There was silence. Then there was a thundering noise – the sound of a heavy body crashing through the undergrowth at high velocity.

The bear charged from the bushes towards me, enormous, unstoppable, an unmistakable glint of malice in her eyes. Then she caught sight of Johnny, skidded hastily to a halt, turned around and legged it back the way she'd come. He helped her on her way with a carefully timed rubber welly-boot up the bum.

"Don't take any shit from this bear," Toby translated the accompanying explanation.

In fact Osita was in a playful mood, owing to it being a long time since she'd had so many visitors. With three volunteers now, Johnny felt he had the manpower for a long overdue clean-up operation. So we'd gathered a stack of tools and one by one squeezed through the open gate into the bear enclosure. I felt a shiver of excitement run down my spine as I crossed the threshold. This is why I was here! We were explorers, young and unprepared, and about to embark on a mission deep into uncharted territory. The jungle surrounded us, vibrant and alive. Anything could happen!

"Watch out for that big turd, mate." Toby was timely with the warning. "Ugh! It's a runny one. Too much fruit," he added.

I could have done without that knowledge.

Osita's enclosure was our finest. Huge steel posts carrying a powerful electrified fence surrounded well over an acre of untamed wilderness. As with all the larger enclosures at Santa Martha it stretched right down the side of the mountain, giving the territory a dramatic gradient. To stand at the top was to be roughly level with the tree tops halfway down; to reach the gate from the bottom was more akin to climbing than walking.

There was a row of substantial trees running along the top edge, separated from the regular *snap! snap!* of the electric fence by a narrow path. Osita loved to climb these trees, but as she was getting bigger so were they. Between them they presented a worrying escape option. If the bear tried jumping over the fence from a branch she'd either electrocute herself and land on her head, or escape to roam the mountainside until she got shot by an overprotective farmer. Neither were cheery prospects.

After a quick conference with the boss Jimmy and Danielo each climbed a tree and unleashed their fury. They were hacking off the thick, gnarled branches about ten feet from the ground, pruning the great trees like they were bonsai. It took a lot of work.

While Ashley set to cleaning the enclosure, I aimed a hosepipe into the deep concrete bowl on the slope below me and began to turn it back into a pond. Toby was controlling the water from a tap near the gate.

"Spray her!" he shouted at me.

"Eh?" I turned around to find Osita standing a few feet away, contemplating me. She approached another few steps and swatted at my leg with a paw.

"Aw! Are you trying to say hello?" I asked her. She swatted me again, but with a little more force. So I turned the hose on her. Just for a second – but she soon shifted her fat ass! It was great to watch the way she seemed to roll as she ran, galloping like a chubby pony away from the spray. It was, I discovered, one of her favourite games. Which was why no matter how ingenious a device Toby fashioned to use as a plug, the bear always managed to remove it and drain the pond. She just loved having us come back to refill it.

It took forever. By the time it was half full I'd fended off numerous incursions from Osita, occasionally letting her come close enough to snuffle at me, but once the batting game began I'd always chase her off with a blast of water.

The Ecuadorians had decimated the trees by this point. Ashley had been gathering dead-fall from all over the enclosure and looked knackered, struggling uphill with an armful of branches. I felt almost guilty that I'd been stood there relaxing, playing with the bear and daydreaming about us roaming the jungle together as man and bear.

"We've just got to do one more tree, down at the bottom," Toby called to me.

I suddenly wanted very badly to feel like I was of use around here.

"I'll do it!" I shouted.

There were slyly exchanged looks between the real men as I scrambled enthusiastically into the tree.

"NOT this bit," Johnny explained, indicating where a branch extended over the fence. I could see that simply lopping that bit off would flatten the fence completely, quite an expensive mistake for me to make so soon after arriving.

"Cut HERE," I was instructed. Holy shit! They wanted me to take the whole top of the tree off, at an angle that would encourage it to fall inwards instead of out. Well, too late to back out now.

I settled myself on a branch and chopped away at the only point I could reach – a spot just below my dangling legs. I could see Toby cringe every time the machete rebounded from the solid wood. "Don't worry, I'm fine!" I told him. Liar. My hands were killing me, and much faster than they were killing the tree. Each chop split blisters left over from my last encounter with a machete and sent the now familiar vibrations shooting up my arm. I changed hands, which involved a rather trapeze-like draping of myself across the branch I was trying to remove. The plastic handle of the machete was slick with sweat, almost impossible to hold onto. "Sorry!" I told Toby as he handed it back up to me for the third time. "Good job you weren't underneath me, eh?"

And then, when I had almost given up, there came an ominous groan from the wood beneath me. I tensed ready to spring – but nothing happened. My heart beat faster as the machete bit home with a satisfying *thwack!* I was getting much better at this!

"I think it's coming mate!" Toby shouted up.

I heard the creak at exactly the same moment.

I shrieked and leapt from the tree.

Now, I hadn't actually put any thought into what to do with the machete whilst leaping for my life, so as I jumped I instinctively cast it aside to avoid landing on it. Unfortunately 'aside' quite accurately described the patch of ground where Toby, Jimmy and Johnny had been sniggering at my efforts until a moment previously, at which point they all saw the blade coming, shouted "SHIT!" in a variety of languages and flung themselves into the bushes in all directions.

The tree, however, refused to move at all.

"Oh, well, I guess I'll have another go then," I valiantly

suggested after picking myself up. I'm not sure everyone was as keen as I was.

When it did fall, it was with a mighty *CRASH!* I remembered to keep hold of the machete this time, with the result that it buried itself blade-down in the soil mere inches from my feet. What I hadn't remembered was to jump clear of the gigantic branch which landed on top of me, connecting with that part of my anatomy currently uppermost, which happened to be my ass. It was the first time I'd been spanked by a tree.

Revenge, Toby called it. At least it gave the others something to laugh about as they hauled the crooked log off me.

"How's your buttocks?" Toby asked.

"Fine." I said through clenched teeth.

"Wow, that thing properly beat your bum cheeks! You got bitch slapped!"

"I'm okay."

"Really? Coz it looked…"

"Stop looking at my ass!" I told him.

Only my pride was damaged.

Brenda brought some sandwiches down from the house for a late lunch. I'd ravenously devoured half of them sitting on a pile of dead branches when there was a rustle in the bushes. The sound of something heavy heading this way. Suddenly Osita burst from the undergrowth and barrelled straight towards me! She pulled up right next to me, the tip of her nose positively quivering.

Very slowly, I held the last half of my sandwich up to her and she gently took it off me. CHOMP! CHOMP! GULP! And it was gone. And I had a new best friend. She was snuffling noisily now and pawing at my legs. I had to work hard to resist the urge to pet her head like a dog, in case she wasn't *that* friendly. In full sunlight, in the open, I could see that she wasn't really big – just very, very furry. Darkest brown, almost black, all over except for her golden brown nose. A fuzzy ring of the same colour ran around each eye, the distinguishing mark of an Andean spectacled bear. It also gave the appearance of eyebrows, which made her upturned-snout 'begging' look almost impossible to resist. I held up another sandwich and broke it in half. She really was keen on jam!

We collected logs and planks from all over the enclosure to contribute to a new shelter. It was seriously hot work. The enclosure was so steep for us to move around, and terraced either by design or nature. Taking a large chunk of wood from the top all the way to the bottom was a good ten minute mission and incorporated all the major Olympic disciplines – throwing, climbing, jumping, balance – not to mention weightlifting. If the pond had been full we could have added swimming, but Ashley was now aiming the hose into the half-full pool. Damn, it took a long time to fill that thing! As each log arrived at the construction site Toby supervised its assembly to match his grand vision. I was starting to wish I could have grand visions and supervise their assembly while he lugged bloody great lumps of tree halfway down a mountainside. Bloody vegetarians. We'd cut enough off the trees to make a good solid lean-to, with the heavier timber supporting a loose screen of sturdy branches. It wasn't much to look at, but would give our bear somewhere to rest out of the midday sun and it was built with tender loving care. I only hoped she would appreciate all the effort it had cost us.

At long last Johnny pronounced himself satisfied with our labours. The pond was finally full. Ashley looked thrilled. Standing motionless on one end of a plastic hose for the better part of two hours was looking like being the booby prize as far as jobs went around here. Hopefully this would be the first and last time it needed doing. All of the trees had been reduced to a more containment-friendly size – still big enough to be fun for Osita, but not enough to bring her within bear's breadth of the fence. She was fed, watered and delighted with the company. She bounded around the enclosure saying an energetic good-bye as we all squeezed back through the gate. I lingered until last, hoping perhaps for a more personal farewell. Perhaps she'd like to thank me for the sandwiches? But no. I think maybe the jam was responsible for the sudden burst of energy which sent her tearing around the enclosure like a fat hairy footballer who just scored a game-winning goal. I ducked through the gate and stretched my aching muscles on the far side as Johnny wrestled with the ancient padlock.

Suddenly Osita found herself on the same level as her new 'cub-by' house. What would she make of this strange and exciting new structure? All eyes turned to watch her investigate. But Osita had done curious. All day she'd been following us around, poking her nose in and pawing at her new friends. Now she was in the grip of a sugar rush. She charged towards the shelter like a giant furry battering ram, slamming into the log wall, smashing straight through it and bursting out the other side without a pause. Logs the size of an Ecuadorian rained down in her wake. Lesser branches came to rest a more impressive distance away. In a tiny fraction of the time it had taken to build, Osita had reduced the shelter to kindling.

I was gutted. Johnny sighed in his best world-weary manner and trudged up the hill towards the road.

"Ha! She wants you to go back in and fix it," said Ashley.

"Why not?" asked Toby. "You up for it mate?" He clapped me on the shoulder. "Fancy a game of Pick-up Sticks?"

That Bear Ate My Pants!

Machachi and Machita

On Sunday morning, Ashley and I made the epic hike down the mountain. As we came out onto the Quito road a bus was rapidly approaching. So was another one, about twenty feet behind the first. Another was just cresting the ridge about half a mile away. And no doubt three or four had just left.

The first bus slowed vaguely as it approached us. The little sign in the window said 'Machachi'. Judging by the random limbs sticking out of every available window it was pretty full.

"Shall we wait for the next one?" Ashley asked.

"Ha!" was my only reply. It was my duty to heap scorn on such a naive idea – nearly three weeks in the country qualified me as a veteran. I knew we'd be more likely to catch a bus to Mars than to find one with enough space on it to breathe freely.

"*Machachi Machachi Machachi,*" called a skinny young lad leaning out the door. I nodded and waved, and the bus slowed even more. The lad reached out and grabbed my hand as I leapt for the step. He thrust me past him and reached out with his other hand to grab Ashley by the wrist. It was over in a flash – two new passengers picked up within ten feet of each other. Useful kid. Though what the hell he'd have done if we'd been three fat chicks with a pram each is anyone's guess.

I was really excited to be spreading my wings a bit. Granted, I wouldn't be able to spread very much at all until we'd arrived and got off, but I had Ashley with me and we were on an adventure into parts unknown. And I'm not just referring to our neighbours on the bus – although it is true I was being squeezed closer and closer to certain parts of their parts than I really wanted to be.

"*Machachi?*" I croaked at a young girl as the bus pulled up ten minutes later.

"*Sí,*" she replied.

"We're here!" I grabbed Ashley and swam for the door.

We burst from the bus like two big bubbles from a mouthful of chewing gum. The air tasted sweet and body odour-free.

All around us was a bustling market like a scene from a film with a very small bustling market in it. A *very* small market. In fact, if there had been two less stalls I would have called it a hot dog stand. That's when it hit me.

"Ashley, I think this is just a hot dog stand."

And it was.

Not to be deterred, we thoroughly explored both stalls and even gazed at the hot dog stand itself for a moment or two. Then we noticed a petrol station a little further up the road. You'd think we'd have noticed it sooner, what with it being the only building for miles in any direction. We wandered over, looking casual, or at least trying to look casual whilst frantically searching the dictionary for the Spanish equivalent of 'market'.

An ancient little woman held court on the forecourt.

"*Hola,*" Ashley began. "*Dónde está el markaroo?*"

It sounded dubious but it was the best we'd come up with.

"*Mercado? Machachi?*" the old woman asked. She seemed to be the only person there, so all our eggs were in her basket.

"*Sí, sí, Machachi!*" we both chorused.

She gestured down the road in an offhand manner. Intense concentration on her hoarse mumbling paid off when I caught the words "*Diez minutos*".

Only ten minutes further down the main road... if the old dear was to be believed. We set off, keeping to the dusty hard shoulder as there wasn't anywhere else to walk. The road stretched on for miles. The hot dog stand slowly receded behind us. Ten minutes later and the view hadn't changed much. The ten minutes after that brought nothing new either.

Twenty minutes after that...

"I think that old crone lied to us," Ashley said.

I had to agree. "Bollocks to it. Shall we try to flag down a bus?"

Ashley considered. "If we don't we could die of starvation here. Or old age."

A bus was charging towards us at that moment. This was hardly surprising, as buses had been charging past us every thirty seconds or so. For a road to nowhere it sure was busy. We waved. The bus charged past. So did the next three. Apparently we'd discovered the one place in the country that buses actually couldn't stop, either due to some primitive traffic law or, more realistically, because they didn't have good enough brakes.

"We could try cars?" Ashley suggested.

Eventually a shiny blue pickup pulled onto the hard shoulder just ahead of us and we piled into the tray back. On a hot sunny day, through flat green countryside, this was the only way to travel. Almost ten minutes had passed when our driver pulled off the main road and turned into a town. Aha! It occurred to Ashley and me at the same time – ten minutes by car, the old woman had meant. Clearly she hadn't expected anyone to be stupid enough to try to walk down the freeway.

Machachi! The place was an assault on the senses from the moment we squirmed out of the back of the pickup. My nose immediately registered the presence of something frying. In garlic. The air was rich with the aromas of strange and spicy foodstuffs a-cooking! The entire town was thronging with people. Everywhere I looked hung racks of crazy trousers, blotched, striped and tie-dyed in dozens of colours, woolly cardigans to match, and thick, blanket-like ponchos. The scent of leather exuded from stalls selling wallets and belts, only to be overwhelmed by cloying floral perfume from the next stall over. For the first half hour neither of us spoke beyond the occasional exclamation of "Woah!" or "Look at this!". My head was a periscope, spinning from side to side trying to take it all in. Dodgy Spanish pop music blared from a dozen sources. An agonised wail seemed to be the vocal choice of the day, overlaid with rapid beats so heavy they made my teeth vibrate. Everywhere were hats and bags, indecipherable t-shirts, ornaments in glass and china and stone-faced stallholders sweltering in the heat.

It must have taken us an hour to do the first full circuit. Lines of people straggled up every alley, pushing through the narrow corridor between stalls shoulder to shoulder with the line pushing the opposite way. Every so often we'd break out into an open space or a junction with a slightly wider street. In the thinner crowds we could pause for a few seconds to wipe sweat the from our brows (I was dripping like a melting ice lolly) and check our pockets hadn't been picked. Then one or the other of us would choose a direction and we'd plunge into the human stream once more. In one of the slightly more spacious areas we came across an old woman frying little cakes on what looked like a big metal bin lid.

I pointed at one and asked "*Qué?*"

They were cheese. I bought one and ate it. It was like the answer to all my prayers! I bought ten more on the spot and started to cram them into my mouth. Absolutely delicious! Cheesy, maizey, fried thing. Ten for a dollar. Why weren't these things more popular? I looked along the row of stalls ahead and realised that every single one of them was frying cheesy maizey things. Popular enough then, just not in Tambillo.

Even without any meat in it my stomach was feeling a lot happier. The meat, when we came to it, looked a little less appetising than it smelled. Another row of stalls just beyond Fried Cheese Row were the source of the delicious aroma. In front of each stall was the ubiquitous metal bin lid, this time fully ablaze; above it a whole guinea pig was roasting rotisserie style. And when I say whole, I mean whole. Eyes, teeth, claws and tail. The sharp front teeth a sickly yellow and longer than my little finger.

Hm. I'll pass on that, thanks.

We wandered through what looked like an aircraft hangar, full of dripping red body parts bleeding onto the floor and fat men waving cleavers at each other. Flies swarmed over everything in sight. I decided not to buy any meat just yet. I could sense the onset of plague. We hurried out into the daylight once more to be greeted by the ever-present sight of yet more crazy trousers. Strangely enough I never saw anyone wearing them.

We found a huge fruit and veg market and an entire square devoted to tool stalls. I'd already passed enough knives and machetes to make me drool. I have a deep-seated love of sharp things and couldn't wait to get a two-foot-long blade all of my own. But not quite yet – I'd better wait until my language skills were good enough to bluff my way out of police custody just in case. The sun was baking hot. We bought an icy can of Coke each from a guy sat on a cooler and let ourselves drift with the flow of shoppers for a while. We washed up in a livestock area and were quickly surrounded by baskets of live chickens, rabbits, kittens, a pair of goats on a leash – it was like a petting zoo with price tags. I could only hope they were intended as pets. I mean, if you were served kitten in a restaurant, how would you know?

In between the forest of legs something caught my eye – a little patch of light brown fluff on the ground. I headed that way, and as the number of legs between me and it diminished, the shape resolved into a tiny ball of fur. Ashley pushed through the crowd beside me, and we knelt down either side of the most pathetic looking puppy I'd ever seen. It was about the size of my palm, and looked as though it had been stood on. It was flat out on its side, eyes closed. I reached down and stroked its head. The creature twitched slightly, but that was all. I looked at Ashley and saw that she too looked distraught. Surely there was something we could do? We were supposed to be animal rescue workers! She tried to persuade it to sit up, and I tried to tickle some life into it.

Then out of nowhere a bony pair of hands thrust down and grabbed the dog, lifting it up to our eye level. We both stood up as a decaying old woman with a wisp of beard jabbered loudly at us. Ashley dug for the dictionary, then stopped and looked at me. "I think she's trying to sell it to us!"

Both of us began to shake our heads, holding up our hands palm outward in that internationally recognised gesture of 'No thanks'. Internationally recognised did I say? Apparently not in Ecuador. The old woman shoved the dog into Ashley's hands and vanished into the crowd. She was gone so fast it was eerie. We scanned the press of people in all directions – nothing. The old woman was clearly a ninja.

Ashley was left holding a half-dead, runty-looking little dog and neither of us had a clue what to do with it.

She voiced the question first. "Should we keep it?"

I stated the obvious. "Johnny will go crazy. He's got about a hundred dogs. What the hell are we gonna say to him?"

Just then the little beast stirred in Ashley's hands. It lifted its head about a centimetre off her fingers and made a pathetic attempt to lick its nose.

That decided it.

"We're gonna need some milk," I said, "and puppy food. Oh God, how the hell do you say that in Spanish?"

"I think I saw a stall up there that had baskets for sale," Ashley said.

And just like that we'd become parents. Of the most feeble, microscopic, excuse for a dog the world has ever known. I couldn't help but love it.

The basket was perfect. A little wicker thing not much bigger than the dog itself, though it was a long time before we could bring ourselves to actually put her in it. Instead we took turns in holding her. Every few minutes one of us would come up with a pressing reason to confiscate her back – "Buy some of those cheesy things," I'd say to Ashley. "Here, I'll hold the dog." And she was mine again!

The cheesy things were a big hit. Nutritionally I'm sure they're terrible food for very small dogs, but it was all we could find that looked edible. I pulled a little bit off one, blew on it for a few seconds, then held it out to her (Ashley had handed me the cheesy things – "Here, break one up for her," she'd said, "I'll hold the dog for you"). I touched the mushy cheese to her nose (the dog's, not Ashley's) and she stirred slightly. Her eyes opened, and her mouth did, and she took a bite. Mmmm, good!

Over the next half hour we took it in turns to feed her two and a half cheesy things. Holy crap, this creature ate like me! She probably could have managed even more, were it not for the twin facts that a) we'd decided not to overdose her on day one, and b) I'd already eaten all the rest of them. But small dogs cannot live by cheesy thing alone. I helpfully relieved Ashley of the dog, on the pretext that she needed to use the dictionary to discover how to ask for puppy food. What we ended up with was milk – only available in litre cartons, and about as fresh as my socks, which is to say it was that everlasting UHT stuff which hasn't seen a cow since they've been domesticated. Ashley took the dog ("Give me the dog while you open the carton," she'd said. Subtle, Ash!) and I held a finger dipped in milk up to her nose.

She sat up and licked me!

Other things probably happened that day, but buggered if I can remember them.

I do remember that despite how crowded the bus was, the people made room for me to sit on the floor with the basket of dog in my lap. I remember wincing as the bus bounced into and out of every pothole. I remember a little lad on the seat above me talking to me and grinning at the dog the whole way home. I didn't need to speak his language to understand what he was saying. And of course, I remember the reactions back at the refuge, when I gingerly handed the basket down to Ashley before jumping out the back of the pickup taxi that brought us up the hill.

"What've you got there?" Toby asked as he wandered over. "Oh my God!" he said, then laughed. "It's fuckin' tiny!"

My sharp eyes spotted straight away that Toby was hooked. Big girl's blouse.

And Johnny who had, quite literally, the power of life and death over the little beast? It wouldn't last a day if he made us leave it somewhere outside the farm. He looked into the basket for a long time, then spoke briefly to Toby, turned and walked off. I looked at Toby for a translation.

He grinned as he told me. "He said she'll have to have her shots!"

"Woohoo!" I hugged Ashley in glee as Toby poked a finger at our new pet.

"So, what DVDs did you get?" he asked me.

Ah. Bollocks.

For the next few days my little dog became the centre of my world. I lined her basket with a skanky t-shirt. I set up a pair of saucers for her, one with milk, one with water. I even introduced her to the cat. She soon learnt to fear that cat. This was only to be expected though – we all feared the cat. He was called Don Juan, though we more often referred to him as 'Satan' – and not without reason.

Whenever I wasn't working I was playing with the dog, or more accurately, letting her sleep on me. I'd have let her sleep in my bed at night but for the results all those cheese things had on her. Her digestive system had been jump-started, with the predictable result that she shit her own body weight every half an hour.

Ashley and me, loving parents, and Toby, already hopelessly addicted, cleaned up every mess without complaint for days. Until one day the mess was in Toby's shoe.

Naming the tiny creature was somewhat more of a struggle. That first evening I'd suggested we call her after the place we'd found her. Machachi had a grand ring to it. It was a name she could grow into (since it was considerably bigger than she was) and it certainly beat calling her Blondie or Spot. Ashley had agreed until the following morning, when she tried out the obvious shortened version we would end up using. The subsequent argument had been fierce.

"We can't call her Cha-chi", Ashley repeated stubbornly, "that's what we call cheesy guys in Canada."

I was torn between making a polite response, or telling her honestly that that was the single most bloody stupid thing I'd ever heard anyone say in my entire life. I settled for "But I like Chachi. She's from Machachi. It works."

"No way! We'd be calling for her, 'Cha-chi, Cha-chi...' it's like really bad. Like calling her a bad word or something."

Oh my God. It was either compromise or strangle her. It took me a full minute to make the decision.

In the end, 'Machita' was the result of some letter jigging on my part. Not perfect, but I could cope. Toby, of course, had a far simpler solution.

"I'm gonna call her Chachi anyway," he announced.

Why didn't I think of that? That'd show her! Me and Toby could train her to respond only to us, and then teach her all kinds of tricks to play on Ashley! Ha! I watched as the tiny little creature tentatively stalked a very small stick, eyes wide with fear.

It was then that I revised my plan as being overly ambitious. We'd be lucky if she could learn her name. During this extended debate it had gradually emerged that my poor little dog was stupid.

Dawn of the Layla

Toby had mentioned that we were expecting another volunteer. Had all his hard work (and partying) in Quito come to fruition? No. This wasn't a new volunteer, it was an old one; she'd worked at Santa Martha for a month already, before being moved by the company that arranged her placement. It was a period of time that Toby never talked about, in much the same way that ex-prisoners of war rarely wish to relive their experiences. Privately my respect for Toby dropped a notch. I mean, afraid of a girl? Really?

I'd been secretly hoping to be joined by an all-girl Swedish volleyball team who were so used to communal showers that they hardly noticed Toby and me jumping in there with them. They all had long legs, longer blonde hair, spoke broken English with an exaggerated Scandinavian accent and giggled when we mentioned words like 'innocent'.

The reality: Layla was short and dumpy. Pasty and freckled. Eighteen years old, a soon-to-be student taking a gap year before university so that she had something interesting to talk about when it was time to make new friends. Her parents had money, obviously, or they'd never have been able to afford the ridiculous fee charged by their 'Placement Organiser'. To my mind rich girls should be prettier than the not-so-rich ones, as they have access to expensive skin and hair products and clothes, personal trainers, et cetera. Alas, Layla's parents must have spent their entire cash horde on feeding her.

She had drab brown hair in a short bob, and a sour demeanour. Toby welcomed her back with an awkward smile and a stiff hug, then went into his room and shut the door. It might have been my imagination, but I thought I could hear him sobbing. I figured it was down to me to make some kind of effort. After all, Layla was going to be here for two months.

"So, how was your last placement?" I opened. Small talk was clearly the way forward.

"Boring."

"Oh! Why's that?"

"Just didn't like it. No-one ever did anything."

"Right. Well we're pretty busy here!" I told her.

"I *know*," she gave me a flat, unfriendly look. "I've already *been* here. You dig holes and get covered in mud."

"So didn't you want to come back?"

"Dunno. Better than the other place. I didn't like anyone there."

I bit my tongue against the obvious retort. "Well, welcome to Santa Martha," I said instead.

"Great. Thanks," she mumbled.

"You can put your bags in there..." I pointed to the dorm room.

"I *know!*"

Ouch. Ashley was just coming out of the shower. "Oh! Hey Ashley! This is Layla. Come and say 'hi!'" I said. And I ran.

Water Polo

Pulling the remains of a long-dead horse out of a swamp; it was jobs like these that kept the glamour alive at Santa Martha. We were in the middle of an epic exploration when we first discovered the bones. I was hacking away with a machete, helping to clear a path through the dense jungle undergrowth above a previously hidden river. It felt so much like I was in an adventure movie that the sudden sight of a skeleton embedded in the riverbank seemed perfectly in place. No doubt some previous explorer, reckless and unprepared, had attempted the exact same journey years before us. But he was not so lucky. I grimly pushed on past the hideous relic until a chilling scream from my beautiful assistant stopped me in my tracks.

Actually it was Ashley and she didn't really scream. She just said "Ugh! Shit! A dead horse".

It was enough to shatter my fantasy though. Probably for the best – the others were surely getting sick of me narrating the whole journey in a bad American accent.

"The group recoiled in horror from the corpse of some hideous beast..."

"Shut UP Tony!"

"Sorry."

The dead horse, or most of it, was scattered around a

clearing we'd carved at the base of a small waterfall. It was hard to believe that all this land belonged to Johnny. Two days ago for no apparent reason he'd decided to discover the course of a river which ran across the farm through a good mile of virgin cloud forest. The phrase cloud forest had conjured up images of infinitely tall trees, ramrod straight, disappearing into the mists in some ethereal dreamscape. Well, before I'd arrived of course. Soon after getting here I'd realised it was just a posh word for jungle. But this made me very happy. I love jungle.

The thick layer of tangled branches and vines started about a foot above the level of the water and rose impenetrably high above our heads. Jimmy had gone first, carving a path with ruthless efficiency. But being Jimmy he had also carved it about four and a half feet high, which left Toby and myself the job of expanding his hobbit hole to fit westerners. We took it in turns, chopping away at the foliage until our arms ached then switching sides. The girls followed, hacking at the undergrowth on both sides to expose a strip of riverbank. I was having so much fun I hardly even cared that my left welly was leaking.

It was the third day of splashing through the river with one boot full of water when it started to bother me – mostly because of the decomposing animal we'd just found. There was something altogether less wholesome about the water now. Ashley was poking at the remains with a soggy stick. "Ah man! There's still skin attached to these bits…"

"If there's any meat left it's mine!" I said.

"Ew, you can't eat horse!" said Ashley.

"Ash, I've eaten more bloody vegetables in the last week than I did in my entire life previously. I'd eat you if I thought I could get away with it."

"Human meat is supposed to be closest to pork," Layla declared.

I looked at her. The truth in her words became

immediately apparent. Don't say it! I warned myself. It's too easy... With an effort I ignored the comment. What I couldn't ignore was the next image that leapt into my mind; Layla with an apple in her mouth and a skewer going in between her bum cheeks for slow roasting... I had to laugh. Oh did I laugh! I doubled over and hugged my knees for support until I could control the guffaws.

Ashley was nonplussed. "What's so funny?"

If only I could tell her! "Oh, I'm, um, laughing about that dead horse..."

That earned me a pair of peculiar looks.

"Anyway, no point flogging the poor creature," I added. "Might as well clear it up."

"I am not touching it," said Layla.

"Well, more for us."

Clearing the river took a good few days. Sometimes it was only Layla and Ashley helping me as we sloshed around pulling branches and rotting leaves out of the water (Toby had conveniently discovered some urgent computer work he had to do). Sometimes the Real Men mobilised, and we had the bosses plus Leonardo, a friendly vet from Quito, and local tour guide 'Falco' Freddy lending a hand. The two were opposites – Leonardo was stout and cheerful, with a wispy black comb-over covering his balding head and the undeniably sharp intellect within. He even spoke occasional words of English, as though to keep us guessing at just how much of our conversation he could eavesdrop on. Freddy was big and dumb; his full head of hair and imitation Ray-Ban aviator sunglasses concealed very little worthy of note. He was working far too hard to project the same image Johnny did effortlessly; his khaki shirt was covered with sew-on badges making him look halfway between a third world military officer and a boy scout.

Johnny directed the mismatched pair in the setting up of

a rope system for hauling the debris out of the river valley. I say 'system'. This is perhaps an overly grand label. It consisted of a rope. Stuff was tied to one end and I was tied to the other. Hand over hand I raised sacks of branches and buckets of leaves. Every so often I'd hear my favourite Spanish word – a sharp cry of "*Cuidado!*" (careful!) – from below, which would indicate that whatever they'd just fastened to the other end of my rope was particularly heavy, or spiky, or sharp. Glass and jagged chunks of metal came up. I struggled at one point, straining with teeth clenched and veins throbbing, until Johnny and Freddy climbed up to lend their combined manhood to the task.

Between us we dragged up the bank an inch at a time a colossal framework of rusted metal. It wasn't until we collapsed in the long grass with the mission finally accomplished that I noticed what it was. Where they'd dug it out from I'd no idea, and fuck knows why it was down there in the first place, but we'd just dredged up half a small car. A Citroën I think.

Bones we had aplenty. Toby guessed that at some time in the past the landowners had simply tipped any animals that died over this cliff, handily disappearing them into the jungle with the minimum of effort. Now Johnny had picked the exact same spot to be the culmination of his grand River Walk, which meant that what went in had to come out.

We found a wolf skull – 'Falco' Freddy identified it, drawing upon his intimate knowledge of wild animals and their environment. I had a feeling he was full of shit and had just made his best guess but I wasn't about to say so in front of Johnny. Anyway, my idea was even less likely – I was still trying to convince everyone it was the skull of a sabre-toothed tiger.

From start to finish the 'walk' was a mile long. We'd cut a lovely channel through the vegetation above it and cleared the river of all debris in both directions. Quite how it was going to become a commercial success as a tourist attraction I couldn't see. There was nowhere to walk other than wading down the middle of the river. Boardwalks would be ideal, but so far out of our ability to buy and/or create that we might as well be considering conveyor belts and escalators. Still, Johnny was enthusiastic and the work was immense fun, so I ignored the logistical issues and struggled on.

There was a reward at the end. We climbed up over a series of small waterfalls and followed the water upstream to a narrow cleft in the cliff wall. Above us the road curved through the uppermost reaches of the forest, but from down below we were totally hidden. Toby ventured into the opening first. He was our fearless leader after all. Something moved in the darkness. Did a bat just fly past my head? The stone walls pressed tight on both sides as we edged sideways through the defile. It was almost completely dark inside. I shrieked as something touched me. Which made Toby snigger, as it was him that had touched me.

"I think it opens out up ahead," he chuckled.

"Fucker," I responded.

What was living down here in the darkness? Something ancient and monstrous, skulking in the jungle and surviving on the flesh of dead horses? Was this a pit of sacrifice to the beast? Just ahead I heard Toby gasp. I quickly pulled myself around the corner behind him. We were in a small, glistening cavern. A single shaft of sunlight filtered through the water that cascaded from the roof. The effect was magical. The walls, wet with spray, reflected the light in a million glittering points all around us. The floor was a stone basin, catching the falling water in a cold deep pool before allowing it to spill out down the channel we'd followed in. I could have stayed there, gawping open-mouthed at the beauty of the place for hours.

"Shit, I'm soaked!" said Toby. "Let's get out of here."

It became a tradition, as each new volunteer arrived, to bring them all the way down the River Walk whilst recounting the adventures and mishaps we'd had creating it. We'd finish by making them go first into the darkness of the cave and see the look of terror on their faces become wonder when they came out again. It was the most amazing thing we ever discovered, tucked away beneath a forgotten pocket of jungle halfway across Johnny's land.

But it never became a tourist attraction.

Pit Stop

"You can drive, can't you?" Toby asked.

"Well, no," I informed him. "I mean, I can, of course, but I can't, you know, legally speaking."

"S'alright mate, I figured you could do it. Just don't hit anything."

He tossed me the keys.

Sweet! I was going to get to drive the white 4x4 all the way across Santa Martha, to the fat puma's enclosure. It was a long, long time since I'd been behind the wheel of a car, and what with never actually taking a test and all, not many people felt comfortable about letting me loose in theirs. But now I was in Ecuador. No licence? No problem! Stuff like that just didn't matter on Johnny's farm – it was one of my favourite aspects of the place. I had to be a man after all, and men can drive – it goes without saying. My only regret was that it wasn't Johnny's own monstrous truck. I'd ridden up the mountain in it often enough to respect its raw power. But then again that might be a bit much for me to handle on my first attempt. I'd be less worried about hitting something and more worried about roaring straight off the side of the mountain! Be calm, I told myself, the time will come. Today I gain their trust with a flawless trip in the white truck. Before they know it they'll be lending me the big one to go on a night out in Quito... Bwah ha ha HA!

The other volunteers were standing around the car looking at me strangely. Had I accidentally laughed my super-villain laugh out loud? Did they know what I was planning? No, impossible! Then what...? Ah. They were waiting for me to unlock the car.

I reversed somewhat quickly out of the barn and screeched to a halt outside Johnny's house. Toby had lingered by the front door to watch this manoeuvre, most likely to reassure himself that he'd made the right decision in giving me the keys. I waved at him through the window and gave him a triumphant thumbs up. He merely shook his head in what I assume was mock despair, and went into the house. Ashley and Layla walked over to the truck and threw their tools in the back. Then they both rather prudently climbed into the cab behind me instead of joining their equipment. Clearly my opening gambit had not instilled much confidence.

"It might be a little bumpy," I warned, to cover my back in case I went a bit too fast. I had to get used to the clutch and the brakes, whilst travelling downhill over a narrow, twisty and seriously knackered farm track. 'Bumpy' was likely to be the understatement of the century, so it seemed fair to warn them.

Off we went. I drove slowly, but not too slowly – you never know when Jimmy might be watching, and even Toby copped shit from him for cautious driving! I had no desire to be told I drive like a vegetarian. I swung round a few corners and bounced off some of the larger rocks in the path. A few minutes later we'd arrived, rattled but essentially undamaged, at Garfield's enclosure. My heart was beating triple time.

"Here we are," I pointed out, trying to sound casual. The girls peeled themselves out of the back seat and reclaimed their tools.

"You can go a bit slower you know," moaned Layla. "We're not on a time limit. Every time you go over a bump our heads hit the roof, and the faster you go the harder we get bashed."

Mental note to self: drive faster. "So sit in the back next time," I told her. I felt that I had the right to be flippant. I was the driver.

Entering Garfield's enclosure was my second adrenaline rush of the day. It was always thrilling to be so close to such a massive beast, though he never seemed even remotely bothered. I'd still never seen him move. I could easily have believed he was too fat to stand if it wasn't for the amount of effort he seemed to put into distributing scraps of chicken carcass all over his enclosure. Chunks were scattered through the bushes, stuck halfway up trees, partially buried in half a dozen locations. It always took a long time to gather the various pieces and finally inter them. Maybe he just liked the company and wanted to prolong our visit? I'd like to think this was the case. Because the other alternatives were that either he fed with a mindless ferocity that belied his bulk, or that he sadistically enjoyed tearing the chickens to shreds.

Eventually the gory duty was finished. All three of us trekked back up to the car and ditched our tools and gloves. I was elated – time for me to take the wheel again!

"Hop in guys!" I said gleefully.

"You've got to turn round first," Layla pointed out.

"Oh, yeah. Do you want to get in now, or shall I go turn around and pick you up on the way back?"

The girls exchanged glances. "We'll wait here," said Ashley.

Women!

I fired up the engine and roared off down the track. For most of its length this path ran around the side of the mountain, with a steep slope upwards on one side and a very steep slope down on the other. The path itself was quite narrow, and there were few places where a car of this size could easily turn round. In fact, as I kept driving, I discovered there were no places where the car could turn around easily. It was going to be difficult wherever I tried it.

'Hm, not there,' I thought, passing another slight widening in the path. Up ahead was the quarantine pen where we kept the ocelot with HIV. The clearing sprang to mind as the perfect location, but the closer I got the smaller it looked. Any overly enthusiastic reversing would send me careening backwards down the mountainside, sealing the fate of the unfortunate cat even sooner than nature had ordained. That would really piss Toby off – only recently I'd witnessed a heated argument when Johnny again suggested we have the ocelot euthanized.

No, better keep looking. After a minute or so I came to the main ocelot enclosure. Sure enough, the track widened quite a bit at that point, enough so that the top fence was set back from the road by a few feet. From there the fences led downhill at a crazy angle, enclosing a huge chunk of land that quickly fell away from where I had pulled up. The place was almost impossible for humans to traverse – regardless of the six-strong pack of stalking ocelots, the sheer steepness of the mountainside at that point negated any possibility of simply walking down. To the cats it was a fantastic multi-level playground, but to us it was pretty close to being an overgrown cliff face. All of which put me in an uncharacteristically cautious mood. I jumped out for a quick look. There was *almost* enough room to turn around, but was there *quite* enough? I couldn't be sure. And my clutch control still left much to be desired. This was a point at which one wrong move, one tiny little wrong move, could be the end of the car – and more importantly the idiot who'd decided to attempt a twenty six and a half point turn in it.

No, there had to be somewhere else.

It occurred to me that the girls had been waiting quite a while by now. At each potential turning point I'd stopped for a few seconds to evaluate the possibilities, and all that time was starting to add up. Pretty soon they were going to get worried, start thinking that I might have had a crash. The smart thing to do was get back in the car, drive a bit further up the path, turn the thing around and get back to them ASAP. So I did.

Except that, the further up the path I drove, the narrower it seemed to be getting. A couple of minutes beyond the ocelots I was struggling to find enough road for the wheels. The track here was carved straight out of the mountain, obviously by someone who was seriously bored with carving it. He'd made it as wide as he could be arsed to, and not an inch more. I held my breath a few times as I eased the truck around tight bends where at least one wheel was hovering over the abyss. Holy shit, I thought, this is a goat track! And for bloody skinny goats at that.

The track was rising, too. I'd passed a ridiculously steep trail which led off to my left, straight up the side of the mountain. Other than that there'd been no escape at all from the rapidly dwindling path. Maybe if I could stay on it long enough it'd lead me right to the top? In any case there was absolutely no chance of backing up. If I didn't find somewhere wider to turn around soon... I didn't want to think about it. All of a sudden a tiny stream of doubt trickled into my mind. Had I missed the right place? Almost certainly. At the ocelot enclosure? Most likely. Was I going to find somewhere else suitable? I shied away from the obvious answer.

One last corner. The path seemed to crest a ridge just beyond where I was. I edged forward, first gear, slower than a slow walk. I climbed up the ridge, and over, and looked down on a great big meadow. Saved! Except that, like most of Johnny's land, it angled downwards so steeply it made my stomach churn.

Bugger.

What to do? By now the girls were almost certainly fearing the worst. And sooner or later they'd come looking for me. That didn't matter – it'd take them a week to hike up here and they'd surely give up before getting this far. For starters they'd never believe I could possibly have come this way in the car. But more worrying was that they might go back to the house for Johnny. My first trip out in the car... I couldn't have them putting any doubts in his mind. So there was only one thing for it. This was a 4x4 after all. Speed down the hill, swing a wide loop at the bottom and use my momentum to power back up. Simple! Then a few narrow corners and I'd be back with the girls in no time. I took a few deep breaths, then caught my face in the mirror. Desperation stared back at me. Was this, I asked myself, a really, really stupid thing to do? Oh God I hoped not.

I set off down the hill in first gear. Straight away the car accelerated so much the engine roared. I approached the bottom of the hill at breakneck speed and hauled on the wheel to spin the truck for its return journey. It slewed around in a massive semicircle and I stamped on the accelerator to blast back up the hill. The car fairly leapt the first few metres, assisted as planned by a shitload of momentum.

Then it slowed. Slowed some more. And finally stopped.

I'd had my foot to the floor the whole time but to no avail. And now, wheels spinning frantically on the grass I could feel myself slipping very slowly backwards... I shit myself and grabbed for the hand brake. Pulling it on as far as I could with all the panicked strength I could muster just about managed to stop the car rolling the rest of the way back down the hill. I was stuck. Halfway up a crazily steep hill. Miles from the farm. Miles from anywhere. And all on my own. In Johnny's car.

"Oh SHIT!" I shouted at the grass outside the window. "Johnny's gonna KILL ME!"

The walk back took a long time. I finally met up with the girls a few bends away from the house. They'd assumed that I'd turned around, then somehow gotten past them on the road and was sitting laughing with Toby about how long they'd wait there before realising I'd abandoned them.

Jeez! How paranoid were they? But it did sound like the kind of thing I'd do. Come to think of it, it was one to remember for the future... If I got out of this alive. I miserably explained the situation to the two stroppy women. An identical incredulous expression grew simultaneously on both faces.

Ashley was the first to find her voice again. "You got... stuck? But... So... Where's the car?"

Clearly I hadn't done a very good job of explaining the situation. I tried again, more slowly this time: "It's S-T-U-C-K. Stuck. As in, can't go anywhere."

"But where?"

This was the crux of the matter. "Well, it's kind of hard to describe. You know the ocelot enclosure?"

"Holy shit! You went that far?"

"Yeah, well, a bit beyond that there's this place where the road gets really narrow..."

"Further? How far?"

"Well, beyond that the road sort of goes up, and then there's this ridge, and below that there's a field..."

"Tony, how far?"

"Um, about two miles."

"WHAT?"

"Yeah, about that. Ish."

"Oh my God!" Layla couldn't contain herself any longer. "Johnny's gonna KILL YOU!"

Toby's face was a picture as he saw us hiking back up the path towards him. Confusion, then disbelief, which gave way to a half-smile as though he thought maybe we were playing a joke on him. He hooked his thumbs in his pockets and sauntered down to meet us. As he got closer he could read my expression. I watched his change rapidly into something approaching horror.

"Where's the car?" he asked fearfully. "What have you done?"

"Oh, nothing much," I tried to grin to put him at ease. "Just got it a little… stuck."

"Stuck? Oh shit! Is it okay?"

"Oh yeah, I didn't hit anything." At the memory of his earlier advice I could smile again. "Yeah, absolutely nothing wrong with it at all. Just got the bloody thing stuck, is all." I braced myself for the inevitable question.

"Where?"

"Well…"

I told him.

"Oh my GOD!" He wasn't impressed. "I don't even know where that is! Are you sure you went past the ocelot enclosure?"

"Yeah, pretty sure yeah."

"'cause that's where I normally turn around."

"Yeah, I thought it might be,"

"So past the ocelots, then."

"And a bit further up the path. See, it gets really narrow, then starts to rise…"

"I don't know that bit," he admitted, "I've never been that far. How far is it in total?"

"What, you mean from here?"

"Yeah, from here. How far?"

It was my favourite part.

"About two miles."

"Two MILES! The farm isn't even that big! That's not

even Johnny's land!"

"Um, yeah. So, can we take the other truck, or something, and pull it out?"

"I don't know. I'll have to tell Johnny." All of a sudden his eyes twinkled. "Oh mate, he's gonna..."

"I KNOW!"

Johnny was fairly pragmatic. Toby had hardly gotten through the first few sentences of his explanation when Johnny glanced over at me, then away again with a muttered curse. That world-weary look he did so well came over him, as though he really wasn't capable of coping with the stupidity of foreigners. He listened in silence to the rest of it, until Toby ran out of words and started to study the tile floor. I'd been doing the same since we'd come in.

I could feel rather than see Johnny's gaze travelling from one of us to the other, then back again, as though weighing up who was the most likely to blame for this disaster. Then, all of a sudden, he walked out the front door. A few seconds later we heard the engine of his truck fire up, and ran out to join him.

"*Más, más,*" Toby shouted from the back of the truck. He was telling an amazed Johnny that we still had further to go. He'd been repeating this at every bend in the path since we'd passed the ocelot enclosure, in response to ever more violent-sounding questions coming from the cab. Jimmy was sitting in the back with us, grinning madly. Nothing could possibly have amused him more, though he was struggling not to show it in front of Johnny. Safe in the back of the truck he'd spent most of the trip asking me to repeat bits of the story, as though he couldn't quite understand my attempt to explain in Spanish. Every so often he would shake his head, then point at me and draw a finger across his throat. The joke was wearing thin.

Even from the back I could hear the incredulity in

Johnny's voice as the truck sat before the final rise in the path. I glanced at Toby and nodded. Mirth was shining in his eyes as he relayed the message in Spanish back through the cab window.

"Yes, up there!"

Johnny muttered a few choice curses and started up the hill. He drove right up, and over, and stopped the car at the top of the meadow. It was several seconds before I heard him speak.

"*Choo-cha madre!*" he thundered. It was a uniquely Ecuadorian way of swearing, invoking certain parts of one's mother's anatomy that are reserved for occasions when no other words are adequate.

Toby stood up to get a better look over the cab. There, far, far below us, facing up, was the tiny white outline of the missing truck.

It was more than he could take. "Oh my God!" he exclaimed in total disbelief. Then he collapsed back into the truck, laughing so hard he was crying. From up here it did look pretty ridiculous. I couldn't help it. I started to chuckle, and before long the pair of us were wetting ourselves, rolling around holding our sides in hysterics. Good God, but it was funny.

Johnny was of a slightly different disposition. Faced with an almost impossibly steep hill and what from this distance appeared to be a two-inch scale model of his white truck parked two hundred metres down it, he positively growled, favouring both Toby and myself with the blackest look I'd ever seen him deliver. I could guess it'd be a while before he'd let me drive again.

Without telling us his plan he fired up the engine and roared down the hill to where the white truck was mired. I surveyed the mess I'd created. Huge muddy tyre tracks had been carved through the long grass behind the wheels by my efforts to persuade the car to keep moving. All to no avail.

Johnny and Jimmy had already set about tying the two trucks together by the time Toby and me jumped out to help. We couldn't do much in any case – neither of us had managed to stop laughing long enough to breathe. Toby was the first to regain the power of speech.

"What I don't get is why you didn't turn around sooner," he spluttered, "like at the ocelots."

"Well," I explained between sobs, "there wasn't enough space! Not for me."

"So why did you... why did you come down here?" He broke into new convulsions of laughter.

"I figured what the hell, it's a 4x4, it can probably make it."

Toby's laughter stalled mid guffaw. "Whaddaya mean?" he demanded.

"I tried to get enough speed up on the way down to swing round and power back up. I thought a 4x4 would be up to it. I guess not."

"Um, Tony, mate, that white truck?"

"Yeah?"

"It's not a 4x4."

A string of expletives from Johnny startled me from the revelation. He was swearing at us, and pointing at the back of the stuck vehicle.

"Oh, I think he wants us to push," supplied Toby. We braced ourselves against the bumper and strained as Johnny gunned his engine. Wheels span. The trucks lurched forward. Toby and me both staggered and fell flat on our faces. Jimmy laughed. Wheels span again. The rope between the two trucks sang. And slowly but surely the white truck began to roll back down the hill towards us. Toby jumped up with a shout, alerting me to the immediate danger of being reversed over. I jumped out of the way, but the car never got near either one of us. Its brief bid for freedom was over almost before it began, arrested by the rope fastening it to Johnny's tow hook. The white truck could never pull Johnny's, even downhill – but neither could Johnny's pull the white. He was stuck too.

A few choice oaths accompanied Johnny's realisation that his prize vehicle was going nowhere. He floored the accelerator and span the wheels violently for a few seconds as a substitute for kicking something. Then he got out and roared something indecipherable at Jimmy. Jimmy quit grinning at us and ran to help his boss untie the rope between the two trucks. It seemed the battle was over – for now, at least – and the hill had scored the first victory.

The Ecuadorians piled back into the good truck, and with me and Toby panting through the twin efforts of pushing and laughing, we managed to get the tyres back onto unspoilt ground. As soon as the wheels stopped spinning and started to bite the truck surged forward. Better prepared this time, Toby and I both stayed on our feet and watched, as without a pause Johnny roared off up the hill. It was a truly impressive display of what a real 4x4 could do, and was marred by only one thing. He didn't bother stopping for us. He gained the crest of the hill, shot over the top of it and disappeared out of sight. By the time we'd jogged to the top ourselves we could just see the tail lights disappearing around a bend a good way further down the road.

"How far you reckon it is back to the house?" I said unnecessarily. I knew the answer.

"Two miles." Neither of us was laughing now.

"You think he's coming back?" I knew the answer to this one too. Toby didn't even bother answering. He just gave me a resigned look and started walking.

Half an hour later we agreed we were almost halfway home. It was going to take a while, but not forever, and it was a nice day. It would have been a lovely walk if I hadn't been more than a little worried about what kind of a welcome awaited me at the end of it. We pressed on, and before long started to hear a noise in the distance.

"What the hell is that? A plane?"

Toby's guess was better; "The chainsaw. He's probably practising for when you get back!"

I noticed he'd excluded himself from the equation this time. Well, it *was* my fault. The noise grew louder. And closer.

"Oh no!" Toby exclaimed suddenly. "I know that sound!" The tractor hove into view round the next bend, heading towards us like a bat out of hell. "It's the tractor's engine!" he finished helpfully.

No shit! So that meant... Toby as usual was almost a whole heartbeat ahead of me. "He didn't leave us! He just went for the tractor!

The same thought occurred to us both simultaneously. I know this because after years of being scared of looking stupid I can instantly recognise the same fear in others. And how stupid would we look having walked all this way, bitching the whole time about being abandoned... As one, we turned and sprinted back the way we'd come.

By the time we made the top of the hill sweat was pouring off us. This morning had turned out to be a lot more work than I'd anticipated.

Jimmy had just finished hitching the white truck to the back of the tractor. He jumped up into his cab and put the tractor in gear. It strained – for almost an entire second – then ripped the truck free of the muddy skid marks and dragged it straight up the hill. The two bound vehicles pulled up next to us as we stood, dripping and panting, on the crest of the hill.

Jimmy leaned out of the cab. "You like to walk, eh? Or you want a ride this time?" Not only could I understand the

Spanish – he'd said it simply on purpose – I could also hear the sarcasm dripping off every carefully enunciated syllable.

Toby's breathless reply brought a snigger from above.

The tractor edged forwards, taking up the slack in the line. "What was that, I didn't catch it?" I asked.

He looked at me with the same resigned expression he'd offered me earlier. "I told him I'd untie the truck and drive it home."

"Oh. Cool."

Toby shook his head. "No. He told me to leave it tied. He said we could ride in the truck, but Johnny doesn't trust us to drive anymore." He sighed. "Either of us."

Training Machita

Over a week after Ashley and I had brought her home, Machita was still trying to impress us. Several times a day she would proudly present us with a curly fresh turd, usually laid right in the middle of the room to allow us to appreciate it more. She tended to wee behind things, be they fridge or bookcase, but she always came racing to fetch me straight away, yipping in anticipation as she led me back to her latest masterpiece. For such a tiny beast she had an unbelievable bladder capacity.

Toby would shout at her, storm and rage, and threaten to fling her out of the house. I would give a loud "Oi!" – but she was always so pleased to show me that her little tail would start wagging, and then I could never stay cross at her long enough to punish her. I'd mop up the mess with bog roll, pausing every now and then to give her a very stern look. This wasn't proving to be a very effective training method. Either she was incredibly clever, and knew she could get away with anything so long as I was around, or she was just too stupid to realise she was doing something wrong in the first place. I had my suspicions as to which theory was correct.

In the end Toby solved the problem by deciding that Machita would be an 'outside' dog. This also neatly solved the problem of her trying to escape every time the front door was opened. Toby opened the front door and Machita immediately bolted for freedom. Toby let her have it. Then closed the door behind her. Machita had moved out.

We found an old wooden crate which was a bit more suitably sized for the rapidly expanding creature. I lined it with my recently ruined fleece, and threw her old t-shirt in there for good measure. It wasn't long before she accumulated a pile of pilfered socks, pants and scarves. If any washing went missing it was a fairly easy guess as to where it had gone. Some days she had more clothes than me.

Every night she whined outside the door until everyone else had gone to bed, at which point I would stealthily sneak over and open it. Opening the door produced a sound like a hundred terrified cats being molested with red-hot pokers, which kind of ended the stealthy part of the operation. It didn't matter how I tried to do it. Opening it quickly just made the cats shriek louder. Opening it slowly just seemed to prolong their agony. Assuming I had remained undetected at this point I would let her in for a little snuffle. I could only risk playing with her for ten minutes or the chances were high that she'd wee all over the place in sheer excitement.

Satisfied that she was okay, and that she still loved me best, I would coax her back outside and lock her out. Then I went straight to bed, put my earphones in and listened to some tunes to drown out the renewed whining.

Poor little critter.

Eventually my dog adapted well to a life outside. But she still whined at the door all night every night for weeks. I felt like a very bad man the entire time.

By morning she would be delighted to see us, yipping, wagging her tail and tearing little celebratory holes in the washing she'd stolen. One of us would feed her from our patented puppy food mix – a margarine tub full of mashed up rice, vegetables and tuna which until recently had been our patented cat food. She also got a handful of dog biscuits and a bowl of water, milk, or hot, sweet tea depending on who was doing the feeding. Yes, the tea was my fault.

It was a huge relief to be free from presents in the form of big puddles of fragrant wee or small piles of vomit cunningly concealed. With the whole area around the house to play with she'd thankfully chosen a less visible toilet. Once or twice she did try to impress us with a dead mouse or bird on the doorstep, but it was painfully obvious they were the cat's kills that she was trying to pass off as her own. She probably thought the cat had privileges, since it came and went from the house at will. The truth was we just couldn't keep the bloody thing out! Not all the windows would shut properly, and while my poor Machita was about as intelligent as a similarly sized chunk of wood, that cat was an evil genius.

We'd feed Don Juan inside and Machita outside. Don Juan completely ignored his own food for half the day, safe in the knowledge that no-one else could get at it. Instead he would breakfast on the best bits from Machita's bowl while the tiny dog looked on, powerless to do anything about it.

We made every effort to shut the cat out at night – out of the rooms, out of the house – all to no avail. We were no match for his animal cunning. I once caught him squirming in through the kitchen ventilation. He would crack the house without breaking a sweat, then commence the terrorisation of the dorm room in retaliation for his exclusion.

Above the dorm room door was a rectangular hole that must once have contained a glass fanlight window. This was the cat's primary means of access. With superhuman leaping ability it could spring from the floor of the lounge to the gap above the door in one go, a distance of at least seven feet. Rather than repeating the feat on the other side however, it had found a far simpler solution. In the top bunk nearest the door, my pillow was an easy jump for the demon-spawned beast. It landed with a very un-feline thump, which I'm sure it had calculated to produce maximum noise. Where most cats would at least have the good grace to slip in silently, Don Juan had perfected the belly flop landing just to prove a point.

Startled suddenly awake I would lie there staring nervously around me in the darkness. About six inches from my face he would always be there, eyes shining with malice. After patrolling his territory by jumping from bunk to bunk all the way around the room he would leap back onto my pillow, climb across my face and disappear out the hole above the door.

An hour later he'd be back.

Throughout the night he would come and go, always using my bed as a springboard, always scaring the shit out of me in the process. And always gone a couple of hours before dawn, allowing me just enough time to get into a nice deep sleep ready for the rooster to start screeching at six.

Sleep deprivation, however, was the least of my problems. It was Layla. In the darkest hour of the night, caught twixt cat and rooster, her caustic comments replayed over and over in my head. No matter what I did, or what order I did it in, I was wrong. Clumsy. Forgetful. My opinions were worthless, my ideas pointless. Even giving her a compliment by way of a peace offering caused her to look at me as though I was something unpleasant she'd stood in whilst cleaning out a monkey cage. Perhaps because she'd been here before she considered herself superior. Or perhaps she always considered herself superior. Either way it was starting to get on my tits.

It had come to a head earlier in the day, during an epic attempt to construct a new tortoise enclosure from scratch.

Johnny, in his infinite wisdom, had decided that Meldrew needed a new home. It required a vast number of post holes dug into the unforgiving rocky ground at the bottom of the valley.

Layla had been delighting me with a running commentary of my shortcomings and mistakes throughout the morning, before deciding it was too much like real work and lying down in the sun instead. But the peace didn't last.

"Not like that!" she shouted as I wrenched the handles of the *excavadora* around. "You'll break it!"

I gritted my teeth against both the pain and the desire to beat her round the face with a shovel. "This is the only way it can be done," I said quietly.

"Jimmy didn't do it like that," she retorted.

That was when I lost it. "You know, I've been here for a month and I've dug hundreds of these fucking holes," I enlightened her. "But if I'm doing it wrong, please feel free to come over here and dig one your fucking self. Then tell me how it's done. Okay?"

Oh, it had felt good! Not quite as good as planting the moaning bitch head first into one of the completed holes and making a fence post out of her, but at least this method bore fruit. She'd grabbed a random tool from the pile and stormed off to misuse it on the other side of the river.

Now, replaying the event in the silent darkness of the dorm, it became obvious just how small a victory it had been. I would never really win against Layla.

It wasn't that I didn't like the girl – more that I wanted to stab her eyes out with a fork every time I looked at her. When she wasn't making a direct personal attack on me she was moaning incessantly about everything else. From the wind to the mud, the work, the house, the conversation – even Machita was too loud or too smelly. Had she been a supremely hot chick I might have expected a little of this – not condoned it, mind, but understood. Santa Martha wasn't a good place for manicured nails and hot pants. Sadly. But Layla was a troll. She must have fallen out of the ugly tree, hit every branch on the way down, and then had the tree jump up and down on her screaming 'Die bitch, die!' As far as I could discern, Layla had absolutely no redeeming features.

And in a few cold hours I'd be shaking off the miniscule amount of sleep and dragging myself out of bed to spend another joyful day in her company. The thought of it made me want to cry.

Shots in the Dark

It was definitely a gunshot that woke me. I've seen enough quality action movies to know. There's something different about hearing one in real life though. It's an ugly, evil sound; it freezes the heart. CRACK! Another gunshot rang out. Instantly recognisable, terrifying, echoing around the hillside. Our hillside. I leapt out of bed, nearly breaking both ankles in the process. God damn that top bunk! I limped into the lounge and met Toby running out of his room. He had a nice double bed, so didn't need to sleep on the top bunk.

"Was that a gun shot? It sounded like a gun shot," his voice was hoarse from sleep and shock.

"Should we go see what's going on?" I asked.

Toby looked at me like I had three heads. "What? Fucking hell no!"

I reviewed the options. One: go outside – potentially get shot and die. Two: stay inside and listen. Well, it wasn't hard to beat option one. The more awake I became, the dumber my idea sounded. "Okay," I said, "so what do we do?"

Outside another gun fired, louder and deadly deep.

"Let's get knives," suggested Toby. So we did.

I'm not a massive fan of violence, particularly when it's directed at me. I was therefore very glad when morning came and the house hadn't been invaded. Toby and I were both asleep in chairs on either side of a dining table festooned with weaponry. I opened my eyes to see Layla, standing alarmingly close and staring at me.

"Morning," she said sullenly. "Why are all the knives out? Are you making breakfast?"

I slowly stirred in my seat.

"Why did you sleep out here?" she asked.

I wasn't in the mood for criticism so I came straight out with it. "We heard gunshots last night. A lot of them, really close by. I think some people were outside." I expected panic or terror. Both seemed sensible reactions to this news. I should have been more realistic.

"Really? Oh, don't be stupid. Is that why you've got the knives? Real mature, guys. I bet there was no one outside."

Oh, Layla! It's a good job I'm not a fan of violence. I reluctantly put the tempting proximity of every kitchen knife we possessed out of my mind. "The body would be found," I murmured to myself.

Toby was stirring in his chair. He opened his eyes and looked straight at me. "We're still alive then," he noted. Then he glanced over at Layla. "All of us," he added with a slight note of disappointment.

Ashley it seemed, had slept through the whole thing.

I raised an eyebrow. "Breakfast?"

Toby went on a fact-finding mission as soon as we'd eaten. He wasn't long with the news. "There *were* people with guns here!" he reported excitedly.

"I knew it! They were definitely gunshots!" I was more relieved that I hadn't been imagining it than I was scared about the implications. But then, it was daylight outside. "So what happened?" I pressed him.

"Johnny just said that he heard some people moving around near our house —"

"What? Our house? This place?" Layla was less than impressed.

"Yes, outside *here,*" Toby drew the last word out as though he was trying to explain something obvious to a particularly dense child. I turned away to hide my smile.

"He said there were three or four of them, and they had hand guns."

This was serious news. It wiped the smirk right off my face.

"He said he heard them moving around, and came out on his balcony to have a look. He could tell they were planning on breaking in, so he got his shotgun."

The story got better! I willed Toby to go on.

"He shouted down to them, and some of them pulled out guns and took some shots. He hid behind the wall of his balcony and fired back. I think they started to run away, so he took another shot – and he got one of them in the ass!"

"Yes!" I enthused. Then the gravity of the situation hit home again. "Those guys were trying to break in here…"

"Looks like. But fair play to Johnny! Shot one in the ass! Apparently the others dragged him away. He reckons they're not likely to come back."

I contemplated this for a few seconds. "How likely is not likely?" It suddenly occurred to me that if my mum knew about this, she'd freak. "I think I'm gonna buy a machete this weekend."

"Not a bad idea, that," Toby agreed.

Layla just looked vaguely sick. "What good is that going to do? If someone breaks in here, and they've got guns, you'd better just give them anything they want. If you try to fight them with a machete because you think you're tough you'll just get killed, and it'll be your own fault." With her final word on the matter said, she stomped off into the bedroom.

"She's got a point," Toby conceded when we were alone

again. "A machete won't scare 'em if they've got guns."

"Yeah, well I've got a plan." I beckoned him closer, as though someone might overhear us. "I'll just grab Layla and hide behind her. If her face doesn't scare the shit out of them, at least she's wide enough to absorb a few bullets!"

That evening Johnny came to see us. It was fairly rare for him to visit the volunteer house, the more so since the girls had arrived, and he caught us a bit by surprise. He just knocked on the open door and strolled in as we were sitting down to dinner. He didn't stay long. We'd spent the day joking with Jimmy about last night's events, imagining the reactions of the would-be thieves when one of their number took a bullet in the buttock. "I wonder who got to pull it out?" I'd said to crack Toby up, "And I wonder if he shit himself as well? I would have. Who got to clean *that* up?"

But Johnny was here with the official word. He strode into the kitchen, turned a chair around backwards and straddled it, as being a man meant he didn't have to sit on chairs in the way they were designed. As he talked, Toby translated for the rest of us. Some words I could pick out, but not nearly enough to make sense of the conversation. Only his tone told me just how serious he considered the matter under discussion.

"Last night some men tried to break into this house," he began. "Not good men. Maybe from the village, I don't know." He paused a little while Toby gave us the English version, then continued in his slow, flat monotone. "From now on I don't want you to be out after dark. Don't leave anything outside at night. Not even washing. If they see things to steal they might come back." He paused again to let Toby catch up. "I've got Danielo patrolling the grounds at night. If there's any trouble he'll find it. But don't go outside. I don't want him to shoot any of you by mistake."

That seemed to be all. He stood to go, and I clearly

recognised him politely declining Toby's offer of eating with us. As he directed a general "*Gracias*" around the room and headed for the door, Ashley looked vaguely sick. I don't think she'd believed our stories until that moment, but there was a grim tension in Johnny that quashed all doubt. I trailed him, not knowing if I should say anything for fear of sounding foolish, but wanting him to be aware that I understood the situation. He stopped at the door with a few last words for Toby.

It was now or never, I decided, and blurted out possibly the stupidest thing I could have said, under the circumstances. "*Este fin de semana, quiero comprar una machete.*" (This weekend, I want to buy a machete.) Argh. Good Spanish. Nice sentence structure. Bad, bad content. What had possessed me? He looked at me and cracked half a tolerant smile. But it never reached his eyes.

"*Buena idea,*" he said, then added something rather lengthier towards Toby. Then he did smile, as though to soften the words he'd just spoken. He clapped me on the shoulder, nodded at Toby and delivered a last "*Gracias*" between us at the girls. Then he turned and left, purposefully closing the front door behind him. As always it gave a hell of a screech.

"What was that last bit?" I enquired of Toby. Toby didn't look too happy. "What did he say?"

"He said it was a good idea. To get a machete, I mean."

"Yeah, I got that part. Then what. Why does he think it's a good idea?"

Toby seemed to be thinking back over the conversation, trying to put his words in the right order. "He said it's a good idea because around here people don't break in and point a gun at you until you give them your valuables. It's too much trouble. Here they just break in and kill everyone straight away. Then they can take their time robbing the place."

We had a quiet evening after that.

A Wise Move

Toby and I had been in hysterics watching Machita's new trick – now roughly the same size as the cat, but still obviously too scared to confront him face on, she'd discovered the most bizarre way of standing up to him either of us had ever seen. When he threatened her she would turn around, presenting her bum, run backwards at the confused creature and sit on him. The cat didn't have a clue what to do about this, with the result that Machita, arse first, had been chasing him around the living room since we'd let her in half an hour ago.

Seeing Don Juan on the receiving end for a change had inspired me to rant about his night-time depredations. Toby's answer was as welcome as it was simple: "Come and sleep in my room if you want."

I was really grateful for the chance to get out of the dorm room. I did feel slightly guilty about leaving poor Ashley alone in the firing line. Not enough to stay though. My paranoid mind had been starting to play with the theory that Layla had recruited Ashley to Team Torment Tony and that the pair of them were ganging up on me. Until one lunchtime when Ashley approached me with a cheese sandwich and a heartfelt plea for help. It turns out Ashley was worried that Layla was ganging up on *her*.

Machita was waiting for me as I moved my blankets into Toby's room and prepared for luxury. I chased her out and started distributing my few belongings between the wicker shelves in the corner and the small square table next to my bed. Toby had a lush double bed with a single bunk above it – the usual construction, tubular steel and springs – and I had a real, one storey, pine single bed. I lay on it and luxuriated in the silence. No rusty springs. No shriek of tortured metal accompanying every inhalation. And no Layla moaning at me for breathing too loud. Paradise.

I chatted a bit to Toby as we lay in our beds. He was telling me about a girl he'd been hanging out with in Quito.

"Alice!" He said the name with relish.

"Skinny and blonde, huh? How come we never get volunteers like that?"

"Alice was a volunteer here," he enlightened me. "Ages before you came. I fancied her then too, but never… y'know."

"Mm." Guy talk. This was much more like it!

"Have you farted?" he asked suddenly.

"Nope."

"Oh. Something stinks in here."

"Sorry, I'll have a shower tomorrow."

"Ha! Ah well. G'nite mate!"

"'nite."

I was woken in the middle of the night by a violent outburst of swearing. Toby was poking round the corners of the room with his MagLight. "Hey man, what's up?" I asked.

"I dunno mate, that smell is back again. There's something… Dunno, but something really stinks!"

I could smell nothing. I left him to it and fell straight back to sleep.

Next morning I lay awake for a few moments trying to place a strange sensation. Rest! Contentedness. I'd had a good night's sleep for the first time in ages, I felt energised and ready to meet the day. I glanced at Toby's clock on the bedside table. Quarter to seven! Which meant... The rooster! I hadn't heard him. Somehow this room was insulated from the little bastard! That was well worth Toby's night-time stink hunt. I'd give anything to be free of that rooster.

Toby himself was just coming awake. "What time is it?"

"Quarter to seven. We've got a few minutes yet."

"Yeah, sweet." He was quiet for a few seconds. Then "Oh my God, that bloody smell! What the hell is it?"

I didn't know what to say. I was wondering if he did this every night. We were living on a farm after all – the air was often what one would politely refer to as 'wholesome'. But Toby was on a mission. "I could smell it every time I woke up. Ugh! Man, it's rank!" He leapt out of bed and started pulling back his bedclothes. "Can't you smell anything?"

I considered this a rhetorical question. Then Toby swore. He grabbed the steel frame of his bed and dragged it halfway across the room in one go. I sat up for a better look as he came round the side to see what had been revealed. There on the floor beneath his bed, directly under where his head would rest on the pillow, was an enormous day-old turd.

"Ah, fucking hell!" he shouted. "A big fucking shit! Look at the size of it!"

It truly was impressive.

"How did the cat —" There was a pause as his brain caught up. "That bloody dog! How did she get in here?"

"Um, dunno mate," I lied.

"All night... I could smell it all night... I can't believe it!"

"Wow. It's a good job she lives outside now."

"I can't believe it!" he repeated. "That shit is bigger than she is!"

Just Desserts...

I loved feeding the big cats. Every week we'd take delivery from a local chicken farm of all their birds that had died since the last delivery. Wherever the place was, either it was fucking huge or there was a frighteningly high mortality rate. I never bothered to ask, since without it Santa Martha would be in big trouble. The dead chickens were free, thereby saving us the single biggest expense our refuge would otherwise face: meat. Fruit and veg, cheap enough even in vast quantities, were also supplied free by various market traders Johnny knew. He was doing them a big favour I guess, taking all their spoiled produce off their hands and feeding it to customers who weren't quite so picky about things like ripeness and colour. If any of these arrangements were to dry up, even for a few weeks, Santa Martha would go under.

Johnny worried about it continually, or so I would learn later. All his money was tied up in land and machinery and the profits from the dairy farm went into his staff or his gas tank. This was the reason why all our tools were so decrepit, patched up and welded back together by Jimmy in an endless programme of recycling. Some he even made from scratch, like his prize hand plough which had blatantly started life as a road sign. Somewhere in Tambillo the speed limit would forever remain a mystery so that Jimmy could turn soil. But the best example of his enterprising DIY skills had to be our two matching ladders. Bearing in mind that a large part of our day job involved erecting tall fences, decent ladders could be considered essential items. Now, I appreciate that aluminium was expecting a bit much. One of those multi-purpose numbers would have been nice, the ones that fold into peculiar shapes so you can use them on the stairs. But this was taking the piss. Jimmy's ladders could well have been recently discovered proof that early man could use tools. They were made of sticks, nailed (and sometimes tied) to a pair of chunky logs. The power to weight ratio left a lot to be desired. Each ladder weighed close to what I did, yet both were noticeably shorter than me. To say that they were falling apart would suggest that the disparate bits even belonged together in the first place, which was a stretch of the imagination. Carrying them from the *galpón* to the car was an exercise in endurance. Using them at all required courage, and the suspension of disbelief. Going higher than the middle 'rung' felt somewhat akin to climbing the steps to the gallows. You have no idea how badly Tambillo needed a B&Q.

This week the chickens had arrived late and been dumped into the back of our white truck under cover of darkness. I'd watched them tumble lifelessly into a heap, fascinated. The next morning Toby hid indoors, only coming out at the last minute to climb into the cab with me and drive our stinking cargo down the track. We would feed the fat puma, then dump a couple of carcasses in to the eagles just opposite, and finally deliver an eagerly awaited feast to our ocelots by throwing the dead birds over the fence.

Toby hated touching the chickens. We'd somehow managed

to bring only three gloves between us, which was unfortunate for Toby as he normally liked to wear two pairs himself. Thus, I took it upon myself to do the lion's share of the dead chicken-flinging. It was kind of fun in a rather twisted way, a gross new sport I'd invented. I threw underhand, lobbed overhand, fired off two at once – dead chickens soared through the air on every conceivable trajectory. I fast bowled a chicken; I juggled a brace of chickens (three being too heavy).

"That should be enough for now," Toby called. He was standing a healthy distance away from the truck and its mangled, feathered contents, and he still sounded sick. I was starting to appreciate why the bosses heaped so much scorn on vegetarians. Although skinny, Toby was a good bit stronger than me, but having a weak stomach around cat food can't have been good for his reputation.

"Last one mate!" I announced, and dug down through the pile for a huge, smelly old bird that was starting to fall apart. I assumed a stance, legs shoulder width apart, knees bent, and tested the wind. Then in an explosion of power I whirled the carcass around and around like the weapon of a ninja, and launched it into the sky above the cage at super-high velocity.

"AAAaaaarrgh!" came the scream from Toby.

"What's up?" I raced around the truck, all thoughts of gold medals at the chicken-flinging Olympics instantly forgotten. "You okay?"

"Urgh!" Toby spat on the ground, and swore at me. "Fucker!" Then he spat again. He was rubbing frantically at his face with the bottom of his t-shirt, pausing only to spit and swear. Then it hit me – or rather, it had hit Toby! Some flying, gelatinous glob of goo from deep inside the chicken had liberally splattered his head at some time during my record-breaking throw.

"In my fucking *mouth*, you sick fucker!" Toby was

muttering.

"Oh, sorry mate! Did I get entrails on you?" It instantly occurred to me just how amusing the situation was to anyone less squeamish. "Don't worry mate, it was only a bit of the juice!"

Toby made gagging sounds.

"It hasn't gone far, just a bit in your hair. Good protein, that."

"Was it… water?" He panted, struggling to control his stomach.

"Oh yeah, the birds were pretty wet from the rain last night," I remembered. "Probably just water."

Toby took a few deep breaths and straightened up a little.

I gave him a moment. "Oh, but that last one though, it was mostly mucus. Coz it was decomposing, you see?"

Toby spewed. I could just make out a weak "You bastard!" between retching.

He was strangely quiet on the drive back.

Toby Makes an Omelette

Toby poked his head out of the door. "I'm making an omelette for breakfast. You want some?"

"Yeah, cheers mate," I replied. I stretched and lay back in the hammock with my little dog asleep on my belly. All was well with the world. Sunny. No work. Two new volunteers had arrived midweek and were settling in quite well. Carrie, a pretty American girl with straight black hair, tanned skin and oriental features; and Richie, a gangly, scruffy white guy with a bird's nest on his head. He could only be English. Though they didn't know it yet, they were a perfectly matched pair. She was open and likeable, with a delightful modesty that complemented her exotic looks. He was crazy. Everything he said made me laugh – hell, even the way he looked made me laugh. I'd never met anyone quite so... rumpled. Fresh out of bed and wearing his cleanest clothes, Richie still looked messier than the rest of us did after a full day scrubbing shit off parrot perches. The guy was born to be a student. Having them around was a breath of fresh air. Two such breaths in fact (which was a rarity, as anyone who has worked on a dairy farm can attest). For the first time in ages I felt comfortable in my own home and to top it off we were having an omelette for breakfast. Why didn't we have them more often? I wondered. We'd last had one… A stray memory clicked in my head.

I sat up suddenly and swore. Poor Machita was catapulted out of the hammock at high speed. Luckily she landed in a pile of stolen socks. She glared at me and yipped, but my mind was fully occupied with the impending disaster.

Toby's omelettes were a clear violation of the Trades Descriptions Act. Because there was no egg in them. Toby didn't like egg, but he did like vegetables. What he referred to as an 'omelette' was inevitably about half an egg drizzled lightly over a colossal pan-full of raw vegetables. And chillies. It tasted even worse than it sounded, and left me with a mouth so burnt I couldn't eat anything else for two days.

If I did nothing else to aid my continued survival, I at least had to remember not to let Toby feed me any more omelettes. My throat wouldn't thank me today, and my asshole wouldn't thank me tomorrow. The foul stuff burned nearly as bad on the way out as it did on the way in. I bolted for the kitchen.

Toby was chopping assorted veg into large chunks. The contents of his pan already looked like a massacre in a market garden.

"How many people are having omelette?" I asked innocently.

"Erm, Carrie, me, you… and Richie. D'ya reckon I should use two eggs?"

"Nah," I said, "I'm not too hungry, I think I'll just get a bit of bread. One egg should do three of you."

Toby nodded his agreement. "Can you pass the chillies out of the fridge?"

Phew! Disaster averted. For me in any case. I handed him the bowl and went back outside to snigger at my cleverness. Well, I'd had to experience it once, I figured, so why shouldn't the others? We could look on Toby's omelettes as a kind of initiation. Classifying them as an experience would also clear up a lot of confusion.

They certainly didn't qualify as food.

The Beaten Track

With so many of us working together we powered through every task that came our way. Two days digging steps into a random hillside? No problem! Six volunteers carving a set of, say, thirty six steps would only have to dig out six steps apiece. Pah! Barely a morning's work. It only took us two days because a) Richie kept telling ludicrous jokes, and b) there was a bloody lot more than thirty six steps to make. As to why we were digging the steps? Not a clue. Why does the wind blow? Well if you were anywhere near the back end of Richie it was probably something to do with his all-bean diet, but that's beside the point. The sun rises and the sun sets, without question; we made steps based on a similar rationale. They were very pretty.

Next we built a path. The procedure was remarkably similar to stair-cutting only on a horizontal plane. Dig a big-assed chunk of the hillside away. Move it three feet over. Pack it down again. Shore it up with dead trees. Then move two paces forward and repeat. Jimmy singled me out to help murder trees for the project which I have to admit was guiltily satisfying. My blade work was definitely improving. As the trail grew longer and more secure I seemed to be finding a rhythm, swinging with a loose arm and relaxing my grip just as the blade bit home. Inevitably I relaxed slightly too early on a couple of occasions and came frighteningly close to turning Jimmy into Stumpy.

Our glorious earthwork, when finished, traced the contours of the hillside roughly parallel to the road far above. It linked the new steps with a small clearing in the undergrowth, where a river sprang from the base of the cliff face and plunged away into the cloud forest far below. A kind of soily beach led down to the water's edge. That at least was the path's geographical location. From a practical point of view it started in the middle of nowhere, and went nowhere in particular.

It could have been a monument to life in Ecuador.

And then there was the bridge. Because that small river had to be crossed. WHY? Why did it have to be crossed? Was there a leprechaun stashing his pot of gold over there? I never found out. But many more trees contributed their promising young lives to the cause.

The trouble was, the more we cut, the further we had to go to find them. It was deforestation on a very small scale. Carrying the first logs across the road, down the steps, along the path and down to the river required an inhuman amount of effort, which was all wasted when they were too short. Hard to believe we were looking for trees when we were surrounded by them, but we needed exactly the right shape of trees. Very tall, yet slim enough to cut and carry. Sturdy enough to walk on without being heavy enough to crush my spine whilst trying to pick the fuckers up.

We managed to make a partial raft-like structure which almost extended to the far bank. Jimmy and I were the first across (being respectively the lightest and the stupidest of the group), and it was on the other side that I had my first introduction to the Spiky Bitch Plant. Now SBPs are, as their name suggests, festooned with a completely unreasonable amount of inch-long thorns that hurt like buggery when they sink into soft, unprotected flesh. The far bank of that river was covered in them. I came to loathe Spiky Bitches because of their knock-on effect – it hurt so much to get spiked by one that I would quite often recoil at high speed, typically stumbling straight into another one of the bastards. And so it went on.

Cutting trees on the far side was much more successful. They had been protected from our other projects by the river we'd just crossed, so there were plenty of big guys left to decapitate. We laid the first few to strengthen and elongate our bridge before it fell to me to carry the first sizeable log across. I made it exactly halfway. That's when the motley collection of saplings underneath me decided to take their revenge. They snapped under the combined weight of me plus log, one leg went through whilst the rest of my body pitched sideways over the edge. My log landed on top of me, an impact not unlike being punched in the kidneys by The Hulk. But I was saved from a dunking by my new favourite flora. As luck would have it I fell through the outstretched arms of a large stand of Spiky Bitch Plants, who proceeded to break my fall by wrapping themselves around my neck.

"Ack!" I managed.

"Are you… are you okay?" One of the girls managed to stop giggling long enough to ask me.

"Argh! I'm… Ow! Fucking spiky little… Ow!"

"Hang on, we'll get you," she promised. "Just give us a sec…" And they all fell about the place laughing.

Bathroom Break

The toilet door was locked. And there wasn't anyone inside. The latch had developed a decidedly Ecuadorian personality recently, choosing who could exercise their bodily functions and when with callous disregard for our comfort. Now the crafty old bugger was in crap latch heaven, and as a parting shot had decided to expire in the closed position. It was a bit of a problem. Six people, including three girls. Well, two girls and a wobblegong. And I have a bladder the size of a golf ball. Not to mention most of the bunch were vegetarians. If we couldn't get to our one and only toilet soon, this place was going to start to smell.

In truth it already did smell. Damn vegetarians.

By a lucky twist of fate, or in fact my tight-fisted boss skimping on building materials disguised as a lucky twist of fate, the bathroom walls didn't go all the way up to the roof. The room was more like a cubicle built in the corner of the dorm room. About eight feet high, the walls were capped off with a wooden ceiling nailed securely into place to keep unpleasant odours out of our bedroom. I knew how effective it was because I was frequently forced to take refuge from the smell of the bedroom by hiding in the loo.

I got a rickety chair and balanced precariously on top. I couldn't get onto the bathroom roof as it was too close to the ceiling proper, and would never take my weight in any case. When I said it was made of wood, I was perhaps being overly generous. Hardboard is a more accurate description. Here again the consistently poor quality of local building standards might act in my favour. This roof was about as strong as Toby's taste buds, or what was left of them.

Richie jumped up next to me causing severe strain to the chair. "Can we pull that off?" he asked.

"Um… Yeah. Don't see why not." I'd been thinking the same thing. I had to grin at the peculiarities of a life which involved two grown men trying to break into an empty toilet. It was very nearly the strangest thing I'd done all week.

With a screwdriver someone found on a shelf in the living room I prised the edge of the roof loose. The nails this exposed, in keeping with most of the nails we used, were very big and very rusty. With the main roof beams less than two feet above the bathroom ceiling we couldn't open it very far. The thin board was fairly flexible, so by bending it upwards we managed to create a slim gap, edged with rusty nails. It looked disturbingly like a mouth. But being hardboard and therefore only a few generations removed from actual wood, the ceiling resented being bent out of shape and was doing its best not to be. So it was a spring-loaded mouth full of rusty teeth. In I went – losing a fair amount of skin in the process.

Once I'd pulled my top half through I discovered another problem. Well, two problems actually; the first was that once off the chair my legs dangled uselessly with nothing to push on. The second was that everyone else found the sight of my legs dangling uselessly out of a hole in the roof so funny that they let go of the ceiling to laugh at me. It sprang shut on my ass with a sensation somewhat akin to being spanked with a cricket bat.

"Oww! You bastards!" I yelled.

Unsurprisingly this caused even more hilarity. Stuck half in and half out of the roof, all four limbs flailing frantically on both sides of the wall with a rusty nail slowly embedding itself in the soft flesh of my left buttock, now was not the best time to laugh. It was also exactly the wrong time to have that thought. I felt a chuckle coming on.

"No!" I called out to the others, "Don't make me laugh you buggers!"

But it was far too late for that.

All I could hear was echoing guffaws from outside, I could picture five people rolling round the floor holding their bellies as my legs protruded from above them, flapping pointlessly.

I started to laugh, so hard I couldn't stop. It was the sheer insanity of the situation. I could imagine Toby explaining it to a bewildered fireman who scratched his head as he looked up at the visible half of me. For about ten minutes five people sat around cracking up. I just cracked up where I dangled.

What a way to go, I thought, stabbed in the arse whilst trying to break into an empty toilet and then bleeding to death because I couldn't stop laughing about it long enough to get out! Must... Control... Myself...

Reaching out with both hands I braced myself between the side walls. I wriggled my ass a few more inches through the gap.

Then my hands slipped and I fell six feet into the toilet.

A minute later the bathroom door clicked open. I stood inside, one hand on the traitorous handle, and looked out at my equally traitorous work mates. The laughter was slowly winding down. A couple of them even managed to stand up.

"Having fun in there?" Richie asked innocently.

"Not too bad," I told him, "except I got nailed."

After a crazy two weeks, Carrie and Richie left within days of each other. Richie had originally planned to stay longer, but true love has a way of screwing up long-term plans. A few days previously he'd come up with the idea of using all our waste wood for a bonfire. Much drunkenness had ensued, and by the end of the debacle he and Carrie had discovered feelings for each other that the rest of us spotted the day they arrived. They set out to travel South America together, and that was the last we heard from them.

Life was often like that at Santa Martha – volunteers came and went, featuring in our lives for a brief time, and just as I was getting used to them they were gone. It was sad in a way, as each passing marked the last time I would see them again, and living and working so closely together forged strong friendships for the duration of their stay. Yet once they passed beyond the confines of the refuge I found I devoted little thought to them. Their lives were no longer enmeshed as were ours in the daily routine of feeding, cleaning, building and freezing at night. It was hard to think about anything other than the work at hand, or the work waiting for us tomorrow. The centre grew to dominate our thoughts, as will anything which becomes both home and work, and hobbies too, all rolled into one. It was not a bad thing – we just all cared about the centre, loved the animals, cursed the work and shared the same petty frustrations. When not working we talked about working, or what crazy task was likely to be next, or discussed the animals and whether we'd get to see them released or not. Our lives revolved around Santa Martha, and anything which wasn't directly a part of it tended to get pushed to one side.

This was the excuse I used when phoning my parents for the first time since arriving in Ecuador, by way of explaining why it had taken me over a month to do so. I'd last spoken to my mother as she tearfully put me on the bus to the airport. Bless her!

She was overcome with joy to find out that I was still alive.

The Trouble with Reptiles

Every so often a new creature or two would show up at Santa Martha – it was just the way of things, and we soon became used to it. The morning feed would often be punctuated by cries of "Hey, we've got a new monkey," or occasionally "Hey, we've got a new… whatever the fuck that is!" Everyone would crowd around for a quick look, then disperse back to their feeding and cleaning tasks. Later that morning either Toby or me would ask Johnny about the new addition, and he would reply with customary inscrutability.

Me: "Um, Johnny, do we have a new *monkey/*ferret/ *toucan/*unicorn?" (*Delete as applicable.)

Johnny: "Yes."

Me: "Oh. Okay then."

And that was that.

Invariably the animals had been brought by Leonardo, our faithful (and brilliant) vet, under cover of night, either because he worked so hard all day at his practice in Quito, or just because he loved to mess with our heads. Not many people knew how good his English really was, and I'm sure he had a few laughs at our expense as we spent a morning after some heavy drinking trying to decide just how many capuchin monkeys were *supposed* to be in a particular cage. "Either I'm still really wasted," someone had famously said, "or these guys are *breeding*!"

Some of the new arrivals caused more concern than the others – one time I spotted a small crocodile in the middle of the little open garden between the cages. It wasn't moving, but had already attracted a few worried stares from the other volunteers. "Toby," I'd asked, "There's a small crocodile in the garden. Are we supposed to have a small crocodile here?"

"Oh," he replied, "I asked Johnny about that."

"And?"

"He said 'Yes'."

Unfortunately, that poor beast didn't last long. It turned out that a farmer had caught him, miles from anywhere he should have been, so most likely he was an escaped pet. He wasn't well, so Leonardo (assisted by an extremely attractive student nurse) had administered some antibiotics. That was a lesson learnt the hard way; our cold climate kept his blood too sluggish to circulate the drugs. The croc was dead within hours. So if you're ever attacked by a small crocodile, and it's a bit nippy out, and you happen to have a syringe full of antibiotics in your pocket, you're laughing.

The tortoises, on the other hand, we were expecting. Well, perhaps expecting is too strong a word. Basically we were told that some had arrived, which was about as close as we got. They spent their days in the same garden that had witnessed the death of the previous reptile, and generally did very little – with one exception.

Twice each day, during the feeds, one of us would do a quick tortoise headcount. I personally considered it more likely they'd have grown another one than lost one. They hardly ate. They hardly moved. As I said, with one exception. On finding only five mottled brown domes amongst the foliage one morning we began to search in earnest. It was a mystery – in the fairly confined space surrounded by cages, where could number six have gone? It was two days later when he was discovered in a scrap pile, slowly burrowing into the rusty junk on top. To get there he'd had to crawl under a variety of fences, down a narrow gap between two monkey cages, under another fence and then jump off a small cliff onto the scrap heap several feet below. Why? We were stumped. 'How?' was another unanswerable question. Along with 'Did he fall – or was he pushed?'

He did it again two days later.

By the third time we knew automatically where to look for him. He must have loved that scrap heap. Two possible explanations sprang to mind: either he really was trying to commit suicide, lemming style, or (and this was my favourite) he'd watched too many cartoons. He thought he was a ninja.

Cross Country

There are things I'd rather be doing at four thirty in the morning. Well, given the lack of suitable female company, only really one thing. Either way, huddling outside in the freezing darkness whilst tying monkeys to a truck was not on my list.

The monkeys of course were in a cage, and neither they, nor I, was alone. Toby, Ashley, and Layla were also swarming around the vehicle, hissing orders at each other as though talking normally might wake the neighbours.

There was only one reason I wasn't pissed off at the ridiculous hour and swearing like a drunken Scotsman; all four of us had asked, nay begged, Johnny for this opportunity. For the next eight hours we would be tucked into the truck, knees to chins and sandwiched between cages as he drove three hundred miles down the spine of the country. Because at long last we were going to release the animals. We were going to the Amazon.

Most of the previous day had been spent capturing the lucky customers. None of our bigger critters would be making the trip; ocelots, eagles, puma and tortoise, all had nowhere to go. Realistically none of them would ever be leaving Santa Martha. Osita was another story. Eventually she'd be off to our sister programme, a bear-tracking project in the northern cloud forests. For now she was an unruly teenager, still awaiting the decision that she was old enough to leave home.

It took over an hour to secure the cages to the truck. They were stacked two and three high on the roof, with rope running across and around, back through and down, up again and over, and over and over... Toby had been doing the tying and in the sheer quantity of knots I could see his desperation that nothing come loose as we bounced along rural roads. Given the quality of paving in Quito I could only imagine what the road was like in more remote areas. My buttocks clenched involuntarily. I would be riding in the back.

We lined the floor with an old thin mattress courtesy of Brenda, and lined ourselves with three layers of clothing and a couple of blankets. Toby, Layla and Ashley squeezed together along the back wall of the cab, with arms and legs folded tightly around themselves. I wedged myself in facing Toby, next to the single biggest cage we owned, and braced my back against the low tailgate. Hopefully it wouldn't open suddenly whilst we were doing a hundred down the freeway. A wooden crate full of small tortoises (including our resident escape artist) was handed in as a last minute addition to our cargo. Every inch of available space was crammed, with volunteers, excess clothing, animals – if Johnny had decided to take a deck of playing cards with him one of us would've had to get out. We huddled and shivered as the last minute preparations were completed. It was almost 6 am, and cold enough to freeze the balls off a woolly mammoth.

Almost as an afterthought Johnny pulled a thick tarp over us. He'd fastened some poles to the sides of the truck without explaining why; now he tied the free corners of the tarp to them, revealing his ingenuity. Our thoughtful boss had given us a roof over our heads, and as though waiting for his permission the rain began in earnest. I hoped the tarp was waterproof. We were essentially sitting in a small steel box which would need very little encouragement to become a swimming pool.

After an hour of speeding through the darkness I realised I could see out. The sky was lightening almost imperceptibly. Shadowy shops and apartment blocks flew by on either side, grey ghosts of some town on the outskirts of Quito. We made one brief stop in the semi-dark, picking up Leonardo, presumably from his home. He didn't find the humour to pass comment on us as he took the spare seat in the warm, comfy cab. None of us even considered getting out – it would have required at least ten minutes of co-ordinated contortion and frankly, we couldn't afford the energy.

Dawn was a beautiful sight, streaks first of silver and then gold flickering through the gaps between buildings. No-one was speaking, or even moving. Wrapped in multiple jumpers, coats, scarves, gloves... four heads were tucked in tight, facing downwards.

As the light grew and the sound of the rain on our tarpaulin diminished, it started to feel quite cosy in the back of the truck. My body had adapted to the temperature as much as possible, and the area around us began to come into focus. Our world expanded from the square metre and a half of mattress bordered by cage mesh, to shrouded views of the trees and fields around us. We were in the foothills of the Andes mountains, heading steadily upwards.

I must have dozed off, because the next thing I knew brilliant sunshine was baking my box. (By which I mean the box we were all sitting in!) Surrounding me on all sides, mountains towered, vast and snow-capped. Beneath the snow line the world glowed green. Every inch of the landscape was heavily forested and glistening from the night's storm. Steam rose from the foliage and heat-haze distorted the distance. The sheer scale of the panorama was mind blowing. Taming it with a road must have been a bitch of job. On one side of the truck the jungle plunged down so suddenly that we couldn't even see it from the road. Cliffs soared on the other side, scarring the otherwise flawless emerald vista. For miles and miles at a time the only sign of human habitation was the ribbon of asphalt, stretching forlornly into the distance or vanishing around the next granite outcrop. Spectacular is the only way I could describe it – there aren't sufficient words to do justice to that landscape.

About nine in the morning the truck pulled over at a roadside café. There was literally nothing else there – just a café, with a bit of gravel out front for cars to park on. It must have been a lonely kind of existence for the staff, working and presumably living there. Not to mention that, if they ran out of toilet roll while someone was taking a dump it would be a long, long drive into town to get some more.

By the time the whole group of us had piled out and massaged some feeling back into our lower limbs, the café staff had woken up to the fact that they had customers. None of them seemed particularly thrilled at the prospect. A laminated menu was thrust in our faces by a big woman with a moustache. It was something of a shock after a couple of hundred miles of unbroken natural beauty.

We sat for a long time, with the waitress walking backwards and forwards across an otherwise empty cafe, glaring daggers at us each time she passed our table. She was truly hideous; forty going on a hundred and forty, haggard and bitter. And quite possibly a man. When breakfast finally arrived it was unidentifiable – certainly to the waitress, as she seemed to have given us completely the wrong order. Times four. Toby drew the short straw for pointing this out. I thought it might be the end of him. He got a short, vicious-sounding reply, and she pointedly removed each plate one at a time. Then she brought them all back at once, and merely placed them in front of different people.

We gave up. The vegetarians ate what food they thought they recognised and I ate the rest. I'd definitely gotten the better end of the bargain, due to my cultural sensitivity and appreciation. Or as Toby put it, by being about as discerning as a wheelie bin. We beat a hasty retreat before the terrifying woman could poison us with dessert.

The journey continued through stunning scenery for several more hours. The road itself devolved from two empty lanes of bitumen highway to one lane of empty dirt track bordered closely by forest. We were descending now. The lower we got, the more humid the atmosphere became, and the foliage became denser and brighter. We crossed a bizarre steel 'bridge' consisting solely of two narrow girders as the proper bridge had been recently washed away. There was no mistaking our surroundings now – it was genuine jungle, straight out of Jurassic Park.

At some point during this stage of the journey the wooden crate of tortoises ceased to be a crate and became a pile of sticks. Somewhere in the bottom of the truck, between bums, bags, shoes and crumbs, were six medium-sized tortoises, probably scared shitless. A yelp from Ashley announced that she'd found one. A further yelp announced that it had decided to be scared shitless all over her. The realisation spread around the truck that at least five more piles of shit were doubtless waiting to be discovered somewhere beneath us, along with their unhappy owners. And there was not a thing we could do about it. I suddenly regretted persuading them to eat so much banana the previous night.

Only a few miles out from our destination we ground to a halt in a traffic jam. I honestly wouldn't have thought more than twenty cars used this dusty yellow track in a year, but there were already that many sitting in front of us with their engines turned off. We took the opportunity to get out and stretch. Over the last three hours my back had begun to conform to the shape of the tailgate. It had two horizontal ridges running across it between my arse and my shoulder blades. My buttocks had compressed into thin pads consisting largely of bruise, and my left arm sported a decorative imprint of parrot cage. But my right arm was getting a nice tan.

Johnny had walked on ahead to see what the hold-up was. We joined him for the sake of something to do. And stood in disbelief looking at the obstacle in our path. It was an enormous plastic tube. Bright blue. Lying right across the entire road. With impenetrable jungle pushed up close on both sides there was no way around this rather unexpected blockage. Several workmen strolled calmly around the area. Could they be responsible for this? It looked like God had been colouring in the sky and had accidentally dropped his crayon.

From behind the huge tube came the rumbling roar of a big digger starting work. Clouds of dust obscured its operation, but I saw enough to make out the plan. The tube was a pipe. And the pipe was going into the ground. A trench of epic proportions was being dug behind it, and until it was finished no-one was going anywhere. If someone listing the potential hazards of travelling by car in Ecuador had suggested the possibility of being severely delayed by a massive blue tube, I'd never have taken them seriously. But here it was, proof again, had I needed it, that this was a very, very strange country. Their priorities were not my priorities, and to them midday on a Monday must have been the perfect time to bury a two-metre high plastic pipe beneath the only road for hundreds of miles. The whole day's worth of traffic was queued up behind this bizarre obstacle, yet no-one seemed in the least bit surprised. I tried to imagine the reaction of rush hour commuters on any road in England if faced with such a situation. Some of them would drop dead of apoplexy just considering the concept. This car-owning community was far more relaxed. They stood around and chatted with other drivers, smoked, drank or just sat on the side of the road. Quite a few had noticed the strange cacophony of sounds emanating from the roof of our truck. Before long Johnny was pointedly ignoring a veritable crowd of onlookers, all reaching out hands to stroke monkeys and poking whatever came within poking distance. I got poked myself a few times.

An hour or so later the situation finally resolved itself. Working amazingly fast, and with typical lack of regard for anyone's safety, the workmen had managed to scrape a trench almost deep enough for their pipe, dump the bloody great thing in, then throw a few shovelfuls of earth back on top. They stood back from their labours, clearly proud of what they had achieved, as the first vehicle moved up to negotiate the bulge. It was some time before we got our go, and I was glad I wasn't driving when we did. Johnny skilfully traversed what remained of the ramp and ignored the frightening way the top of the pipe seemed to sag and groan under our weight. Then we were across, and home free. As we followed the procession of beat-up trucks and 4x4s deeper into the jungle I swear I could smell the anticipation in the animals. Or wait – no, it was just more tortoise poo.

Removing the cages from the car was a whole lot easier than putting them on. In minutes we had close to twenty separate cages of every possible size and style arrayed around us like Christmas presents. And about a mile and a half of rope. Johnny had driven us down a succession of progressively smaller dirt tracks until the car wouldn't fit any more. From where we'd parked a footpath was scuffed into the grass, leading off downhill. I really hoped we weren't walking the rest of the way. See, you can put eleven large parrots into one enormous steel cage for travelling purposes – assuming you survive the process of catching them – but such a burden doesn't lend itself well to being dragged for five miles through virgin rainforest. It would give even Jimmy pause except that he'd stayed at home to feed the cows – a choice which suddenly made much more sense.

Instead we caught a canoe. The footpath led to the edge of a wide river and by the time we'd hauled every cat carrier, bird cage, box, basket and crap-filled crate down a short dirt slope to the water's edge, a boat had already appeared as a dot on the horizon. It still wasn't substantially larger than a dot when it arrived. If primitive canoes could be described as hollowed out logs, this just about qualified as a hollowed out stick. It had an engine though, which sounded considerably older than the boat.

The pilot threw a long mooring rope at me, which I caught instinctively before realising that there was nothing remotely close enough for me to tie it to. I stood there dumbly for several long moments with the end of the rope clutched pointlessly to my chest, wondering if he was expecting me to tie it to my head. Then Johnny, with a grunt of disgust and a shake of his head for the foolishness of Englishmen, snatched the rope out of my hands and hauled on it with all his might. Sluggishly the canoe responded to his efforts, and by the time it had dawned on me just what had been expected of me Toby was already helping to pull the narrow boat in to shore. The front of the canoe ran a little way up the slope and the pilot, a silver-haired, wrinkled old man wearing tattered jeans of indeterminate colour and nothing else, jumped out onto solid ground. He exchanged a few words with Johnny, punctuated with a sharp bark of laughter, that honestly didn't require translation.

"He thinks you're an idiot," Toby supplied helpfully.

"Yeah? Well I think he looks like a sack with a smiley face drawn on it." I stomped off towards the cages, grumbling to myself.

The trip upriver was exhilarating. Going against the current now rather than with it as before, the canoe skipped over its own bow wave sending sheets of spray high into the air. We got soaked, which clearly didn't agree with Layla, but for me it was all part of the experience. The motor growled, the propeller churned, and the boat sped upriver between banks thick with jungle. Trees leaned out at crazy angles over the water, testament to the ferocity of the river in spate. Vines hung down and draped over logs submerged in the shallows, seamlessly blending the green-tinged water into the lush foliage.

Twenty minutes of strenuous motoring brought us to a much more recognisable dock. A few old stumps of posts jutted out of the water, and further up the bank there were log-framed steps leading off into the undergrowth. The air was alive with insects as Sack Man guided his canoe in to land. A ripple of excitement ran through me. Somewhere beyond those steps was our final destination, and a new home for my furred and feathered friends. It was known in the trade as a 'soft release space', though by all accounts it had better facilities than we did. And lots – and lots – of jungle. It was called Amazoonico.

Tony James Slater

Ama"Zoo"nico

Refuge, tourist attraction and education centre; Amazoonico was all of these things. It most closely resembled the Ewok village from Return of the Jedi. Everywhere was logs. Log buildings, log stairs and walkways and a truly impressive roofed bridge that carried the path from the beach over a narrow gorge and waterfall. It was through this structure that we came, staggering under the weight of our assorted burdens. Around us monkeys shrieked and birds warbled. Cicadas kept up their incessant drone, occasionally swelling in volume then dying down into the background again. Every now and then a more elaborate call would sound, echoing out of the jungle in a complex series of hoots and cries; it could have been the mating call of the Yeti for all I knew.

The air was so humid it had substance. I couldn't tell if I was sweating into the atmosphere, or it was sweating onto me. Climbing the timber-framed steps, like taking a tunnel directly through the rainforest canopy, had taken my breath away in more ways than one. I instantly regretted my gallantry in selecting the two heaviest cages to carry. Who'd have thought we'd have to climb a quarter-mile of stairs with the bloody things?

Amazoonico was alive. I'd been looking forward to

seeing the place for weeks, and I wasn't disappointed. Jungle plants grew between the structures as though the forest was determined to reclaim the place. Parrots sat here and there on branches and roofs. Monkeys hung and swung in all directions. Humans emerged from one of the log cabins to greet us. Then chaos erupted, drowning out the sounds of nature as all the Ecuadorians in both groups began to introduce themselves at volume. Cages were stacked, hands were shaken, and every few seconds the party grew larger as more people ventured out of the buildings to see what was going on. Our little group of volunteers was sort of swept off to one side by the commotion, where we stood in silence eyeing our animals protectively.

Eventually Johnny, Leonardo and what must have been their opposite numbers from Amazoonico managed to wash up together in the midst of the human maelstrom. Once they understood each other they ducked inside to conduct their business. Toby got involved too, weighing parrots and struggling to determine the sex of our kinkajou. Another of the gorgeous creatures was gazing placidly at us from a big cage backing onto one of the huts and our little fella, if deemed compatible, could be introduced to his new room-mate straight away.

Meanwhile one of Amazoonico's volunteers, possibly an Austrian, led the rest of us off between the wooden buildings. "So, we can go on ze tour now," he told me in his very precise accent.

"I've never seen so many monkeys!" I was hoping to stir some enthusiasm in him, as he didn't seem thrilled to have been handed this duty.

"We have released a lot of monkeys in zis area." His explanation lacked passion. I was hoping to engage him in some friendly banter and compare notes on our various experiences, but he seemed less inclined.

"You have a lot of capuchins," I observed.

"Yes," he said, "watch your hat."

My hand went instinctively to my head, which was unexpectedly bare. "What? Where...?"

I twisted around to look behind me. Nothing! Then I glanced up. My hat was dangling from a nearby monkey. I made a grab for it which the monkey casually evaded.

"Don't worry. He'll drop it," said the man.

As if on cue the monkey threw the hat at me and scurried off into the canopy.

"And watch your shoes. And valuables. These monkeys will steal anything."

The tour progressed through a bewildering variety of animal enclosures. They had everything we had at Santa Martha, and so much more. Their 'caiman', small crocodiles identical to the lucky guy we'd inherited and inadvertently executed in the same day, were flourishing in an artificial lake complete with its own island. There were five or six of them at least, looking closer in size to 'real' crocodiles than our poor specimen had. Another lake, dammed at one end by the wall supporting the path, contained the weirdest looking things I had ever set eyes upon. Even Snotty (our blind coatamundi) looked like a regular denizen of planet earth next to these fat grey monsters with bristling moustaches. They looked like the demon offspring of a rat and an elephant seal.

"Capybara," our guide answered my question. So. I'd heard of them, and consider it a matter of pride that I can even spell the word. But I'd never imagined them to look like that; huge, sleekly-furred, with flat stubby noses. When we wipe ourselves out in World War Three and the rodents rise to rule the planet, these guys get to be T-rex.

There were plenty of ocelots. Too many apparently, which is why we couldn't bring ours. The release programme seemed unnecessarily drawn out to me, since they were effectively wild animals that had been captured and imprisoned for varying lengths of time. Months of quarantine and rehabilitation were followed by studies to determine the most favourable time and site for release. But as our guide explained to me there were many things to consider before sending a large number of animals back into the rainforest. "Stability of ze existing population iz most important," he explained. "Some monkeys will fight to ze death to defend zer territory, so if we release zem in ze wrong place many will die. And ocelots, zey are predators. We have already released so many monkeys here. We don't want to watch zem all get eaten!"

The point was a good one. It begged another question, one which our guide certainly wouldn't be able to answer. If we couldn't release a group of ocelots here, then where could we release them? I knew our existing population had been with us for some time. Johnny had explained to Toby and me why they were so difficult to set free in my first few days at Santa Martha, pointing out that surprisingly few people wanted a whole pack of big hunting cats released near their property, but at the same time he'd told us that eventually the release centre would take them. Now here we were in the Amazon, sans ocelots, being told that the release centre didn't want them either. The future looked a little bleaker for the beautiful felines.

We moved on deeper into the jungle, following narrow tracks lined with half-buried tree trunks in what must have been a mammoth project of trail-blazing. Everything was so much bigger and more professional here, it really put our little farm into perspective. With our weird and wonderful array of creatures and awesome enclosures I thought of Santa Martha as a really big deal, and was proud to be associated with it. Amazoonico was clearly in a different league. They were open to tourists, they charged an entrance fee and everything. They clearly had access to more funding than we did (which meant they had access to any funding at all, which we didn't) and that gave them both the ability and the necessity to appear more professional. Every enclosure was securely concreted into place, often with decorative stonework pressed into the cement. All the enclosures were roofed in sturdy wire mesh, which meant they had access to something else we didn't have – a decent ladder. Still, though on the one hand it made me feel a little like a slack-jawed country bumpkin faced with the marvels of New York City, it did mean that our animals would get the best treatment here. I had to assume that the quality of the staff would at least match their facilities.

"You've given me a lot to think about," I told our guide.

And it was true.

Toby had finished helping with the weigh-in. All our new arrivals had been processed and transferred to temporary holding pens ready for admission. The kinkajou, its sex having been determined suitable, was already sitting quietly in the cage at the opposite end from its new cell-mate. It looked a little confused, and my heart went out to it as always.

"You'll be okay," I told the cuddly beast, as much to reassure myself. I'd put so much energy into caring for each animal that I felt I knew them all as individuals. With some I had formed a very strong bond. And some I loved. It was going to hurt, leaving so many of my friends behind.

"You coming for a swim?" asked Toby.

"Yeah man! Why not?"

"You up for it?" he enquired of the girls. "Swim? In the river?"

"Eew! It's probably full of bacteria and parasites." This was from Layla. "You shouldn't go in there. You'll get really sick."

Well that was hardly surprising. And to be honest if she had gone in there, I probably wouldn't have wanted to.

Ashley just shook her head and went back to staring at a truly massive boa constrictor coiled in his pond in an enclosure behind us.

"Sweet!" Toby exclaimed. "Let's do it!"

We stripped off on the pebbly beach where the canoe had docked, put on our shorts and waded gingerly out into the river. The rocks underfoot were slippy, sharp and unstable. And then we were in – swimming in, if not the mighty Amazon itself, then surely one of its biggest tributaries – the Napo river!

There were times when it struck me, just how different and amazing my life had become since I left home. This was the king of all those moments. Not adjusting my tie as I answered the phone in some stuffy back office, or queuing up to buy a CD in HMV, or sitting in my flat eating chips and watching crap on TV. No – here I was in the middle of the Amazon rainforest, floating downstream amidst leaves and clumps of algae, while the lungs of the world stretched endlessly in all directions.

Butterflies flitted just above the surface, and I didn't want to think about what might be below it. But just for a moment I had a sense of my own potential; that if I could be here, doing this, then I could be anywhere, doing anything. The insight left me feeling indescribably powerful; confident, relaxed and free.

Toby was also enjoying himself. "Wanna swim all the way across?" he suggested.

"Hell yeah!" I said.

So we did. It was a tough swim to the opposite bank, swimming more diagonally upstream than straight across in an effort to stay level with the beach. We spent a few minutes on a muddy bank on the far shore, playing Tarzan (well, that's what I was doing. I'm sure Toby was too, but I didn't force him to admit it). The swim back was immensely difficult, as we were both knackered from the first crossing.

It seemed like forever, with the beach getting further away rather than closer as the fierce midstream current dragged us way off target. By the time we hauled ourselves up the bank, mindless of the sharp stones and coated with thick mud, everyone else in our party was stood there waiting for the boat.

It was time to leave already.

Home

The return journey was considerably shorter.

Monster

Two days after the Amazoonico odyssey we'd recovered enough to return to work. Exactly what we were going to do was an interesting question. Before the trip we'd been working like mad to expand and upgrade the centre, building new enclosures and fixing the old ones. But most of them were empty now. The feed took us a fraction of the time it had previously and we were still accidentally making far too much food in the morning. Surely no more building needed to be done?

"So, what're we up to today?" I asked Toby. As usual our co-ordinator seemed to have his finger on the pulse and supplied the information without hesitation.

"Dunno mate," he said.

But he was enthusiastically donning wellies and the girls had emerged too. It was clearly time to do something. We headed around the house and found Jimmy and Johnny standing by Snotty's old enclosure. It had been empty since the release, with the blind coati relocated to somewhere more suitably sized. The cage was big and sturdy with a mesh roof and a well-made door. I'd figured that we'd be filling it when we finally got to go on the elusive 'animal rescue missions'. But the boss had other plans.

He explained to Toby and Jimmy what was needed. I

could follow a little of the conversation, and my intense focus was rewarded when I picked out the word '*lobo*'. Had I heard right? Were we really getting *el lobo*?

Toby confirmed my suspicions. A wolf was on the way. Our mission, should we choose to accept it, was to suitably reinforce the cage to take the beast when he or she finally showed up. Awesome!

Now, this did present a couple of problems. Wolves are, like domestic dogs, fond of digging holes. And if a lifetime of trashy horror movies is to be believed, they are vicious slavering monsters, likely to escape through said holes and devour chickens, parrots and pretty much anything that's small, cute and doesn't want to be eaten. Whether or not that would include small dogs I wasn't sure, and I didn't want to find out. So today Snotty's old home would become wolf-proof.

We discovered several huge rolls of thick wire mesh in the 'huge rolls of thick wire mesh' pile opposite the *galpón*. We blokes dragged them over to the cage, while the girls started digging trenches. As I took my turn at digging I asked Jimmy how deep the trenches had to be. He told me they had to be at least a metre deep and pointed out where they had to run – down the whole length of three out of the four sides of the cage. That sounded like a lot of digging. Was I surprised? I think not.

The others took it in turns on pickaxe and shovel, working on two trenches between the three of them and taking regular breaks, but for some reason I was in the mood for graft. The release trip had given me renewed commitment to the cause, re-affirmed my belief in what we were doing. I wanted to achieve, to impress, to associate myself with good strong work and to be remembered for it. I dug hard and fast, moving from the front by the door back towards the wall of Johnny's house, which formed the fourth side of the cage. The first half went quickly. Not so the second. I'd cleverly picked the most difficult place to work, crouched right under a low log perch which ran all the way across the back side of the cage. Every time I shifted position I'd get poked in the back by a sharp branch, causing me to shout, recoil and bang my head on the log. Then I would swear and start digging again, scraping with the tip of the pick as there was no room to swing it.

Slowly the trench took shape. It was well over half a metre deep and looking very impressive when the others decided they'd finished. I investigated their efforts, and casually informed them that they had a long way to dig yet.

Jimmy, however, disagreed. In his opinion they had all simultaneously achieved the perfect depth for anti-burrowing wire mesh implantation. His idea of a metre differed radically from mine. All we had to do now was fill my hole back up to the correct depth and we'd be ready to start putting the wire in.

Three people took only minutes to solve the problem I'd spent the last two hours carefully creating.

Layla turned to tell me they were done, and got poked in the back by the sharp branch. "Argh!" she cried, and smacked her head on the log. It almost made it all worth while.

The wire was an absolute bitch to get in. It was bent, and the trenches were bent, but not in the same way. Pushing one end of the mesh into place inevitably liberated the other end of the piece, which had until recently seemed securely buried. With one person digging out the trouble spots and two forcing both ends into position it was just possible for the fourth person to fill in the trench and bury the wire. I dug, Toby pushed, Ashley pushed and Layla buried. Success! One down.

But adding the next section meant it had to be tied to the end of the first with wire, leaving no gaps for a cunning *lobo* to exploit. Arse biscuits. As we dug up the end of the first piece we decided that next time we would attach the sections together before we buried one of them.

By late, late afternoon we were done. I was positive we'd made all the trenches plenty deep enough – or more accurately, I was damn sure they weren't about to get any deeper! The last section of the wire had been buried and fastened to the mesh of the cage all the way around. It was all double thick, except for the first section which we'd just finished re-burying when Johnny explained he wanted all sections to be double thick. As far as he was concerned we knew what he was thinking even before he decided to share it with us.

Telepathy was a useful trick during my time at the centre.

Though sadly about as psychic as a cheese, I was becoming a master of bullshit. A case of When In Rome... And I was learning from the masters.

The heavily fortified cage didn't get filled that day. I almost didn't think it had been filled the next day either – but then I looked harder. What had caught my eye? In the shadows something moved. Could it be...? I crouched down for a better look, my face pressed dangerously close. There it was! In the corner furthest from the light, trembling with barely contained rage – or... shivering? In fear? The longer I looked, the more I could make out. Huddled beneath a low feeding platform was a very small, very bedraggled, somewhat pathetic-looking fox. His fur was matted, his long tail wrapped protectively around his quivering body. I think the poor creature was cold. In the ferociousness stakes he must have ranked somewhere between Don Juan and Machita. Maybe even that was too dramatic. In a cage built to contain the Hounds of Hell we had imprisoned a creature that looked like he would lose a fight with a stuffed toy.

And he was a girl.

That Bear Ate My Pants!

Rescue

There was an aura of evil around the circus. I could feel it, or maybe smell it, as we approached the sagging canvas of the big top. Johnny and Brenda, Toby and myself, accompanied by a crack squad of Quito's finest Animal Police. No, seriously! Presumably international pressure on the country's ecological policy was responsible for their creation. I could see them as a sort of lip service sacrifice, the minimum effort and expense needed to make it look like the government was taking the issue seriously. There was only one group of them and I doubted if they knew any more about animals than any other coppers. But interestingly enough we were also being followed by a film crew from one of the local TV stations – they'd sent their star reporter to cover the inaugural rescue of the Animal Police. It meant Toby and me got to ride in a military-style covered wagon with the cops, which they seemed to find very amusing.

Close up, the enormous main tent was dilapidated, dishevelled, and the painted wooden signs were battered and flaking. The place felt like a ghost-circus, some relic of a bygone era inhabited by the tortured souls of those who once cavorted for entertainment.

Inside was worse. A couple of squat, ugly guys were debating with the police in subdued tones. Their anger was apparent, as was their lack of hygiene, but there was little they could do about either with a squad of armed officers surrounding them. One biggish guy with enough bling over his stained shirt and jeans to suggest comparative affluence, was shaking a finger at our short-sleeved cops. There was grass underfoot. Gigantic logs that made our fence posts look like twigs supported the roof. The underside of the canvas was dark blue and painted with gaudy yellow stars.

Along one wall ranged an assortment of cages on pedestals. Each one contained a creature, all looking subdued and sorrowful. A couple of pitiful capuchin monkeys, a few small green parrots – and right at the end was the prize pet of the freak show. A huge scarlet macaw, his beak so grossly overgrown that it must have been almost impossible for him to eat. The bottom jaw, thick and massive, curved up in front of his face and ended above his head. The top jaw grew round and down, crossing the bottom one scissor-like, with its tip digging into the feathers of his neck.

He looked like a monster yet behaved like a mouse. Brenda eased her hands carefully around it and drew it slowly from the cage. As she held it gingerly, both hands cupped around breast and wings, we clustered round in disbelief. The same sense of fascination with the macabre that kept the circus selling tickets was present in all of us. It made me feel unclean.

Johnny held open the gate of one of the cat carriers we'd brought with us. Between them the husband and wife team sealed the freak show parrot away and carried him off to safety. Toby and I stood silently in disgust and glanced sadly from cage to tiny cage.

Off to one side, under the eaves of the tent, there was a wheeled wooden carriage. The cops had clustered around it and were staring intently at something. Our height advantage gave us a glimpse inside to where a fully grown lioness lay on a pile of filthy straw. Lions? I caught the same look on Toby's face. What the hell were we going to do with lions?

Unfortunately that problem solved itself in a most unsatisfactory manner. All Ecuadorian wild animals are illegal to own. We could confiscate them on sight as long as Johnny reported the rescue to the appropriate authorities. But lions don't come from Ecuador. Wherever this stinking flash bastard had gotten his hands on a lioness, it was none of our business. The crack squad of Animal Police didn't look likely to start any kind of investigation into the matter. They seemed happy with their haul, and happier still not to have to risk life and limb to rescue a lion. We confiscated all the other parrots and monkeys one by one, and left. I tried to send an apology to the lioness with my eyes and heart. She didn't even move a muscle. Her cage was less than three metres long anyway – what was she going to do, turn back flips? We rejoined the cops in their wagon, but none of us shared their triumphant mood. They laughed and joked with each other, and poked fun at us, pointed and jeered and laughed some more. Toby and I sat in silence.

Until, going around a tight corner, the steel bench holding half the cops collapsed sending them flying in all directions! Watching them all trying to get back up when every pothole the truck hit sent them sprawling across the metal deck again was at last something for me and Toby to laugh about. Even half the cops joined in, cracking up at how ridiculous their mates looked falling all over the place. By the time we reached our next house call we were both in much better spirits. And I was determined to do everything I could to help in the rescue. Brenda and Johnny displayed such passion for helping these animals and I really wanted to be part of it.

Two small monkeys were chained to equally small trees in the middle of a paved backyard. Knocking on the offender's door hadn't produced any results, so it was lucky that there was access round the side. Surprisingly the police weren't allowed to enter anyone's home. All four sides of the yard were bordered by buildings; bricks and concrete completely surrounded the tiny patch of open ground where the twin trees sprouted. Each monkey had a chain about two metres long fastened around its waist with a leather band – cat collars as it turned out, designed to go around the neck with an ID disc on. The monkeys must have long since outgrown them, and become so wild due to the constant pain of constriction that their owner had never dared get close enough to take them off. By now, after God knows how long in that cramped courtyard, they were deformed and dangerously unhinged.

"I'll do it," I said. It was my motto now.

The look Johnny gave me was at once measuring and concerned. Could I do it? I could see him weighing the odds. Then he shrugged and nodded. "Okay," he told me. "*Cuidado.*"

Careful. Really? I was wearing long black welding gloves and a t-shirt, which was the sum total of our protective equipment. The nearest monkey was already screaming its pain and defiance at me. Quite how I could incorporate 'careful' into my capture tactics was beyond me. Should I have been approaching on tiptoes?

I spread my arms like a vampire swooping in for the kill. The chains were just short enough that neither of the monkeys could reach the other. It seemed a cruel jest on the part of the owner, but it did at least mean I could deal with them one at a time. My first target raced around his tree in a manic blur. Every time I got close to him he'd slip away – largely because I was too scared to grab him. He moved so fast and I was terrified of grabbing him badly and hurting him. In the end though I just went for it. Nothing else I could do, and before long Johnny would have stopped me anyway. So I lunged and the animal fled but his chain, already wrapped twice around the trunk, wouldn't allow him enough height to get away. I closed a gloved hand around his body. Instantly he writhed around in my grip and sank his teeth into my fingers. Again and again he bit. Shit, I was glad of those gloves! I felt every bite like catching my finger in a door, but hopefully nothing was breaking the skin. I adjusted my grip to hold the back of the monkey's head – something I'd had plenty of practice at recently – and suddenly the ordeal was over.

Well, half over – I still had to get the other bugger! It was an action replay moment and soon both monkeys were howling at us from the safety of their cat baskets.

Johnny actually looked proud when I handed him back the gloves. "Monkey Man!" he pronounced me. I've never been as proud of a nickname in my life.

From that moment on I had no fear. I faced down a bunch of dogs at the home of some wealthy government official; the specially trained squad of animal cops wouldn't go near them. I just walked through the gate, right up to the snarling animals and eventually they gave in. The cops came strolling casually in afterwards, congratulating me as though I'd just defused a bomb.

The film crew followed us through a couple more raids, then all the way back to the vet's surgery. There Leonardo anaesthetised the monkeys and carefully cut away the cat collars, revealing angry pink scar tissue beneath their malformed ribcages. The camera lens was mere inches away from the action as he carved away at the monster parrot's beak with an angle grinder. But their star reporter wasn't even watching; she was quite busy chatting up Toby! Since our first arrival on scene she'd been stuck to him like shit to a blanket. Apparently she was some kind of local celebrity. I had to admit that she wasn't bad looking and Toby of course didn't have the same fear of speaking Spanish that characterised my few fraught exchanges with the opposite sex. It'd be a fair coup for him if he started dating Ecuador's answer to Victoria Beckham! Though I couldn't really see her wanting to spend the night in the volunteer house...

She did however get him to star in his own little drama. The film crew asked the cops to reverse back up the road and drive their vehicles into shot with full lights and sirens blazing! It was (in my view) a rather feeble attempt to add excitement to the piece, but if it made better TV of our efforts then it was all for the greater good. So the cops screeched to a halt and out jumped Toby, determined expression on his face and empty cat basket in hand. What a star! I had a jealous moment when I wished they'd filmed me taking on those monkeys, but what the hell. So long as Johnny had seen me I was happy.

And thus, Santa Martha was restocked. Chains were removed, wounds salved and we repackaged several of the critters to take back home with us. The parrot with the huge beak, still enormous but now passably functional, would be coming along with two gigantic blue and yellow macaws that we'd discovered in an illegal private zoo. They'd been so distressed by the sight of the transport cages that they'd ridden all the way home on our shoulders!

We pulled up at the centre completely exhausted. A chorus of shrieks and squawks from the back of the truck announced our arrival. I was bleeding here and there from odd bites that had missed the gloves and heavily bruised from all the ones that hadn't, and everyone present stank like the floor of a monkey's cage. But it was a good smell and it was a good tired. Today we had done good. And that was all that really mattered.

Exorcism

The girls had their turn on rescue missions the next day. I stayed behind with Toby helping to redistribute all the new animals and help them settle in. It was immensely satisfying. What with all the major events recently I really felt like I was helping to make a difference. I'd even made a small collection in the *galpón* of all the chains, leashes and other barbaric restraints I'd taken off various creatures. I was minded to suggest we made a display of it for the visiting school groups to see, so that they could appreciate just how cruel people could be to wild animals. Without exception our new arrivals took to their enclosures with enthusiasm. After months or even years in tiny cages, restrained with ropes or steel shackles, starved, deformed and miserable, the chance to swing free, or fly a little, or even hop around an area bigger than a plastic crate, was gratefully exploited by all. I was already well on my way to making some new friends.

When the girls returned they looked glum. I hardly dared to ask them if they'd had fun. I didn't need to anyway. Layla had only been back a few minutes when she started complaining about it.

"We just sat in the truck while they drove and sat in the

truck when we got there. It was a total waste of time. Then they dropped us in a field and we stood around for ages while they chased after this deer. Like they could ever catch a deer! All we did all day was drive, sit around... so boring."

"Did they catch the deer?" I dared venture.

"Ha!" She scoffed. "Of course not! Why did they even bother?"

I itched to ask her the very same question.

Ashley was strangely quiet on the subject until later that evening. She might have had fun, she all but growled at me, had it not been for Layla whinging and whining, refusing to take part at all and hanging around Ashley like a fart in a space suit. Result: she couldn't take part either, as everyone else had lumped the pair of them together as useless observers. Poor Ashley was every bit as eager to be involved as I was, and twice as hard a worker. And now she was thoroughly pissed off.

The next few days were really tough, with no chance of escaping the tension in the volunteer house. Layla had been excused from working with the rest of us and someone, probably Brenda, had arranged for her to spend her time painting murals on the outside walls of the house. She painted a butterfly, and a picture of Machita, in a rather childish cartoony style. It made the place brighter of course, but it started to look a bit like a crèche. Evenings were spent trying to ignore the awkward silences that grew between us and I often hid in Toby's room until the others were asleep. On the upside, I was getting a whole lot better at chess!

Later that week, Layla was 'transferred for personal reasons'. Her gap year co-ordinator, after negotiations with Johnny, had decided that Layla was homesick and would benefit from a change of scenery. Personally I couldn't have cared less; whether she'd benefited from winning ten million dollars on the lottery, or been repeatedly run over by a steamroller. I was just happy to have her gone from the centre, and I don't think I was alone.

Toby walked with less caution, lost that 'hunted' look and began to strut once more. Ashley smiled continuously in the way that she had previously reserved for watching Machita play. I felt like one of those battered dogs, rescued from a life of misery by the RSPCA and restored to a kind and loving home with children who fed me biscuits and ice cream.

Occasionally Toby and me would catch ourselves grinning at each other for no immediately apparent reason, and at least one of us would spontaneously burst into a few lines of "Ding, Dong, the Witch is Dead!"

Poor spoiled little Layla. Obviously raised with a silver spoon between her butt cheeks, and hovering around 'that difficult age', she just wasn't ready for the wide world. And the wide world wasn't ready for her. Perhaps in a few years she'd learn some tact, earn a little wisdom and humility, maybe even develop a less abrasive personality. Then ideally join a gym, stop eating all the pies and get some plastic surgery. But she'd still be a pain in the arse.

Unfortunately we'd no sooner gotten rid of Layla than it was Ashley's turn to leave. In her case the departure was long arranged, and she'd probably been looking forward to it in the recent atmosphere. It did seem a shame though. She'd suffered less during Layla's reign of terror of course, being more of an ally than a target however unwilling, but it still didn't seem fair that she should have to leave just when we were getting used to having fun again. I told her to keep my tarot cards (I'd brought them to enhance my mystique; Ashley had adopted them after giving Toby a reading so scarily accurate he'd banned the cards from his presence) and embraced her warmly. I felt rather silly for ever worrying that she was joining in some imaginary campaign against me. She said a last tearful farewell to Machita before climbing into the taxi to be whisked out of our lives for good. Toby and I both took a few calming deep breaths but neither of us could afford to cry in front of the other. After all, this had happened before and would surely happen again. But for now it was the end of an era.

And once again we were two.

Bear Faced Cheek

After a fairly lonely weekend, Toby and I were eager to start work again when Monday swung around.

It started like any other day. As it happened, it finished like any other day too, but that's not important. The fact is, between those rather ordinary times, it was not at all like any other day. Well, the morning was different.

It was a day with a different morning.

We were halfway through the 7am feed when the alarm was raised (which happened fairly frequently at Santa Martha, and usually took the form of someone shouting "SHIT SHIT SHIT!" at top volume).

Toby and I legged it down the road to see what was up, leaving a cage full of hungry monkeys beating each other with our wooden spoons. The problem wasn't hard to spot. Around the corner that led down to Osita's enclosure there was a tall tree growing halfway down the hill – with a large bear cub at the top of it. Now, even in Ecuador bears don't grow on trees, and anyway those native to our area had long since been endangered into endangerment. Sitting coolly up that tree with a triumphant grin on her face was *our* bear cub.

Oh bugger. My first panicked thought: What the hell was she doing out of her enclosure? Answer: Simple.

Climbing a tree. Idiot. Next thought: How? How had she gotten out? Had I locked it properly yesterday? Of course! Even I'm not that dumb. Well, not twice. Had she been let out in the night by someone else? Or jumped somehow, despite the electric fence? Not that any of this mattered. There was only one pressing problem which definitely merited a Triple Shit Warning; how, in the name of all that smells fruity, were we going to get her back?

We joined Johnny, Jimmy and Danielo in a meeting of minds (which I appreciate is a bit of a contradiction in terms). I was thinking containment. Whilst Osita looked quite at home in the tree, more worrying was the prospect of her getting bored with it and climbing down. She could romp over the whole valley, and there wasn't a thing we could do to stop her. If she ended up on some other farmer's land she'd be shot without question, and there were no boundary walls or fences – at least nothing that would give her more than ten seconds pause. Osita was a master climber, which was another difficulty in itself. She could hide in the trees in the most impenetrable areas of forest, and be gone again by the time we cut our way through to her. All in all it didn't bear thinking about. To my mind we simply HAD to keep her in that tree.

Jimmy spoke up. "Let's get her out of that tree," he said.

I stared at him, amazed.

"No!" I groped for some pidgin Spanish phrases. "I... sit at tree with food. Fruit. She loves fruit and... she likes me. She come to me?"

"Ha!" Jimmy wasn't convinced. Logic wasn't really his style. The whole group headed for the tree while I suggested loudly that someone go get some food. No-one did of course, and I was too afraid of missing what would happen next to go myself. I had a nasty feeling it would all be over by the time I got back, and probably not for the better. Jimmy's more masculine approach to problem-solving was about as subtle as a kick in the bollocks.

I wasn't disappointed. As we neared the tree the Ecuadorians ploughed through the undergrowth, shouting at Osita as they went. The bear, not being blind and deaf, quite predictably saw them coming. She had two options; stay or go. She went. Out of the tree and down the side of the valley with breath-taking speed. It took rather more breath for us to follow her, not to mention time; as we cursed our way down the steep forested slope she was already climbing the one opposite.

Neither Jimmy nor Danielo seemed to appreciate the flaw in their tactics. They raced across the bottom of valley like two ten-year-olds about to lose their football. I was buggered. Even running downhill at this altitude was really difficult. Running uphill would be almost impossible. And running in any direction through heavy undergrowth was guaranteed to result in a big mouthful of ground.

It wasn't like I could help much. Osita had already given the others the slip. She loped along effortlessly, a big dog playing chase in a field. She changed direction a few times and ended up back at the bottom of the valley, leaving two heavily panting Ecuadorians stuck halfway up the far slope.

From where I stood panting I could watch the whole drama unfold. Bear run up. Men run up. Bear run down. Men run down. Bear run sideways. It was like watching Scooby Doo. At any moment I expected to see Danielo run past wearing a bear head and chasing Jimmy, or Osita tiptoeing along underneath an enormous vase.

All of a sudden the shouts drew nearer. She was heading in my direction! Then... she wasn't. I'd almost recovered, and the small surge of adrenaline powered little cog wheels in my head. I decided heroically to stay put and wait, figuring she might come towards me again. It beat the hell out of running back up the hill, since I was (inevitably) at the bottom. And then she did! I was ready. She thundered towards me, I mean right *at* me – then right past me and shot on up the hill. It was only then it occurred to me – what the bloody hell was I was going to do to stop her anyway? Rugby tackle her? Spank her with a rubber welly? We all know what happens when a bear hits you doing over thirty miles an hour. We were a long, long way from the nearest A&E department.

Then, looking up the hill I saw the Tractor Driving Dude, driving cattle for a change. Unfortunately for him he was driving them along the road right above me, and that meant he was about to have an unexpected visitor. I bawled at the others but they were still miles away. I could only watch in horror as Osita crashed through the herd like a giant hairy bowling ball, scattering cows in all directions before plunging back down the hill. The air filled with moos of dismay. But as she barrelled back past me we finally had the break we needed. She ran not into the main part of the valley, but through an old gate into a disused enclosure. It had previously been a deer paddock, so it was huge with a ridiculously high fence – perfect! I jogged casually over and swung the gate closed behind her. I had enough breath left for one yell of triumph and then I parked my ass on the grass.

By the time the others had arrived, I was reclining comfortably and there were cows everywhere. Toby turned up last. He'd been back to the house for a net and a tarpaulin. He even had a couple of bananas! It was good to know one person was thinking, and even better that it was Toby. Jimmy would have come back with a chain mail vest and boxing gloves.

The bosses held a hasty conference before entering the paddock. I nodded grimly at the serious tones of their voices, without actually understanding what was being said. Not like it mattered – from past experience I doubted they were crafting an ingeniously subtle, yet infallible scheme.

Meanwhile, Osita was climbing the fence. It was this new danger that finally broke up the meeting, prompting us to pile into the enclosure, yelling. Losing her was suddenly less of a problem – the fence she was climbing led into the fat puma's enclosure next door, and that was a disaster just waiting to happen. King Kong's love child versus the Godzilla of couch potatoes. Even Jimmy wouldn't dare to break that up. We attacked the fence to scare her away, so she bolted across the enclosure. As we gave a collective sigh of relief Osita found the bottom of a massively tall, extremely skinny tree, and effortlessly ran all the way up it. From the top she seemed to grin down at us, clearly pleased that she'd remembered just how crap we two-legs were at climbing trees.

It didn't improve Jimmy's mood any. Did I mention his general lack of subtlety? He called for someone to fetch an axe.

"NO!" I shouted. It struck me as a fairly bad idea. I was pissed off too – we all were – but I kinda wanted to keep the bear alive. Jimmy explained that she'd soon get out of the tree when she realised it was being cut down, but I was worried that she might not quite understand the process involved in using edged tools. She was very clever for a bear, and she'd soundly beaten all of us so far, but Jimmy seemed to be crediting her with more intelligence than he had himself!

Then I caught my name. "What?" I asked, suspiciously.

"You like to climb trees," Johnny said. "Climb the tree."

Oh shit, I thought. Johnny had actually read my application form? I knew I shouldn't have put that on it. Unless he was referring to that time in Osita's enclosure when I cut down a tree whilst still in it.

This tree was about as thick around as my forearm, and about as tall as a million of me stood on top of each other.

Well okay, maybe that's a slight exaggeration, but it was a very tall tree. The bear at the top of it looked more like a cuddly toy than ever.

Except that she weighed more than I did, was significantly stronger and had four legs and a head full of sharp things. And if she did decide to come down she would have to go through me to do it. I tried not to think too much about this as I stripped off my shoes and socks. Actually I was thinking about the nettles I was standing in.

Must look hard, I thought. Must be a man.

I took firm hold of the tree and spiked myself on a sharp bit of bark. Bugger.

Then Toby offered me one end of a piece of old rope. He must have brought it from the garage to tie the bear up. For a few seconds I thought he was expecting me to spontaneously knot up a complete safety harness from scratch, or display knowledge of some tribal rope-climbing technique. But as I stared in confusion at the grubby rope in my hand a light bulb pinged on in my head. I'd never felt more like Indiana Jones as, ignoring the oil stains and sawdust, I clamped the rope in my teeth and laid my hands on the bark. And with all the grace of someone who is unbelievably crap at climbing skinny trees, I climbed that skinny tree.

About a third of the way up, sore and sweating, I heard a cry from Johnny. I risked a glance down and saw him waving. I was shaking, just about clinging on for dear life, but I'd made it. I'D MADE IT!

"Okay, tie the rope on there!" Toby called.

I was glad the bosses didn't speak English.

"Are you fucking kidding me?" I growled around clenched teeth and a mouthful of string. I couldn't take even a finger off the now smooth bole of the tree. I needed two hands and two feet just to stop myself slipping right back down the bugger. But down below they were clearly waiting for me to do something. How I'll never know, but I coughed the end of the rope towards one hand and working entirely with my thumbs I made a half-assed knot. That was it for me; my sweaty hands slipped and I slid inelegantly all the way to the ground. Straight into the damn nettles.

And so began my first ever tug of war with a tree. Four people pulling back and forward on the rope while the boss called out the timing. "Pull, pull!" Johnny shouted.

We pulled. The tree shook. And the bear grinned down at us all, obviously delighted with this new game.

It wasn't long before we gave up. It had been a good idea, but yet again the bear had bested us. She was just better at holding on to a wobbly tree than we were at wobbling it. I suggested food again, and even stood at the bottom of the tree for a few minutes with a handful of slightly squashed banana, but apart from looking vaguely stupid and getting my hand all sticky I achieved nothing. The ball was back in Johnny's court.

By the time I'd cleaned the goo off, Danielo was already up the tree as far as my rope, running up hand over hand like a partially shaved monkey. He deftly picked at the knot with two fingers as his whole body hugged the tree, then taking the rope in his teeth he swiftly climbed another body length before tying it back round the now alarmingly slender trunk. I have to say it – I was really impressed. I half expected him to grab the free end of the rope, bellow his triumph and swing out of the tree on it.

In fact he also slid down, without substantially more control than me. I guess it just isn't possible to look skilful when sliding out of a skinny tree.

So the rope was ready again. We had almost five feet of extra leverage, clearly an important factor when squaring off against a hundred-foot tree. But this time even Johnny was lending a hand as we tried out the latest scheme from the great minds that brought you 'Chase the Bear' and the ever popular sequel 'Chase Her Some More'. For our next trick we were no longer Movers and Shakers. We were Benders.

Five bodies twined themselves into the rope and prepared to take the strain. A collective deep breath was taken. And Lo! The top of the tree did begin to bend. But that was just the wind. We hadn't started pulling yet.

We took the strain and began to pull. No grunts of exertion were necessary at first, and the treetop was clearly moving. Bear and all it swayed, then edged closer to the ground. We pulled harder. The tree was really bending now, as our superior strength (or perhaps the extra height in the rope) began to tell. Feeling like my arms would cease to be permanently attached as soon as anyone let go, I gritted my teeth and pulled on. The top of the tree was making a crazy angle with the ground, and the bear was scrabbling around to stay upright. I would have cheered, but my whole body was taught with the effort. Slowly, the scant foliage inched closer. And closer. And closer! We nearly had it! All of us were at maximum effort, five grown men throwing their entire weight onto this rope. So very close! If any one of us could've taken a hand off, he could almost have touched the matted fur of our quarry. Slapped her ass maybe, or poked her in the nipples.

Osita noticed this too. She looked around her for inspiration, and quickly formulated a plan. With a speed born of desperation – or perhaps born of being a bear – she ran down the almost horizontal trunk of the tree to the ground. Across the ground for a short distance. And up the next tree over.

You'd think we'd have seen that coming.

I started to see the funny side of it straight away. Along with the equally amusing prospect of all but one of us letting go of the rope in dismay, only to see the last person twanged into the air by the rapidly unbending tree and disappearing into the distance like Wile E. Coyote. Chuckle!

Starting to laugh at this moment was not a good idea, for precisely the reason described above. Recognising that somehow made it worse, and I suddenly realised that I really had to let go of this rope Right Now.

"Let go?" I hissed through clenched teeth.

"After three," came the reply. "*Uno, dos, TRES!*"

Five bodies flew through the air as we dived wildly away from the rope.

The tree didn't move an inch.

Well okay, it wobbled a bit. But it stayed exactly where we'd left it. In our Herculean efforts we'd bent it past the point of no return! This tree had something in common with a bloke I knew in college. It would never be straight again.

I stood up and brushed the grass off my jeans, feeling a little sheepish. Around me everyone else was doing the same, except for Jimmy. Jimmy was spitting out mouthfuls of nettles.

Toby grinned at me. I grinned back. Then we laughed. Boy did we laugh! Even Johnny joined in. Danielo walked over to the tree trunk and reached up to untie the rope, now hanging from a spot just above his head.

And still there was the problem of the bear. The tree she currently occupied was just a little taller than the one she'd recently vacated. Bending was clearly not the answer. I could really only see two options; either sit at the base of the tree and wait, or… wait whilst sitting at the base of the tree.

Johnny had other ideas. He gathered a handful of small stones and started to throw them at the bear. I figured he'd give up soon, as his aim was tragic. But he didn't give up. He just threw bigger rocks. I was starting to get worried, as a sizeable rock to the head could well result in bringing her down rather more quickly than we anticipated. She was awfully high up and there was no way she'd survive a fall. Killed whilst trying to escape? What was this, a P.O.W camp now?

Then Johnny connected. A couple of decent boulders bounced off her ass in quick succession, and just as I decided to make my complaint more vocal she decided that discretion was indeed the better part of valour, and abandoned the skinny tree – looking annoyingly skilful as she did it. The chase was back on! It was time to start being clever.

Nah, who'm I trying to kid? It was time for a bit more chasing her round the enclosure with no plan or strategy. About three quarters of an hour later, with still no sign of the bear tiring, then it was time to be clever. The only problem being that no-one had any particularly clever ideas at the moment. Chase her with the tarp and the net? Throw them over her and capture her? Wow, good plan. Let's try that. Again. The bear was not only outrunning us, she was outwitting us.

It was my laziness that saved the day. Instead of following the bear back down the paddock I just stayed where I was, gasping for breath. So when she made a break from her pursuers and ran straight towards me I held my ground, causing her to veer back – surrounded! The net was thrown – and missed.

Then, as if by magic (but in fact by the actions of a midget with a bad moustache), the tarpaulin sailed through the air. Jimmy had made a clean throw. And more by design than luck, as he assured us later, it settled completely over her. Score!

Johnny grabbed for her back legs and got a sliced forearm in the process. I grabbed her round the waist, as this seemed furthest from all the sharp bits, and Toby tried to capture her head. This was a mistake. She bit a large chunk out of Toby's palm. I couldn't see the extent of the damage as I was too busy trying to avoid a similar fate. Johnny was shouting at me to watch out as she could easily turn her head and take a chunk out of me. Then Jimmy managed to grab a hold of her nose, and suddenly it was all over.

Well, there were a couple of times when she managed to struggle to her feet and drag us around a bit, all frantically holding on, until we got our weight back on top of her and forced her down again. Eventually and after about a hundred cries of "*Cuidado!*", Jimmy and Danielo got the rope around her as I pinned her to the ground. They passed it around her again and quickly fashioned a harness, sort of like you might buy for a really big dog. And on the count of '*Tres*' once more, we all abandoned bear, leaving her cunningly leashed and Jimmy alone on the end of the rope. Looking remarkably composed considering.

Osita seemed to have chilled out a bit during her time under the pile of people. Perhaps all she really wanted was a hug! In any case, she was now ready to go home. Jimmy still held the lead and I walked beside her with a leafy branch, shaking it in front of her and tapping her nose whenever she tried to leg it into the trees lining the road – roughly every thirty seconds.

We passed her enclosure, Johnny having decided to rehouse her until we could find out how she escaped, and walked back up to the main house in a surprisingly calm manner. It must have made quite a sight, overgrown bear cub leading the way like a gigantic dog on a bit of string, me shaking a branch like a cheerleader and three guys following slowly and trying to look macho whilst bleeding all over the place.

Where do you put a rather large bear cub in a very bad mood? Hang on a minute – didn't some bunch of idiots spend a whole gruelling day reinforcing an enclosure not too long ago? An enclosure now strong enough to survive a direct hit from the Death Star? Perfect.

One rather sad-looking fox was evicted, and placed in a

cage previously used to house a monkey we'd known as 'Mr Personality', because of his lack of it. Osita was happily ensconced in her fortified new abode, and the fox could see the chickens. Literally, as his new cage faced their favourite scratching ground. Maybe we'd see a bit more life out of him now.

What a morning. And it was still only 10am!

The rest of the day, thankfully, was fairly quiet.

Flight of the Lobo

The next morning brought some unfortunate news.

After spending a full day reinforcing the coati cage to hold a ravening wolf, it was working remarkably well as a cosy little holiday home for Osita.

The ravening wolf, however, was gone. The somewhat thinner chicken wire of the monkey cage we'd transferred him to was about as far distant from Osita's heavy security as could be imagined. To be fair I think I could have chewed through it given time. With one whole night in which to work our cunning *lobo* had made good his escape, leaving a pathetically small fox-shaped hole in the mesh. We were so surprised – his demeanour as I'd tried to persuade him to eat a bit of chicken the previous night had been so timid, so withdrawn. He honestly didn't look capable of escaping from a wet paper bag.

Later that day though he did put in a brief appearance, trotting along the path in front of us as we headed down to feed Meldrew his bucket of fruit. Far too far away for us to chase him, and anyway how the hell would we catch a fox? Isn't that the very definition of impossible? At any rate, he looked considerably happier, stopping every so often to loll his tongue at us as though daring us to come after him. His sleek fur shone orange in the bright morning sunlight. He looked well fed too – no wonder there'd seemed to be fewer chickens than normal scratching around between the cages. Cheeky little bugger! If only he'd eaten that bloody rooster then I might have gotten an extra hour's sleep. Perhaps I could arrange something…

So long as our pet fox limited himself to poaching food from our farm we decided to consider him rehabilitated. If he chose to roam further afield then he'd be taking his chances with the surrounding farmers, all of whom were likely to own a disturbing array of guns. All we could really do was wish the little guy the best of luck. There are far worse places than Santa Martha to be a wild, wily Ecuadorian fox. Up ahead our quarry vanished effortlessly into the cloud forest. I felt sure he agreed with us.

Trip to Esmereldas

I couldn't see much out of the bus windows as we pulled into the southern resort town of Esmereldas. This was for two reasons; one, dawn was still a little way off, so it was dark outside; and two, I was lying on the floor of the bus. Toby and his girlfriend Alice had the last two seats. The gruelling seven hour journey had been punctuated by toilet stops, because the rest of the bus was filled with screaming school kids. Every time the vibrations of the engine started to lull me to sleep there came a squeal of brakes, the hiss of opening doors, and twenty five children stampeded over the top of me to get to the loo. There were footprints on every part of my body.

So our arrival at the seaside was cause for celebration on the part of all of my parts. It also meant that we were the furthest it was possible to be from beginning the journey home; thirty hours on the clock and counting.

We'd been invited by Jimmy's wife Nancy, to accompany her and her two children on a school trip to the beach. It was the real deal; an authentic Ecuadorian holiday resort, where people came from all over the country to let off steam. A week off of work would have been well worth the trip, but nothing so sensible was on the cards. No, a weekend at the beach was the plan – in spite of that fact that it took almost an entire weekend just to get there and back. There was only one golden lining on this horizon. Sitting towards the front of the bus was a goddess. Both Toby and I had noticed her as we fought our way onto the bus back in Tambillo, though he'd sensibly waited for Alice to doze off before discussing it with me. He was understandably gutted that he'd brought his girlfriend on this of all expeditions, and he heartily encouraged me to try my own luck. I'd watched her turning back occasionally to deliver a mild rebuke to one of the kids, allowing me a glimpse of her soft brown eyes, full lips and flawless complexion. She was the youngest of the teachers, hardly more than a teenager herself, but seemed calm and in control despite the chaos crashing all around her. Presumably she was intelligent too; as the list of her potential qualities grew my confidence shrank in direct proportion. She was way too hot for me – what could I possibly offer such a glamorous, gorgeous, sensual young woman?

I clambered off the bus and stood with Alice and Toby, shivering in the pre-dawn breeze. We seemed to be standing outside a hovel. It didn't look anything like the glossy brochure we'd been sold on.

"Here we are!" Nancy enthused, confirming my suspicions.

"No swimming pool?" I pointed out.

"Oh, that place is booked up. This is another place."

Quite when she had first been informed of that fact I didn't know, but I had a sneaking suspicion it was a good while earlier than when she decided to pass it on to us. But after a night impersonating a floor board I was too far gone to care.

"So we're staying here?"

Nancy's voice was soothing. "It's cheaper here. Only ten dollars. Nice place." She pointed across the road at the sea, obviously suggesting an alternative venue for swimming.

Definitely no swimming pool then. And a little more worryingly, as we explored the tiny rooms crammed with bunk beds, no towels, no pretty little packets of soap and shampoo...

"Shit, man," said Toby next to me, "maybe we should have brought some soap and shampoo."

"Towels," I added.

"Yeah, and toothpaste."

Toothpaste? He was supposed to have the toothpaste!

"I thought you were supposed to have the toothpaste!" I was indignant. How was I going to endear myself to the stunning mystery woman on the bus? Bad enough that after a day at the beach I'd stink of salt and have hair like a toilet brush, but three meals of seafood and not brushing my teeth? I'd be able to knock her out with my breath alone.

"Alice will have toothpaste," he consoled me.

Alice did have toothpaste. Which we could borrow (though a loud "Bollocks!" from Toby in the bathroom announced rather eloquently that he had in fact forgotten his toothbrush), and a towel big enough for us all to sit on, though it seemed a bit of an imposition to ask if we could dry ourselves on it.

Breakfast didn't disappoint. A huge plate of rice and salad dominated by a great big tasty fresh fish fillet, or in Toby and Alice's case dominated by even more rice and salad. So what if the owner demanded that we pay, despite us explaining that the food was included with our accommodation? The sky was... well, grey, but it was hot, and we were at the beach! Even Toby was happy, having discovered a large pot of chilli sauce.

And best of all we had a boat tour. For a dollar. You can't complain at that price, though fifteen minutes into the tour I really wished I could.

"Here," explained the guide as the boat chugged past

some rocks, "are some rocks. Birds live on these rocks. This rock is shaped like a submarine. We call it The Submarine."

Argh.

Luckily several other holidaymakers on the boat were equally unimpressed, and since for many of them a dollar was actually a decent chunk of cash, they felt fully justified in giving the rock expert a piece of their minds. The only problem was that they seemed to be demanding more for their money, whereas I clearly wanted less. "Just back to shore asap so I can do some sunbathing and swimming, please," was fine by me. But no. They had paid for a good, long tour and they wanted it.

As the professor reluctantly turned his boat towards a rather more distant, yet equally unpromising-looking formation of rocks, I suggested jokingly to Toby, "Race you to shore?"

"Absolutely," Alice replied instead, reminding me a little of Angelina Jolie in Tomb Raider with her cut glass delivery of that most accommodating word. She shrugged out of her life jacket (I hadn't been deemed worthy of wearing one) and we both stood.

"Sit down!" called the boat man. No doubt he had some special rocks in store for us.

"Bugger this for a game of soldiers," I said, though clearly it wasn't, and as one we hopped up on the edge of the boat and dived in. Or out, should I say.

I wish I could have seen the expression on our genius guide's face. With nothing more he could do or say on the matter, he gunned the engine and the boat swung away. The rest of the group sat and glared at him – presumably in stony silence.

We had a lovely swim back, once the pretence of a race had been abandoned. It really was quite a long way. Alice told me all about her job, which she loved. She'd left Santa Martha to teach English at the university, which she'd now been doing for half a year. It was one reason why her language skills were so advanced, as instead of spending all her time chatting to other volunteers in English, most of her friends and co-workers were native. I told her about my aspirations towards being an actor and about the primary obstacle to this goal being the fact that I couldn't act to save my life. It was bonding of a sort and I was pleased to be getting to know Alice so effortlessly. It would make hanging out with her and Toby that much more fun, though I had to admit to feeling a pang of jealousy. This was already the closest I'd felt to a girl since leaving home, and she was Toby's missus. The only female in my life was Machita.

We beat the tour boat back by about half a minute, them having explored several fascinating geological formations around the bay. They all looked thrilled to have stayed with the tour the whole way. The guide's face was like a thundercloud. Clearly he'd hit rock bottom.

The rest of the day was fantastic. I was dragged into a beach football match – "You don't want me to play," I warned the others, "I'm crap." We played for hours; I took crapness to new levels. We tanned and, predictably, burned. We shopped for stringy beady things, ate ice creams, (and in my case hot dogs, more ice cream, a burger, ice cream and a strange frozen jelly thingumy), and then returned to the restaurant for lunch.

The meal was exactly the same as breakfast, except the fish was traded in for a chicken breast fillet. And it was equally delicious. The vegetarians started to wake up to the fact that they'd be eating a lot of rice on this holiday.

The afternoon we spent at a different beach further round the coast, one full of holidaying Ecuadorians having the time of their lives. As the only three gringos in the whole resort we got quite a lot of attention, especially Toby and myself. Everywhere slender beauties with copper skin and long brown hair were smiling shyly and giggling to friends, or staring openly at our glowing red bodies. Cool, I thought, don't have to be a stupendously muscular surfing dude to do well here...

And then, almost before I knew it, I was alone. Toby had gone back to the hotel with Alice to get some 'rest' and I didn't actually know anyone else in the group well enough to recognise them. I stood on the beach, obtrusively white (and red) in a sea of brown.

I was debating my next move when, from a short way out in the sea, a big group of girls started waving. Pushing each other, and giggling, and waving. At me. Panic washed over me. Surely it was someone behind me they were waving at? I checked – no-one there. Who were these girls? Why were they interested in me? Feeling more than a bit foolish, I risked a slight wave of my own.

And they responded! I could hear laughter and some of them were definitely calling to me. For want of anything better to do, I waved again. The calls increased in volume. Waving hands became beckoning hands, signalling me into their midst.

What to do? Indecision paralysed my leg muscles. These chicks were way out of my league, even individually. Together they could quite possibly eat me alive. Except that I couldn't communicate with them. They'd be asking me things, suggesting other things, and I wouldn't understand a word of it. I'd just be stood there, grinning like an idiot, until they got bored of looking at me and waved me away again. Damn this language that everyone said was 'so easy to learn if you went and lived there!' I started to wave again, then thought better of it. Who was I, to wave at a whole bunch of babes when I couldn't say a thing to back it up? I was no mouth and all trousers. I put my ridiculously flapping hand in my pocket, flashed what I hoped would be interpreted as a knowing smile, and walked off up the beach. I'd done the right thing.

"You did the wrong thing there mate," said Toby helpfully.

We were sitting in our room making up a plastic coke bottle full of vodka and coke in the hopes that we could sit outside a bar and catch some tunes while the sun went down. And drink all night for the $3 the vodka and coke had cost me.

"Yeah?" I asked. "What could I have said? Hi, I'm Tony from England, me love you long-time?'

"Ha, well, would have been a start! No mate, just try to speak Spanish to them. If they like you, they aren't gonna care if you sound like a dickhead."

"Thanks for the vote of confidence," I told him. By way of punishment I offered him the vodka and coke to try. I'd been doing the mixing, and the buying come to think of it – and if the $2.25 price tag on the vodka wasn't warning enough of what was in store, the smell certainly was.

Toby still had a cold. And in a few seconds his mouth was on fire too.

"Fuckin' hell! God that's awful!" He coughed violently. "Tastes like fucking meths!"

"Well, you know me and reading labels, I hope I didn't buy meths..."

"How much did you pay for it?" he asked.

"Erm... like, five dollars, maybe," I lied.

"It's fuckin' awful! I can't drink that!"

Oh well. More for me.

The sun was down. The beach bar was wicked – a little serving shack with a thatched roof, surrounded by stools. It was all ours; we had the only actual table, and joining Alice, Toby and myself were several parents of the various hordes of kids we'd dragged along, and – wait for it – yes, the stunning teacher from the bus. Against all the odds she was amongst the five other people from our party who'd dared to venture outside the hotel in search of some nightlife.

Sipping her bubblegum pink cocktail through a straw, she looked so wildly exotic. It was hard to believe she'd come from a place as unrefined as Tambillo. I couldn't talk to her, of course, that having already been established as Not a Good Idea. So I sat, and looked, and listened... A peaceful balmy evening in a paradise location at a grass-roofed bar with a beautiful girl, and I was doing the Green Cross Code.

I could hardly believe it when she asked me to dance. So enraptured was I by the beauty of the scene, and by the fact that the vodka and coke bottle was half empty and only I was drinking it, that I hadn't noticed the salsa music kick in. Now it was time to dance, the sensual swish of salsa for all those with Latin blood in their veins, and that curious shuffle from foot to foot vaguely in time with the music if you come from somewhere near Manchester.

I accepted the invitation, but only because all eyes around the table seemed suddenly to be on me, and it was just about possible for me to look more awkward in refusing than it was actually dancing. But not by much. She avoided stepping on my toes despite some alarmingly fast footwork which seemed to flow around me. I avoided neither stepping on her toes, nor stepping on my own, which was actually quite a feat of contortion, and certainly made me wish I hadn't worn flip flops.

Fairly quickly I realised I had to sit down again. Hell, I was drunk.

Over the salsa, a new music had started to intrude, fast, rappy hip hop sort of stuff that would intrude pretty much anywhere. Its source was the shack next door, and its culprits, well... it was hard to tell, because the first one I saw was upside down. He landed on his feet in the middle of the path, and stepped back to give his mate room to try some moves. It was a small group of locals, practising their breakdancing, and damn they were good. As the next guy span on his head so fast that watching made me feel motion sick, I started to plan out what to say.

Because my mystery girl was sitting next to me! Instead of grabbing the outstretched hand of another partner and spinning away into the (admittedly rather small) crowd, which is what I had expected would happen, she had followed me back to the table for a chat. And now we were alone.

I watched an impressive back flip from one of the guys opposite and wondered if his head was sweating inside his woolly hat. I was sweating. Buckets, and not just from the heat. Right. I turned to face her, and delivered my opening line —

"*Estás bien?*" (You okay?)

She was. "Oh yeah, she's fine alright!" said the voice inside my head. I was at a conversational impasse. Jeez, and I thought it was hard to talk to English girls!

She said something utterly unintelligible, and smiled. I did that kind of half laugh, a fairly safe response to most things said with a smile, then smiled myself so she'd didn't think I was laughing *at* her. "*Sí*," I added, to be sure.

She smiled again – and was it my imagination, or did she lean closer?

Bollocks to it. I was five thousand miles away from anyone who could ever bring this up in the pub and remind friends and strangers alike of just how badly a man can make an arse of himself. Well, except for Toby, and he did that anyway.

I leaned over and kissed her.

At least I'd brushed my teeth.

She looked a little shocked, though not in an altogether bad way. She glanced around, as though vaguely embarrassed, but no-one seemed to have noticed. Then she beckoned me with a finger in a way which completely transcends language. I followed her as she stood and walked to the other side of the bar. There, in the shadows, she turned and let me walk into her, grabbed me tightly and kissed me again. Things were looking up.

She must have noticed that things were looking up, as she glanced at them then smiled mischievously at me.

"I'm a lady" I heard her say.

Quite so, I thought, kissing random strangers in random bars notwithstanding. She held me close, kissing me with an unexpected urgency. I pressed my body into hers and was rewarded with a whispered enticement. It had the word *'playa'* (beach) in it. I felt that up until now my responses had been doing very well. If it ain't broke, don't fix it.

"*Sí,*" I replied with feeling.

So she took my hand and led me off down the beach.

Now, I could leave it at that, were I, for example, a lady. But in case you're in any doubt about the matter, I'm not. Suffice to say that fun was imminent – she finally came up with a phrase I understood. "*Sólo sexo.*" Now, that could really only mean one of two things, and I was fairly sure she wasn't walking half a mile down a totally empty beach just so she could watch.

She found a piece of beach which seemed to be more to her liking than the rest, and there I'll have to leave it for decency's sake – other than to bemoan the lack of a condom in my back pocket, a habit I'd gotten out of due to the total futility of carrying one. In my experience up to that point, it seemed to act as a magical female-repelling charm, almost as if to take one out with me was to tempt Sod's Law into proving just how unrealistic my chances of needing it were. Not so this night. So whilst fun was had, and sand worked its way into crevices not often occupied by a granular substance, there was even more fun that was not had. Damn it.

(Toby had an opinion to offer on this subject much later

in our room. Between explosions of laughter he told me, "You should always keep a condom in your back pocket, mate!" He never seemed to run out of this vital, if a little untimely, advice.)

We emerged from the darkened beach to find the party much reduced. Toby had headed off for the night, as had all but two of the parents. We sat back at the table with Alice, and gazed into each other's eyes. Then she glanced around the (now even smaller) crowd a little nervously.

I tried to kiss her again, but she leant back out of reach and smiled instead. Huh? She looked around again, then said something to Alice. Again I picked out the word 'lady'. Alice introduced herself in turn, and it finally trickled through my drink-addled brain that the Spanish word for 'lady' was nothing like the English one.

Alice turned her attention to me "So, what have you been up to then?" The way she stressed the word 'you' made it clear she didn't need me to answer. Plus she was giving me knowing eyebrows. My lady kissed me quickly on the cheek, then glanced around guiltily.

I was so confused by this stage, with no idea what was going on. "I don't think she likes me anymore," I mumbled at Alice. The glory of the night was evaporating quicker that the foul spirits in my glass.

Now Alice looked sympathetic. She turned and chatted to Lady for a few minutes. Lady glanced around again in that conspiratorial manner, then replied. I was closely watching Alice's face, trying to read the news before it arrived, and I caught the exact moment of comprehension as it dawned. Her eyes widened just a little, her forehead creased and her jaw loosened somewhat. She said something back, then turned to me.

"And?" I had to ask.

In fairness to Alice I feel that at this moment, had Toby been in charge of this revelation, he would have pissed himself laughing. To her credit Alice merely looked a little concerned.

"Okay, for starters the Spanish word for 'lady' is '*mujer*'. What she was telling you is, her name is Lady.

"Ah! Yeah, I just got that!"

"And she's not a teacher. She's here with her two children."

I choked on my drink. Meths and Coke dribbled down my chin.

"And she's nervous about kissing you in public," Alice continued, "because some of these people know her husband."

Return of the Red-Eye

The journey home from Esmereldas was considerably more comfortable than the journey there. I was still sitting on the floor of the bus, but this time my mind was occupied with happy memories. And wild fantasies. Every few minutes I stole a look at the back of Lady's head, half a school bus away, and imagined what it would be like to run my fingers through that lustrous shiny black hair, when it wasn't covered with sand. Occasionally I caught her sneaking a glance back at me, and when our eyes locked even I blushed at the intensity of our combined desire. This was the perfect distance – from here I could admire her, and picture her naked, and not have to speak to her. Why oh why had I been so slack in my language studies? Well, now that would have to change. The prospect of seeing her again without a drastic improvement in my conversational skills frankly terrified me.

We stopped for lunch at another beach, and Lady subtly signed to me that we should sneak off. We walked hand in hand through empty streets looking for somewhere, anywhere to be alone together. After last night's drunken antics she was determined to be more circumspect. Her last whispered comments to me before I'd staggered off to bed had left me in no doubt that she wanted us to be together, and a passionate embrace outside the hotel had rekindled my desire for the same. But this was a big deal for Lady. Her children were on that bus, along with probably half the people she knew. I was immune to local gossip; she would have to cope with it every day.

Eventually we wound up sitting in a tiny café, fingertips still touching, drinking coffee with our free hands. I stared into the hypnotic darkness of her eyes and tried to think of something, anything, to say.

Then a horn blared. A voice shouted. I looked up.

The bus was parked directly outside the cafe. It was fully loaded – kids, teachers and two very amused gringos stared down at us from dusty windows. The driver honked again, and some of the kids started to bang on the windows. The shout came again, evidently from whoever was in charge of the expedition. I looked back at Lady to see her face frozen in shock. She'd gone pale – no mean feat for someone with her complexion. Suddenly she lurched to her feet and grabbed for her purse. I dropped a few coins on the table and followed her out of the cafe. We were greeted outside by a chorus of catcalls, whoops and sniggers from an entire bus full of comedians. I just grinned like an idiot and pretended not to notice it was anything out of the ordinary. Poor Lady seemed mortified. I could only guess at what was being said to her, as Alice felt it too vulgar to translate. And anyway she was laughing too hard.

"When you're trying to shag another man's wife," Toby advised as the bus lurched towards home, "you should try to be a bit discreet, mate. Just a little bit."

How – Are?

It was a long time before I lived down the events of the holiday. It probably didn't help that I developed a habit of daydreaming, fantasising about Lady in the middle of the most random tasks. Even Jimmy joined in the teasing, with a predictably macho thrust. "Be careful," he warned me, "I've seen her husband. He is a very big man."

One of the few benefits of being a gringo finally came into play for me. "Big man, eh?" I held a hand across my nipples. "So he's about this high then?"

Luckily something came along to take our collective minds off my romantic complications.

I was walking past Johnny's truck when it growled at me.

I froze instantly. This was unusual behaviour even for Johnny's truck, though it had been known to cheep or chirrup on occasion.

The growl came again – deep, guttural, filled with menace. It was the kind of sound that, if you hear it from less than three feet away, means its time to shit yourself because you're about to die. I took a few cautious steps back from the truck. Either we were about to inherit a tiger, or someone was sitting in the back watching the Discovery Channel with the volume right up. Shivers of fear and excitement rippled down my spine as the deadly noise replayed once more, quieter this time and all the more dangerous-sounding for it.

I had to stifle an impulse to reach over the side and throw back the covering tarpaulin. The war between curiosity and sensibility raged within me for several seconds until the first surge of adrenaline wore off. I noticed that I was shaking, and not from the cold. Well maybe a little from the cold. The truth was, I was getting through my first aid kit fast enough already. And there wasn't much for loss of limbs in there. Instead I sought out Toby, the wellspring of all knowledge – or at least of some knowledge. Occasionally. I managed to deflect his request for a game of chess by recounting my last few minutes.

"I think it's a tiger!" I told him breathlessly.

"Woah... Dunno mate!" Toby replied. "I heard from Johnny that he was getting something today, dunno what it is though. Something South American. 'How-Are' it sounded like, with a rolled 'r'."

"How Arre?" I mimicked. "How Arrrrrre?"

"I'm not bad mate, thanks. How are you?"

"You're an arsehole," I told him.

The mystery was solved the following morning. There was, of course, no tiger. It was a jaguar. Full grown, adult female, almost two metres of magnificent golden jungle cat, spotted all over with dark brown rosettes – and in a really bad mood.

"Man that jaguar is pissed off," said Toby.

"*Tiene ambre*," explained Johnny. The cat was hungry.

But we couldn't feed her much as she was. Leonardo arrived to tranquillise her, and the rest of us set to creating a new home. Johnny had obviously been making enquiries of his neighbours, because moments later a truck rolled up with an enormous cage, brown with rust, perched precariously on the back of it. The bars were as thick as the ones on a prison cell. God only knows where it came from. I couldn't imagine any reason why anyone would own such a cage, other than for torturing people who'd seen something they shouldn't have. I made a mental note never to visit this particular neighbour. It took the whole team of us to pull it off the truck and move it a few steps at a time all the way to the *galpón*.

That's when Jimmy winked at me and fired up the welding machine. Oh shit. I made myself busy carrying twisted metal bars over as he donned the ridiculous mask and started blazing away. He was a pro though. It only took him a couple of hours to turn wreckage into... well, wreckage, but four sides of wreckage and a roof that were all cleverly fastened together. I'd had one more go at welding in the meantime, accidentally burned a small hole where two bars were supposed to meet and gone stomping off to sulk. Even Toby was better at it than me. The git.

The jaguar was fast asleep. How long for was anyone's guess – even Leonardo couldn't say for sure. Ketamine was notoriously unpredictable in its effects and it wasn't like he anaesthetised big cats on a daily basis. We hauled the cage a few feet at a time around the front of Johnny's house, past cages full of curious monkeys, and manoeuvred it into position on a plot of scrubby grass beyond the parrots.

Toby sighed. "I was saving this area. I really wanted to make a garden here. Grow some veg, you know. It'd save loads of money." Poor Toby. Not only was he vegetarian (which was already a recipe for disaster in my book), he was vegetarian in a country that just wasn't ready for it. And to top it off, he couldn't cook vegetables. Basically he was screwed.

Now that the cage was in place I was more than a little confused by it. It looked like a relic of the Spanish

Inquisition and was very nearly as scary as the jaguar herself. Johnny had explained that it would only be a temporary home, as he'd ordered enough materials to build her a brand new enclosure to rival our best. That was an eye-opener in itself – Johnny buying something new! I'd believe that when I saw it. But for now this evil prison would be the cat's home. To my mind it seemed to be missing something. Like, oh I don't know, a front! I had a nasty feeling Jimmy was going to wait until the cat was inside and then produce a roll of duct tape to seal off the end with.

Carrying the Jaguar was an altogether more exciting experience. I took her head, marvelling at the deep grunt every time she drew breath. Not as many hands could be brought to bear as on the cage and the cat weighed a tonne. And it goes without saying we couldn't stop every ten seconds and drop her for a rest! We staggered over to the cage and lowered her massive golden body to the grass. I had to move away before allowing myself to collapse – there seemed to be some primitive survival instinct that just would not let me lie down next to her. Especially when she kept twitching violently. Probably tearing us all to shreds in her dreams...

The cage was manhandled across and dropped over the top of her, the bottom edges coming to rest in shallow trenches Johnny had dug whilst Jimmy was welding. Finally it all made sense! Four sides and a roof, grass underfoot... and no door.

"Um, how we... get inside?" I haltingly asked Johnny. He took a step back and looked at me as though I'd just sprouted a large penis from the top of my head. I think his expression could best be described as disbelief.

"We DON'T!"

That Bear Ate My Pants!

Cat Food

Lunch was disturbed by a screech from the front door, followed by Johnny's head poking through. "Okay. Jaguar is awake," he told us. "Now we feed her. You want to watch?"

I did. Of course we did.

"Can we feed her?" Toby asked.

Probably not without crapping myself I thought.

"No." Johnny was very direct about it. He obviously had our best interests at heart. "She is very dangerous. I will have to feed her."

He pantomimed the actions, to save talking to me in baby language. It was a powerful performance – first he became the pair of us, bravely approaching the cage and with exaggerated caution, placing the food on the ground outside the bars. Then he was the mighty jaguar itself, coiled for the spring, and with brutal directness he pounced on the fence, shoved his mighty paws through the bars are dragged his prey inside. The look of abject terror on his face as he became us again clearly demonstrated our unsuitability for the task.

It was quite an act. I almost applauded.

"He puts the food outside?" I checked with Toby, since he'd been the sole beneficiary of the audio commentary accompanying our little play.

"Yep," he confirmed, "he says she'll pull it inside herself."

Interesting! This really was something I had to see.

Outside, I stood with Toby, eyeing the caged jaguar in awe. Even motionless, curled up on her side in a corner, the beast radiated power. When she was up and pacing the smooth, sinuous motions and rippling of the muscles beneath her sleek hide screamed danger. This was not a beast to mess around with. She was without a doubt the most beautiful animal I had ever laid eyes on. And she was totally, utterly deadly.

Perhaps that explains the attraction. Johnny snapped me out of my reverie. "*Listo?*" (ready?) he enquired. I nodded.

He swung his arm in a couple of loose practice arcs, then gently lobbed the dead bird towards the cage. It was a perfect shot – the meal landed exactly at the base of the cage, on the opposite side from the jaguar herself. It really was a big chicken, and made an impressive thump as it hit the ground.

We held our breath and waited.

The jaguar looked up, slightly puzzled by this turn of events. A second later I could almost see the moment when the scent hit her nostrils. An electric shiver ran through her whole body. In an instant she was transformed from curled relaxation to coiled spring. An audible heartbeat passed before she pounced.

One spring carried her clear across the cage. Before we'd registered the leap she had both paws through the bars, claws fastened in the chicken's flesh. She pulled and jerked back, flinging her entire weight into the motion, once, twice, and on the third time the chicken gave. It was like watching the bad guy in some sci-fi movie getting sucked out into space through a tiny hole in the spaceship's hull. The chicken was torn in two, the sections buckling in on themselves with a series of sickening *cracks*. In less time than it takes to tell it had been dragged back into the cage, through a pair of three-inch-square gaps in the bars.

Amazing.

We stayed to watch while she fed, pinning her meal down with her forepaws and ripping strips off it with her teeth. It took only a couple of minutes to dismember and consume the entire chicken.

"Man. She was hungry." It was all I could think of to say.

"Yeah!" Toby enthused. "That was fucking awesome!"

Johnny rolled his eyes at our childish glee, but the light in his eyes said he'd been excited too. He straightened up, turned and strode away without saying anything more.

Toby looked after him briefly, then turned to me with a conspiratorial smile. "I'm gonna feed her again later. Did you see that? Oh my God, she's fast!"

Johnny evidently didn't want her feeding again so soon. "*Ten cuidado*," he warned us when we asked. He sighed at our obvious enthusiasm. "*Ella es muy peligroso!*" (she is very dangerous!). But I was entranced by the beast. A short while later I slipped out of the house, camera in hand, and warily approached her cage. She was lying on the far side of it, apparently asleep. "You are so beautiful," I told her, and was rewarded by a flick of her tufted ears. I crouched down to put her on eye level and crept a tiny bit closer.

Mistake.

As she exploded into motion my own much slower reflexes kicked in to throw me backwards. For a second I was hung up on something, then fell back as it was pulled free. I landed on my arse a good two metres from the cage. It was a second or two before I even realised what had happened. My blood, too, seemed to be caught off guard by the speed of the attack. It took another long moment before it welled out of my hand and ran down my fingers to drip onto the ground.

In that split second blur of motion the jaguar had crossed the cage, shot a leg through the bars, and raked me with a single claw before I could tumble out to safety. I'd thought I was well outside her reach, at least a metre or more from the bars. Somehow she had managed to get her entire limb through a tiny hole. Deadly she was indeed, I reminded myself as I shakily rose to my feet.

I backed away another few steps just to be sure. The jaguar was pacing the cage, agitated. I didn't want to stir her up any further. Far enough away to finally feel safe, I started to calm down. I dared to look at my injury and discovered it wasn't too bad. One solitary claw seemed to have hooked me, tearing a small chunk out of the back of my hand. Blood was flowing freely from the hole; it looked deep, but not wide. Thank the Goddess, I thought, that my hand had been the closest part of me! If I'd been pushing my face closer to get a better view… it didn't bear thinking about.

I shook the worst of the blood off my hand and headed back to the volunteer house. Hopefully I'd get it cleaned up before anyone noticed. Toby was just coming out as I went in. "You alright?" he asked.

"Yeah, man."

"Oh. Sure you're alright?" he asked again.

"Yeah, fine, why wouldn't I be?"

"Ah, well… your eyes are massive! And you're white as a sheet, and…" he trailed off as he glanced down at my feet. I followed his gaze.

"And you're bleeding on the floor," he concluded.

"Seriously? The jaguar?" Toby sounded impressed. Once he'd persuaded me to let him examine the wound I'd felt inspired to tell him the tale.

"Um, yeah. I couldn't believe it myself! Shit, she's so fast. I can't believe how she got her whole arm through the bar! I was miles away. Well, far enough that I thought I was well out of reach. Unbelievable."

Yet the evidence was there, painfully obvious.

"Johnny won't be happy," I thought suddenly.

"Johnny?" Toby thought about it for a second. "He'll probably piss himself laughing!"

Just what I wanted to hear. Probably true though.

"Only you, mate!" he went on. "I've never known someone get injured so much! Is there anything here that hasn't bitten you yet?"

"It's not my fault," I said defensively. "I don't know why it happens to me."

"But seriously. I want to know – is there anything here that hasn't bitten you?"

I was forced to think hard for a response. Machita? Bitten me. Don Juan? Bitten me. Monkeys, cats, even my beloved Snotty McSnot. And as for the parrots… it did seem rather excessive.

"Is there anything?" he prompted.

"Yes actually, there is," I told him. "The horse!" And with that I stalked off to bleed in the dorm room.

Language of Love

Life had been lonely since the girls left. Every once in a while I'd be invited to Jimmy and Nancy's house along with Toby, and we'd sit on the edge of their bed and watch a pirated DVD from Machachi market. Maybe we'd share a beer or a bag of crisps, but apart from that our social calendar had been kind of bare. I worked with Toby, I hung out with Toby. I'd moved back into the dorm room as it seemed almost incestuous to sleep with him as well. We couldn't really party together, as Johnny's edict forbidding night-time manoeuvres meant that anyone going to Quito would be staying there, and that meant they wouldn't be around to feed the animals at seven the next morning. Sitting around the dining table, drinking the local rum whilst wrapped in five blankets, was about as exciting as life got.

All that changed with the onslaught of the Irish. Emer arrived first, a tough lass from County Cork with wavy brown hair and a savage sense of humour. She talked fast, talked loud, talked constantly; occasionally she talked in Gaelic. She was a lot of fun, and in my opinion was a few bites short of the whole cracker. But meeting Emer was like a taster of the full experience; it helped prepare us for the arrival of her sister. Because Marie was insane. Her permed hair was wild, her chuckle wicked and her volume knob stuck in the 'full' position. She swore like a trooper, smoked like an active volcano and drank like a bottomless pit with lips. If she hadn't already been engaged, I'd have been sorely tempted to ask her to marry me. Between them, the pair were a force of chaos to rival nature herself. Jimmy had better watch out.

This meant that we finally had enough people to organise a massive night out. But first I had something else to attend to. After much prompting from Toby, and even more prompting from Alice (via Toby), I'd finally set up a date with Lady.

I was about as nervous as it's possible for a person to be. It was one thing to brag about having a stunning Ecuadorian girlfriend, but quite another to actually go on a date with her. The phone call earlier in the day had brought back all those fears of awkwardness. She didn't speak English. I spoke almost no Spanish. It was as simple as that. And yet now I had to entertain her for a whole evening. I just had to hope that talking wasn't a big part of her plans for tonight.

Ha! I pretty much hope for that on every date anyway.

I am, after all, male. Though on behalf of my gender I feel I should point out that this is a fairly simple, and by now surely quite obvious, intention. Whenever I hear someone warn a girl 'Careful – he's only after one thing!' I think – no shit?! It only took several thousand years of evolutionary evidence and a lifetime of precedent to make that giant leap of intellect. It is, after all, what we're biologically programmed for.

If, however, his one desire is eventually fulfilled, the average bloke is then immediately satisfied – he wants for nothing more and is happy to oblige his partner with almost anything s/he could desire in return. The average woman (speaking only from my limited experience of course), goes out on a date expecting a man to be strong yet vulnerable, tough yet sensitive, honest without being painfully honest, nice but a bit mean with it, funny yet able to hold serious conversation, not too desperate and clingy, yet to immediately agree to marriage and children as soon as she decides she's ready, and – best of all – to know *exactly* what she wants, without ever having to be told. Thank God I was born a man. I don't think my head is big enough to hold all the contradictions involved with being a woman.

I left to a chorus of jeers and 'helpful suggestions' from the new arrivals. Toby had taken it upon himself to enlighten the Irish girls about the circumstances surrounding my first meeting with Lady. He hadn't spared a single detail – he'd even added a few to spice the story up. So when he asked if I 'needed to borrow anything' it was met with even more hilarity. Luckily this time I would be well prepared in that area.

I hiked down the hill, trying not to exert myself too much as I didn't want to sweat in my nice clean shirt. For weeks I'd wondered why the hell I'd been stupid enough to bring nice shirts to work in a zoo. Now at long last one of the pair had been liberated from my rucksack, shaken out, and was currently trying its best to absorb every scrap of moisture from my skin, so it could cling to my back and smell.

It was a beautiful day. Damn that hot, sweat-inducing sun. As I carefully climbed the odd barbed wire fence along my route, I pondered the ordeal ahead. Belatedly I wished I'd done what I promised myself I would do, straight after agreeing to this date – study more Spanish. I'd always meant to, yet somehow events always conspired to keep me from doing any.

Okay, so that's a bit of a lie. The truth is I just couldn't be arsed. Damn my laziness! And damn my cowardice. If one of them didn't screw up this opportunity for me, the other one would. Because as I reached the foot of the mountain, where the highway marked the border of Tambillo town, my dream woman was nowhere in sight. And the voice in my head screamed 'Run away!'

I took a deep, calming breath. I could wait, I decided – for as little time as possible – before bolting back up the hill to safety. I'd tell the others I'd arrived late and must have missed her. Everyone would commiserate with me; Toby would tell me it was her loss for not waiting, and that she obviously wasn't worth worrying about, the girls would agree with him and secretly think I was a bastard for being late and standing her up; and everything would be all right. The world would carry on turning, each new day bringing me closer to finding that perfect woman. Who, knowing my luck, would only speak Chinese.

Hard to believe, but after ten minutes I was literally preparing to run for the hills. In fact it was more like five minutes.

I was seriously on edge. When a car horn beeped nearby I jumped about three feet into the air. Along with everyone else on the planet, when a car beeps I automatically assume it's meant for me. But unlike everyone else, this time I was right. Lady beamed at me as she jumped from the passenger seat of a tiny square car that looked decidedly pre-cold war era.

I grinned back, and she approached until we were face to face. Good God she was gorgeous! In all my panic over the language barrier, I'd almost forgotten. Her smooth, coffee-with-cream complexion, big brown eyes, sensuously full lips and long, straight midnight black hair – and yes, she had a body to die for, but do you really think I'd forgotten *that*? Not likely. We gazed into each other's eyes like they do in movies, and all of a sudden it didn't seem that awkward.

"Quito?" I said.

"*Sí*," she agreed, and smiled again.

Luckily there was a bus there at that exact moment. Two

of them in fact, with a third on the approach. But staggeringly, amazingly, this bus wasn't full. It had to be fate, I thought as we took two seats together.

We said nothing as the bus pulled away, just looked at each other. I can only imagine that my expression must have matched hers perfectly – she looked at me like I was made of the tastiest chocolate in the world. Emboldened by her silent attention, I reached up and brushed the side of her face with my fingers. She closed her eyes just briefly. I leaned towards her and kissed her.

Half an hour later as the bus bounced through Quito, we stopped kissing long enough to look for our stop. Amazingly we hadn't even missed it. The driver slowed down so much to let us off that he very nearly stopped completely. Without a doubt, it had been the best bus journey of my life.

I wrapped my arm around her, and we set off through the streets of Quito. I had no idea where we were, and no idea where we were going. Though I suspected Lady knew our current location, I was fairly sure that she didn't have any particular destination in mind either. We hadn't exactly talked about it on the bus. My mind had been on other matters, and I have enough difficulty speaking with one tongue in my mouth.

Sooner or later though, the question would have to be asked. And since I probably wouldn't understand it if she asked, and couldn't answer it in any case, I decided to be the one to broach the topic.

"Where do you want to go?" I asked.

"I don't know," she replied. "Where do you want to go?"

This was not going to be easy. I didn't care though – I was ecstatic that I'd understood her! Okay, she'd used almost exactly the same phrase as I had, but we were communicating, baby!

"It's very cold," she mentioned. She was right.

"I'm not cold," I said, by way of proving my resilience and manhood.

"I am," came the reply.

A complete exchange of dialogue! With the most beautiful woman on the face of the earth. My feeling of triumph made me bold. "It's warm in bed," I said.

She let out a surprised gasp, then started to laugh. "*Bandito!*", she told me, "You are *bandito!*"

"I'm not!" I protested. It wasn't hard to guess what I was being accused of.

"*Sí, sí, estás bandito!* You are very bad!"

The truth will set you free.

"Yes, a little," I admitted.

She stopped in the road and turned to face me. "Good," she said, and kissed me. "Let's go."

There was a hotel nearby. I steered us towards it, through the doors and into an incredibly expensive-looking foyer. Marble floor, wood panelled walls, brass fittings everywhere. The hotel was called 'El Ambassador'. I felt a sudden pain in my wallet. It was far from the first time my eagerness for sex had gotten me into trouble. I very much doubt it will be the last. But this had all the hallmarks of bankruptcy. If I blew my entire bank balance on one night's accommodation I wouldn't be able to eat for the next two months. Or worse – I'd have to call my parents for a loan, and explain to them I'd spent all my money on sex. I could think of few more embarrassing things to do in the whole world, but I was going to have to apologise to the concierge, who was now staring expectantly at me, and to the beautiful woman on my arm, plead poverty and walk back out into the night. In Spanish.

Lady had other ideas.

"How much for a room for the two of us?" she asked.

"Twenty-five dollars," I caught the reply.

What? Really? Lady glanced back at me, uncertain what

to say.

"Twenty-five?" I asked her. She nodded.

Pretty cheap.

"We'll take it!" I said, perhaps a little too triumphantly. I didn't care. I felt powerful again! Ug! Man strong. Man make fire. I paid up and handed over my passport for the concierge to examine. He gave me a check-in sheet and slid my passport back to me. Bold again now that the problem was over, and feeling cheeky as I anticipated what was to come, I pocketed my passport and signed us in as Mr and Mrs Smith. I'd always wanted to do that!

Lady had been asking questions, and I think she'd established that we had our own bathroom. I took her hand and led her off up the wrong staircase. A shout from the concierge brought us back to his marble counter, from where he pointed us in the right direction. Not caring in the slightest about looking foolish now the goal was in sight, Man took Lady back to his cave. Ug.

And what a cave it was! Enormous double bed, delicate little table lamps, thick carpet and a complete en suite bathroom the same size as the bedroom! A TV with cable. Wouldn't be needing that. And a stack of towels on the bed.

"You want a shower?" I asked her.

She did.

The next couple of hours I will leave to the reader's imagination, save to mention that we had to call room service when our hot water ran out. I enjoyed that evening immensely.

We nipped out for food a bit later on, holding hands and not saying much. I have no idea what we ate, or whether it was good or bad. We returned to our room for the night, and the morning found us very happy and very tired.

Lady had to work, so I kissed her good-bye and put her in a taxi. I promised to ring her later on and she disappeared into the city. I turned to head for home.

Or would have, except I still had no bloody idea where I was.

Several hours later I returned to Santa Martha. I didn't know what time it was, but I'd obviously missed the feed. I'd been in for about ten minutes, trying to decide whether or not to get changed and go looking for the work party, when they arrived outside and started to take off their boots. Oops! I'd skived a whole day's work.

Toby walked in first and did a double take when he saw me standing in the middle of the living room. "Alright mate!" he said, "Been workin' hard?" He went past me into the kitchen as the girls walked in one at a time behind him. They each wore a sly smile and had a couple of comments for me, though none witty enough to be memorable. I had that strange combination of profound embarrassment and heady pride that can only result from your mates taking the piss out of you after you've pulled.

"I'm going to bed," I announced to no-one in particular, which caused laughter all round.

"Will you be up for the afternoon feed?" Toby asked.

"Oh, yeah sure," I said. "I've got to ring Lady anyway."

And with that my blood froze. Sex was all well and good, but now we were back to square one. And I had to call her.

The Fear followed me into the dorm room and climbed into bed beside me. How had I gotten myself into this ridiculous situation? I hadn't been thinking. At least, not with my brain.

Eventually I fell asleep.

Shocking Behaviour

On the day we were due to return Osita to her proper enclosure, Leonardo arrived bright and early. He'd decided to weigh and measure her as part of his ongoing monitoring of her development, and to give her a few precautionary shots. The darting was routine, as Osita knew him well; he didn't even need to use his primitive-looking tranq gun. We took her in the back of Johnny's car, slowly, and it took six of us at full capacity to carry her in a sling of tarpaulins and blankets.

We deposited the sleeping bear just inside her enclosure. Leonardo immediately grabbed his gear to check her vital signs as the rest of us scurried around trying to make her comfortable.

Johnny stood back from the chaos, presumably thinking deep thoughts as his eyes roamed around the perimeter of the enclosure. With all hands on bear, I was feeling a bit surplus to requirements, so I took the opportunity to wheedle a few answers out of him. If knowledge is power, there could be no doubt about who held both. And Johnny was not big on sharing. I should have known it would not end well.

"So was the electric fence broken then?" I asked. It had been the subject of much debate after the escape, since Osita had blatantly climbed out, yet as far as I knew there had been no attempt made to find and fix the problem. The fence no longer gave off its ominous clicking. Had she known? Or had she managed to jump from one of the trees in spite of our earlier efforts to reduce them?

"I don't know if it's broken," Johnny told me. "This is what we must find out."

"*Sí*," I agreed. "But how?"

He grinned at me. "Easy. Touch it."

I laughed at the joke. Johnny smiled. And beckoned me towards the fence. He was serious.

"*Chooch!*" I swore. "You touch it!"

Johnny roared with laughter. I loved to surprise him, and vulgarity was rather more likely to do the trick than dazzling him with my expanding vocabulary. It didn't sway him from his plan though. "Touch it there," he gestured.

"No way!"

"You can do it," he told me. "Be a man."

And that was it. The one challenge that could not be refused. Any threat to one's masculinity had to be immediately negated, no matter the cost. I'd worked very hard to build up my current level of respect, losing a fair amount of blood and skin in the process. But this? I'd never live it down if I refused.

I contemplated the wire. There was no way out for me now; it was obvious that I'd been called on to prove myself, and had no choice but to see it through. I wondered briefly what a bear-repelling jolt of direct current would do to my manhood. Give my pubic hair an afro at the very least. Slowly I extended both hands, palms open. The threatening wire was now only centimetres from my unprotected flesh. I shrugged a few times to loosen my shoulders and took a deep breath. Then another. "Okay," I announced, "here goes!"

But then I did nothing. False alarm.

"Okay, this time I'm gonna do it…"
One more deep breath. Hopefully not my last.
A wiggle of the fingers (very important).
And I grabbed it.
Nothing happened. No blinding flash, no searing pain. I was alive!
"Not working," I reported to Johnny, who had been watching my preparations with a tolerant smile.
"No," he frowned in response. "Not working. Hm." Johnny looked thoughtful. "Then we must find out where it is broken. Touch the next section."

It was three quarters of the way around the enclosure that I got my first shock. I'd become complacent by then, having long since gotten over my initial fear. Thirty-plus sections of fence had surrendered themselves to my embrace with less drama than a Quito football match. My ears had registered the slight 'click' as I stood at the lowest point of the enclosure, surrounded by bushes on the bear's side of the fence, but my mind paid it no heed. I'd convinced myself that this whole ridiculous task of scrambling around the enclosure 'testing' the fence would come to nothing. There was probably a burnt-out generator somewhere that needed a good kicking, but nothing more.

I reached lazily out towards the wire. There was a massive BANG! and I was lying in a bush a few feet away, impaled on thorns and utterly confused as to how I'd gotten there.

Johnny helped me up and put his finger to his lips.
I plucked a thorn from my backside and listened.
Click. Click. Click.
"Click! The fence is working!"
Johnny nodded. "*Aquí*," (here) he pointed. There was a short pipe jutting out of the closest fence post, with a strip of rubber wrapped round the end. The electric wire was looped

tightly around the pipe, only not around the rubber bit. It had slipped down a fraction, and was now directing the rest of its voltage straight through the metal post into the ground. We studied the problem in silence for a few seconds. It was obvious what had to happen to solve it – just not how to do it. Not to me anyway. Johnny had that worrying look in his eyes, like he was about to explain something he considered very simple to me. He made a gesture that I'd used in high school to signify sex, then pointed to the offending pipe. There really was no need for any more graphic illustration. The horror of what was expected from me was already sinking in. I felt the blood drain from my face.

"Can't you… turn it off?" I almost pleaded.

"Ah, no. But it's okay. Be strong, uh?"

"But… why? Why can't you turn it off?"

"Ah. Because, the power, it comes straight from the house."

Aha! From… the house? Johnny's house? So… it was wired into the mains! Holy Shit! "Big… um, *grande electricidad!*"

"*Ah, no problemo,*" he soothed. "Stand on one foot!" He pantomimed to aid the translation. Except it wasn't the translation I had a problem with.

"*UNO pie?*" I struggled to put my amazement into words. "*Matar… Mato…*" I couldn't quite conjugate the verb for death. Which was surprising, given how long I'd been at Santa Martha. "*Quiere mátame!*" I finally came up with – literally "You want to kill me!"

Johnny laughed and waved a hand vaguely. "It's okay, stand on one foot. You have rubber boots!"

I looked down at my wellies doubtfully. I had a feeling this wasn't going to end well. "One foot," I muttered as I turned to face the wire. It clicked maliciously at me. No amount of deep breathing was going to help me this time. So as Johnny urged me along, giving constant advice from just behind my left shoulder like a biblical devil, I fixed the electric fence.

I held the dead end, hauling on it to give sufficient slack, then coaxed the wire loop back over the rubber strip. BANG! A flash accompanied my return to the thorn bush this time, as did a string of four letter words in a selection of languages.

"Let go more quickly," was Johnny's suggestion. Of course, the instant the wire became insulated from the fence post, the fence was effectively fixed – leaving me holding it. The wire had of course slipped back off the rubber as I flew backwards, putting us both back to square one.

"Quickly!" Johnny reminded me as I lifted one welly-boot off the ground and reached for the fence again.

It was a long, long time before that fence was fixed. I was so dazed I could hardly remember what was going on around me. Time and again I'd looped that wire, sometimes letting go too quickly, sometimes holding on far too long. Eventually there came a time that it stayed.

"Finished," I reported to Johnny, and I didn't just mean the job. I swear there was smoke rising from my boots.

Together we trudged back up the paddock to the gate. The Irish girls were helping Leonardo pack up his gear. They'd obviously spent most of the morning refilling the pond, since Osita's last act of defiance before escaping had been to cunningly extract the latest plug Toby had fashioned. Scraps of rag balled up in plastic shopping bags had been pushed back into the outlet pipe and seemed to be holding for now, though once the bear was back to normal it was only a matter of time before she managed to fish it out. Again. It was a good job we loved her so much. Toby was still checking her progress as she tried groggily to sit up.

"How is the chubby monster?" I asked him.

"Good mate, good. Whatcha been up to?"

"Oh, we fixed the electric fence." My weary sarcasm must have alerted him.

"Erm, nice one mate..." He eyed me for a few seconds. "You alright?"

"Just ready to lie down," I told him.

He clapped me on the back and turned to follow me up the hill. "You look fried, mate."

Men in Black

The day's shocking events had driven me to drink. My feelings were a mixed bag; gratitude that I had survived, vague triumph that I had done so against all the odds, and a weary resignation that it was bound to happen again. The alcohol, building on these emotions, had brought me a sense that I was invulnerable – well, temporarily. Regardless, outside, at 10pm, was a seriously hostile environment. The last of the rum, which had sustained me inside and dared me to venture out, was long gone. It had been dark for hours already, and it was colder than a penguin's testicles. I stubbornly sat there anyway, looking up at the stars, and wondered why they were trembling.

Ah. It was because I was shivering so violently that my head was shaking. There was no two ways about it – I was going to have to go back in. I'd been completely defeated by the cold, which is only fair seeing as how it's bigger than me. I glanced idly over at the main house. No lights were showing upstairs. Even the boss didn't have central heating, so he was likely in bed by now too.

But someone was standing in the doorway looking over at me. That was a surprise. Had Johnny nipped out for a last cigarette? I looked at the shape. The drive and doorway were a tangle of thick shadows. I couldn't make out a face –

in fact as I looked closer it actually seemed like the person there might be facing towards the door.

That was very unusual. And not in any way good news. Then I caught movement. A second person, dressed in black, was squatting beside the truck a few feet away from the door.

Oh shit. Invasion. I froze in the hammock – not a difficult task in sub-zero temperatures – and stared at the silhouettes. Please, I thought, please let it be Johnny. Neither figure seemed to be moving. They obviously hadn't noticed me. I had some thinking to do. If these were bad guys there was no way I could let them get into Johnny's house. His horror stories of normal burglary procedure in Ecuador were whirling through my mind at high speed. If they were the men who'd tried to break into our house previously... they'd definitely be armed.

Spiders, scary music, even lawyers, hold no fear for me. Beautiful women? Well, that's a bit touch and go. But I'm shit-scared of guns. It must be due to my desire to keep my internal organs internal.

My mouth was dry. Neither person had moved yet. I had to do something. Shout, raise the alarm? Johnny and Jimmy could handle these guys for sure, if only they were awake...

Very, very slowly I slid one leg over the edge of the hammock. I had to challenge them, at least vocally. I would shout '*Hola!*' at them. Both men seemed to be facing away from me. If they weren't friendly I would have the time it took them to turn around and draw their guns to get behind the porch wall. If I made it, hopefully the gunfire would wake Johnny – if not, my screaming would.

I'd managed to get both legs over one side of the hammock. All I had to do now was stand up. "Jesus Christ," I thought, "I'm going to die." Nothing flashed before my eyes.

I stood up and opened my mouth. *"Hola,"* I croaked. Hardly any sound came out. Both men spun to look at me.

"Hola," whispered the figure in the doorway. It was Johnny.

He motioned at me to be quiet. Not a problem. My arse had done the talking for me anyway - time to wash my underwear tomorrow.

I edged along the side of our house, then tiptoed to the gate. Johnny was coming to meet me. The figure crouched near the truck approached too. He was wearing full body armour, overalls and a balaclava, all in black. It looked like Johnny had hired the SAS.

"There are people here," Johnny told me without preamble. "We're looking for them."

The highly trained counter terrorist lookalike proved to be Danielo. Both men had shotguns. I suddenly felt very glad that they were on my side.

"Do you need help?" I asked. I was wired on adrenaline.

"No," Danielo told me. "Go inside and lock the door."

It was the most sensible thing I ever heard him utter. I did it straight away. "This weekend," I whispered to myself as I once again took the biggest kitchen knife to bed, "I am going to Machachi and I am bloody well going to buy that machete!"

Though sleeping with one of those came with a high risk of waking up circumcised - or worse. I thought I'd scared myself sober, but apparently not. A deep, drunken sleep soon enfolded me.

And this time I slept through the gunfire.

A Method to the Madness?

Work on the new jaguar enclosure was taking forever. The poor cat was still stuck in her fiendish steel cage, and no matter how much time we threw at the project it just didn't seem to be getting any closer to completion.

It had taken days just to dig the post holes. No prize for guessing who did that. My skill with the big spoons was now legendary. (They needed no skill at all to use by the way. It's just that no-one else was dumb enough to want to dig post holes, and they all pretended I was better at it to avoid having to do it themselves.) I could now wrench the *excavadora* around all day without getting a single blister. My hands were so used to the tool that they made unconscious curling motions when I wasn't looking. I had the feeling it made me look like I was continually contemplating murder by strangulation.

The site for the new enclosure was halfway down the hillside, a bit further around from our carefully carved stairs. It was in severe danger of giving a purpose to our previously pointless path. If asked, Johnny would be sure to claim it was the result he had intended all along, as though his superior logic had predicted the need to house the most dangerous predator on the continent. So I didn't ask. Quite a way back from the river and the pitiful remains of our attempted bridge was a clearing of sorts, which we had enlarged by the simple expedient of cutting down everything in sight. This still left the ground at quite a steep angle though, and it had taken one day of colossal effort to turn the sloping hillside into a two-tier enclosure like a pair of enormous steps. We would enclose a bit of sloping ground at the left and right edges to allow the beast to move freely between levels.

The difficulty lay not just in the size, but in the complexity of the structure. To feed such an impressive creature without becoming the meal yourself required some clever planning. 'Clever' and 'planning' are two words which don't translate very well into Ecuadorian. Eventually Jimmy had surprised me with his ingenuity. He'd come up with the idea for a cage within a cage, controllable from the outside. Well, theoretically it was controllable – I had my doubts. He wouldn't explain exactly how it worked, and it goes without saying there wasn't a technical drawing sitting at home in a filing cabinet. What he had done was pace out the area it would occupy on the side of the main enclosure, and asked me to dig post holes around it.

After a week of hard, hard graft from everyone (except Toby who had suddenly remembered some urgent website work that needed attending to halfway through the second day), we were almost ready to attach the wire mesh. Jimmy and me were hauling the last few logs up to the site – so big that we had to carry them between us. Even Jimmy had taken a good ten minutes to cut one of these giants down, and for once he didn't even suggest I carry it on my own. The lightest of them weighed as much as a medium-sized volunteer. The biggest ones, like the one we were carrying now, were heavier than the both of us put together. It was the biggest piece of wood I'd had since my arrival, including the night I met Lady.

We tried three times to pick it up without success. We

just weren't strong enough. In the end Jimmy managed to get his shoulder under one end and I crouched under the middle and, legs shaking, stood up. The effect was immediate. It was like walking balls-first into a concrete bollard. The breath was instantly gone from my lungs. My body just wanted to fold in half. Instead I leaned forwards and staggered a couple of steps, hoping that the motion would allow some air to slip into my flattened chest. Jimmy matched my first few stumbling steps and we turned it into a kind of rhythm. I found I could breathe a tiny amount as I rolled to the log-side and took a step with my opposite leg. Not a word from Jimmy, which was totally unprecedented. I could only imagine he was struggling for oxygen too. Somehow we made it up the hill. Even with the steps it was incredibly steep, and our repeat passages earlier carrying so much weight had abraded them quite dramatically. We now shuffled up a kind of dirt ramp we'd worn through the middle. This probably helped – at least we didn't have to raise our feet very far. By the time we got to where the path branched off, and there was a little patch of level ground, I was seeing stars. Coloured blurs danced around the edge of my vision and the back of my scalp was tingling. Jimmy gasped enough breath to wheeze "Down."

We dropped our left shoulders and the behemoth tree trunk rolled off and hit the ground with a thud. In its passage it rather casually stripped the skin from the top of my shoulder. Then it lay still beside us as we both stood panting, heads down. The sudden rush of air into my lungs was bliss. The next second my head span, as though I'd stood up too fast. I tried to breathe slowly, deeply, and the feeling passed without me fainting. It's the altitude, I reminded myself. We were well over ten thousand feet after all. Quite why Jimmy had decided to cut logs from the bottom of the hillside instead of the top was a mystery. Pure sadomasochistic glee? It was as good a guess as any. Jimmy was looking at me as I straightened up, back to normal at last. He mugged a half-impressed look at me, then planted one booted foot on the titanic log. "Now you're a man," he said.

It was as close as he ever got to honest praise. It meant more to me than a thousand thank-yous. I was still glowing quietly when the others arrived to see what was happening.

"Jesus, that's a big bugger," Marie commented.

Everyone helped to move the enormous log down the path to the enclosure. Marie impressed the hell out of me with her keenness to get stuck in. Technically she didn't work here – we only had her for a week, until they were ready for her to start volunteering as an English teacher in the school in Tambillo. She'd still be staying with us though, and she'd promised to muck in after work, on her days off, and at weekends. Her mad enthusiasm for life spilled over onto our mission, and she went at it like a woman possessed. Emer too demonstrated a surprising strength and determination. Plastered in mud up to the knees, scratched and scraped by logs and spiky bitch plants, she still insisted on wearing shorts to work. But most delightfully of all, neither of the Irish girls would take any shit from Jimmy. Comments on the general frailty and loose morals of womankind, which I translated with mock outrage, would be met by vicious comments on the circumstances of his birth or the likelihood that his parents were related (which I chose not to relay back to him, since he seemed to consider me an ally in this battle of wits).

Emer would take everything he said, turn it on its head and throw it right back at him – normally with a couple of four letter words in the mix. I had to admire her for that.

Marie mostly found him funny. But then Marie found everything funny. She was often to be found on her knees, cackling madly at the vehemence of her sister's comments, whilst digging an extra post hole with her bare hands. I left her to it.

The big log was supposed to form a central support column in the middle of the enclosure. That meant it needed another, much bigger, hole making – which the others had thoughtfully left for me to do. There was a brief moment where Jimmy almost decided that the trunk was too big to make a fence post. I made damn sure it was in the ground before he finished thinking about it. Yet another sun set as the half-finished enclosure inched towards completion.

The next morning we were greeted with several massive bales of brand new wire fencing mesh. It looked expensive, an indication of how seriously Johnny was taking our recent efforts. It was green, plastic coated and very, very heavy. We man-and-woman-handled it onto the truck with a squeal of protest from the suspension. It took a concerted effort from everyone to get it out at the other end and down to the work site. We now had everything we needed to turn this forest of poles into a house fit for the King of the Jungle. In theory.

It was a fairly simple process – unroll the mesh, drag a section of it upright, and nail it into place on the fence posts. The difficulty was provided by the weight and flexibility of the material, and its tendency to rapidly unroll itself downhill with an effect not unlike a green plastic-coated steamroller. By the time we'd learnt that we needed a separate person completely devoted to controlling the stuff on the ground, quite a few people had been violently flattened by the runaway bale and were looking a bit pissed off. And decidedly two-dimensional.

A smoke break had to be called to let frayed tempers recover. The job wasn't getting any easier with practice. In fact it was about to get harder. We'd taken our break when we reached a corner, and our next task was to continue the fence down a forty-five degree incline for the length of the enclosure's short side. Whichever way we did this we still ended up with a triangular flap of mesh left over, which Jimmy with his usual practicality simply nailed back to the post in as many places as he could reach. I think his philosophy on life was that you could fix anything if you threw enough nails at it. Which probably went some way to explaining his rather spiky relationship with Nancy.

An unprecedented amount of swearing accompanied the erection of the final sections of fence. Three people were hanging off the fence by their fingertips trying to put tension on it from every possible angle. Everyone left was frantically nailing it to their nearest post over and over. The swearing came when the hangers-on released a section too soon due to arm fatigue, or on time only to find it wasn't as securely nailed as the nailer had led them to believe, or released a securely nailed section only to watch it spring back into its natural shape – leaving a rather unfortunate gap along the bottom of it. By the time we were nearly finished, the super-secure perimeter of the enclosure looked like nothing so much as an enormous, green... well, pile of shit sprang to mind.

I pointed out a few jaguar-sized holes where the mesh met the ground. The entire fence sagged like a pair of eighty-year-old boobs. No-one was particularly impressed with the fruits of our labour.

"Jimmy, this isn't going to work," I said.

He looked around the enclosure and shrugged the criticism off. I hated to admit it but I had a feeling that we'd wasted a lot of time, and a huge amount of that bloody green mesh. We'd had better days. Meanwhile the jaguar brooded. In a cage ten feet square there was sod all else she could do.

It was another day of work to put the roof on. Working with yet more mesh we cut off strips, each as long as the cage is deep. Or, in hindsight that's what we should have done. It would have resulted in far fewer casualties. What we actually did was fasten one end of the roll to the top of the fence on one side, then three willing volunteers hefted the bale over their heads and walked across the enclosure, paying it out as they did. Every few seconds two people would pay out a length of mesh that still had the third person's fingers threaded through it. A scream would split the air, usually followed by a variety of choice oaths and a round of increasingly frustrated apologies. Then the process would begin again, and continue until the loose soil slid out from under someone else, bringing the whole bundle down on top of them and their co-workers, and pulling the fingers off the poor sod who was coming along behind them stitching it to the top of the fence. This was my job. I still bear the scars.

Sewing neighbouring sections of roof mesh together with bendy wire was also rather tricky. The seams would naturally come in the middle of the enclosure, where they were all several feet out of reach, and there was nothing to lean our ridiculous ladder against. It fell to the others to take turns at being the thing to lean the ladder on. It was a job that invariably involved being stepped on quite a lot and left its mark in the form of two top-of-ladder shaped bruises on the upper torso. For me, frantically bending wire on a wobbling ladder of extremely dubious construction, high above the head of an unwilling and rapidly tiring volunteer, the major concern was not to shit myself with every sudden lurch as there was someone below me who might notice.

It was a long day. By the end we had a completely mesh-covered enclosure, though it was still sagging like a bouncy castle with a puncture. Despite the variety of minor injuries no-one was bleeding beyond their ability to control it. No-one was dead. And I hadn't shat on anyone's head, which I guess qualifies it as a victory. The feeding cage, an extra section which could be shut off from the main enclosure by a gate worked from outside, was a triumph. Unless the rope toggles used to operate the gate fell inside of course, at which point it'd be down to drawing straws to see who went in to fetch them.

As for the rest of the structure, I still had my doubts.

"Imagine I'm a jaguar," I said to Jimmy. I had a sneaking suspicion he wasn't taking this seriously. "Really," I said. "Me – Jaguar." Best not to look for his reaction. I backed up, and trying to avoid looking too much like a complete pillock I pantomimed throwing myself against the fence. To prove my point I followed up by prodding the same section with a stick I was carrying. It bellied out alarmingly. "The jaguar is much stronger than me," I finished.

Jimmy thought this was hilarious. I had a sudden urge to dig a post hole on his head.

"He's not taking it seriously," I complained to Emer, who was watching the exchange in fascination.

"Ah, yer man doesn't give a shite. I know what you mean though," she agreed. "This cage is slacker than Marie!"

As we gathered our tools and made our way back up the hill I offered to take bets on the length of time the jaguar would remain in captivity once we let her into her new enclosure.

"On the bright side," I pointed out, "next week we get to do something really cool. Catch an escaped jaguar."

Emer chuckled. She hadn't been here during the Great Bear Hunt. One thing was for certain – if that jaguar climbed a tree there was no way in hell I was climbing after it.

A Class Act

"Hoo-jah, hoo-jah, hoo-jah!" The noise issued from a room full of throats. "Hoo-jah, hoo-jah, hoo-jah," it came again.

"Very good," said Alice, addressing her class in English. She was standing at the front of the room next to a cheap table of the designed-to-stack variety you only see in schools. I lounged back in my matching plastic stacking-type chair, trying to look nonchalant without really understanding the meaning of the word, and shook my head at the peculiarity of the situation. I had to hand it to Alice – whether by fortune or design, we never met in what one could call conventional circumstances.

She pointed to the blackboard where a simple phrase was neatly and precisely written. "Hoo-jah go out with last night?"

"Hoo-jah go out with last night," the students chorused.

"Very good," Alice said again. "Now this one – Ware-jah."

"Ware-jah, ware-jah, ware-jah!"

"Ware-jah go last night?" She indicated the board again.

For an English teacher she was teaching some pretty weird English.

Alice had invited me to guest star in one of her lessons.

Actually, to say she'd blackmailed me into it would be more accurate. I'd accidentally stood Lady up on a date in Quito, on account of me throwing up several pints of blood on the way into town. The rest of the volunteers had had a whale of a time, after laying me to rest in a darkened room in a youth hostel. They'd had so much fun that none of them had remembered to meet Lady and explain my predicament to her. Alice, who saw Lady quite often in town, had very kindly offered to make amends – saving me a truly difficult and stressful phone call. Her price was my body; she wanted me in her class for one whole afternoon, for her pupils' viewing pleasure.

Alice had a room full of university age students to entertain for several hours a day, and the last time she'd told them she was bringing a friend to class it had turned out to be a stuffed toy monkey. And not just any monkey – it was an English-speaking one. The students had been understandably underwhelmed when she'd announced another visitor to their lessons, so she was determined to make the most of me. It had gone well so far...

First she'd instructed me to create a character. Not that Tony, penniless backpacker from England working as a volunteer because it was cheaper than staying in a hostel, wasn't an interesting persona, but she wanted to add some genuine interest to the lesson. Or fake interest, since I'd be making it up on the spot.

Enter: James Anthony Romeo. Actor, lover, action hero; my alter ego was all the things I pretended to be whenever I was trying to pick up a hot chick in a night club. With one major difference – this time I'd be talking to someone who actually gave a shit. About twenty of them in fact, all with questions to ask and reports to write, and I was to be the subject of all of it. God, I hoped I'd do better than that stuffed monkey.

My dramatic entrance couldn't possibly have gone

better. Following Alice's directions I'd arrived at a locked door surrounded by a handful of her keenest students. Both they, and I, were early. Alice herself had been stalking the surrounding corridors vainly looking for someone to unlock her classroom door. She didn't look happy.

"They're so bloody disorganised here!" she complained. "My class is here every weekday, but half the time I still have to find the bloody supervisor to open the door!"

The supervisor's office was the barest I'd ever seen. One chair, one table, one filing cabinet. No artwork, no carpet and no supervisor.

"So what can you do?" I asked her.

"Nothing. Just wait till he shows up. This is so annoying, my students are paying for their lessons too, and they get to spend half of it stood around in the corridor."

We walked back to the classroom and stood outside the door in question. The window above it was open as if to taunt us.

"Shame you can't open it from the inside," I said, "or I could just climb in through that window."

Alice looked surprised. "You can open it from the inside! It's a like a Yale lock. Can you get through that?"

I took another look. The window was a decent size. "Easy," I said. A quick glance around the gathered group told me that most of them were already waiting, and more than a few were studying me suspiciously. I could hardly believe how perfectly the circumstances had conspired. I waved a couple of guys away from the door, made a quick show of stretching and flexing my arms, then jumped up and caught hold of the window frame. In what I hoped was one smooth motion, I pulled myself up and through, swung my legs around and dropped to the floor inside. It was like breaking into our loo, something I'd practised several times since the first, largely because every new volunteer managed to lock themselves out at least once on their first day. Some learnt straight away never to close the toilet door with no-one inside, whilst some (no names mentioned!) always seemed to remember this rule just after they'd done it. Either way, I was getting good at breaking and entering. And it had all been for this moment. I flipped the latch and held the door wide for the surprised students. By now they were really confused. My legend was growing.

I'd been sitting in a corner listening to gibberish ever since. It had never really occurred to me before just how difficult it must be to learn English as a foreign language, when even the natives don't speak it properly. Whereas the beginners class would obviously start by learning questions with the words 'Who, where, when', they'd be screwed if they came to England and expected to be asked a perfectly enunciated, and thus understandable, question like "How are you this morning?" Just listen to yourself one day; "Ware-ya bin bro?" or "Wossyername?" – questions completely unintelligible to the untrained ear. The whole language is so laced with contractions and slang that most of us don't even know we're using them. First we complain when foreigners don't speak English, then when they try to learn we move the goal posts. Aren't we a bunch of bastards!

Surprisingly enough the English aren't well-liked abroad.

A last chorus of "Wenja wenja wenja," followed by glowing praise from Alice, seemed to wrap up this utterly bizarre section of her lesson. Now it was my turn. Alice glanced over at me and I stood up to join her at the front of the class.

Twenty confused faces looked back at me. Some of them were cute too. It's official, I thought. I'm going to hell.

"This is Mr. James Anthony Romeo." Alice told the class. "He's an actor from England. He is very famous there. And because he's my friend, he's offered to come here and let you interview him."

Silence descended in a heartbeat.

"Hi!" I waved.

No-one spoke. Tough audience.

"My name is James Anthony Romeo," I said by way of getting into character. "Do you want to ask any questions?"

I really hoped this wasn't going to be a bust. Alice had been so looking forward to it. As had I, to be honest. I needn't have worried. She was more than up to the task.

"Carlos. You have a question. Ask it." Her tone brooked no argument. This was a side of her I'd never seen before – Alice the teacher, all grown up and responsible!

One of the lads took a deep breath and started speaking halting English with a slightly shaky voice.

"Why are you in Ecuador?"

Good question. Even the real Tony didn't know the answer to that one. I launched into my planned story about shooting a big movie in the jungle. I picked the cheesiest title I could come up with in response to another question. "It's called 'The Jungle of Death'."

The rest of the class relaxed once they realised they weren't being tested. They asked about my home, my life, my past glories. I told them about my countryside mansion in Cornwall (lies), my hobbies breeding horses and driving sports cars (more lies) and my recent success at the box office with films like 'Tomb Raider 3', 'Space Explorer' and 'The Assassin' (lies, lies, lies!). It was so much fun. I couldn't tell if they all believed me or if none of them did. That Ecuadorian inscrutability must develop from birth. One group of lads seemed to be holding a fierce debate in Spanish. In the lull between questions I caught the occasional word or phrase from them. 'Full of shit!' was amongst the more dramatic declarations. How right they were!

Finally though, they caught me in a lie. When asked if I was married the power went to my head. Any one of the gorgeous celebrities I lusted after could be my wife. I suddenly remembered my first meeting with Alice, swimming ashore to escape the world's worst boat trip.

"Angelina Jolie," I answered without pause.

I mean, you would, wouldn't you!

At this a flurry of questions broke out, and a few of the poker faces at the back cracked a little. I described our recent meeting on the set of the new Tomb Raider movie, our whirlwind romance, her divorce and our quiet marriage ceremony back in England. This was one bluff too far and it was promptly called.

"What nationalities are her children?" The question came from a grinning lad at the centre of the unbelievers. They'd obviously spent their time picking out a question to trip me with.

I had no idea. "African?" I guessed, and the game was up.

Slightly ruder questions about the nature of our relationship flew aplenty now that they'd realised I was a fraud. Alice brought the session to a close by shouting until everyone else shut up.

"Thank-you very much," I said.

Laughter and a few thank-yous rolled my way as the class packed up and headed for the door.

"And you really don't speak Spanish?" The lad who'd outed me at question time had approached me instead of leaving.

"No," I told him.

"Really?"

"Not a word of it," I said in Spanish.

His eyes widened a little, then he laughed and headed for the door, calling out to his mate. "Manuel! He did hear you call him an asshole!"

A Cold Stretch

The rooster went off at 6am. It was only still alive because at 6am it was still far too cold to get out of bed, much less go outside. Ordinarily I would spend the next forty-five minutes fantasising about taking the bloody thing's head off with a machete, while trying in vain to get back to sleep. Not so this morning.

Last night, after a few glasses of rum to celebrate my successful infiltration of Alice's world, and then a few more glasses of rum because, well, there was still some rum left, Toby had hatched a grand-sounding scheme. Every morning from now on, we resolved to get up at 6am (since we were always awake already) and brave the cold like the men we were, to do an hour of calming, meditative yoga. Like the women we weren't.

No, that's unfair. I love the idea of yoga – strength, balance and flexibility – I really do! At any time after about midday. Preferably in a warm room. Somewhere with a carpet.

At 6am, in sub-zero temperatures, there were things I'd rather do than lie balls-down on a tiled floor and try to bend my legs back the wrong way. In fact I'm very hard pushed to think of anything I'd less rather do. But a deal is a deal. I'd offered to learn, if Toby would teach. His back was in bad shape due to a nasty diving accident years before, and he needed an excuse to stretch it out more often. I on the other hand was merely incredibly foolish and needed punishing. That ravine-sized opening in my head, kindly termed my mouth by those that have never suffered its consequences, had struck again. In its wake my life was about to get even harsher; clearly I wasn't learning my lesson fast enough. How many times did I have to remind myself? If I must drink half a bottle of rum of an evening, I should at least have the foresight to cocoon my head in duct tape and drink through a straw.

I dropped off my bunk onto the icy floor. There was one thing I was sure to learn, I reflected, Toby's teachings notwithstanding: not to do anything, much less yoga, the morning after drinking half a bottle of rum.

Toby joined me in the lounge looking equally upset with himself. But being men, and therefore extremely stupid, neither of us would admit what was surely obvious to both of us – we'd rather be in our beds, dreaming up an unpleasant demise for that bastard rooster.

"I think we'll do some 'sun salutations' first," Toby explained.

What sun? I wanted to ask. It wouldn't even be visible for another hour. There then followed a very cold, very calm half hour of bending, stretching and breathing.

"Enough for me," I said at the first natural break point. I mean, I wanted to help Toby and all, but I was literally bending over backwards for him.

"Yeah, me too," Toby agreed. "We'd better get ready for the feed anyway."

I went back into the bedroom and climbed straight back into bed. The feed could wait until some feeling returned to my legs!

The next thing I knew were the clangs and squeals of protest from the bunk beds as the Irish girls leapt out. We were late! For the first time I'd managed to get back to sleep post-rooster. Well what do you know, yoga was good for something.

The next morning dawned dark and frigid.

Or rather it didn't dawn, because it wasn't dawn, and I had the desperate desire to prove the meaning of true darkness to that rooster by choking the daylights out of the fucker. He was bang on time though. 6am. I swear that bird had a digital watch. And the damn thing was set an hour fast.

It was the do-or-die moment. If I didn't force myself to get up straight away, I wouldn't get up at all. Come on! I told myself. So it's cold and it's early! Hardly the end of the world is it? I should cultivate a positive mental attitude. Yoga is not something which can be done by halves, I thought, unless of course one is quadriplegic.

I grudgingly de-bunked and went into the lounge. Not bad – I was the first to arrive. I sat cross-legged on the floor and wished my pyjamas were thicker. It was kind of like sitting naked on an ice rink, but with no-one watching.

Toby was late. Not a problem, I thought. I'm not more perfect than him, just a little more dedicated. I assumed a tranquil, meditative air to prove I wasn't ruffled by his lack of commitment.

Fifteen minutes later I realised he wasn't coming. Bastard! I'd sat here freezing my backside off to keep my end of his bargain while he stayed wrapped up in bed! It was a betrayal of monumental proportions. Okay, so perhaps I was overreacting a little. I tend to do that when my ass gets so numb I can't stand up. Why the hell hadn't I tried to look tranquil and meditative in a chair? I hauled myself up onto the coffee table. Whilst I massaged the blood flow back into my buttocks I considered my options.

I could go and wake Toby. With ice and very, very cold

water. I could go back to bed and stave off hypothermia. I could go outside and kill the rooster. Three brilliant plans! Alas, being neither vindictive, or a murderer, I decided I would have to limit my revenge to staying in bed an extra five minutes so the others started work before me. Ha! That'll teach… absolutely no-one. But it would make me feel better.

A full three quarters of an hour later I struggled out of bed again and into my disgusting clothes. As I entered the lounge Toby came out of his bedroom. I could tell he'd only just gotten up. He looked like he'd had a nice, long, restful sleep.

I felt like a complete knob for getting up at all. Luckily he didn't know that I had. Or that I'd been crouched in here slapping my own ass vigorously, in an attempt to restore sensation. I intended to keep it that way. Some subtle misdirection was called for.

"Did you get up for yoga, then?" I asked casually.

"Nah," came the reply.

"Oh, really?" I tried to sound surprised. "How come?"

This was it, I thought. He better have a bloody good excuse.

He shrugged. "Well, I dunno, I just… couldn't be buggered really."

Not Suitable for Vegetarians...
(You have been warned!)

It was a long time since I'd made the Sunday pilgrimage to Machachi market; between the rigours of dating and the Irish girls dragging me out to party at every available opportunity, I'd spent most Sundays recovering either at the centre or more often than not, in Quito. Whereas previously I'd spent most of each week looking forward to buying junk food (ie. meat) in Machachi, recently I'd been eating my fill of dubious meals from the wide variety of cheap takeaways that dominated the capital's backpacker district. So far I'd survived the experiences. Mostly. But now the allure of Machachi called to me once more. I was finally confident enough to handle a solo mission, and without the need to shepherd other volunteers around I was also free to pick out my dream machete! For as long as I could remember I'd wanted one of my own, but always felt vaguely ridiculous to be considering buying one. Would they even sell such an instrument of death to a lone scrawny white dude adrift in a sea of tough weathered faces? I now felt sure they would. A blade would be mine! And socks. I needed socks. I'd been hoarding my one clean pair for my next date with Lady, until Machita had found them. Their remains were now amongst her proudest possessions.

Socks were everywhere in Machachi. Every time I looked at a pair I imagined Lady exclaiming in delight as I took them off. What would she find funnier? Pink socks? Odd socks? Suddenly I was nervous. This ridiculous indecision typified the chaos that whirled through my mind whenever a meeting with Lady was imminent. She was so beautiful and so... intimidating! Without a stern bone in her body she still managed to scare me more than every animal in the refuge. Because I cared, so very much what she thought of me – and I was painfully aware that I didn't have a lot to offer her. She had this whole exotic beauty thing going, a real job in the city and... did I mention she was beautiful? I was... well, just me. I'd never had a 'real' job. I'd trained as an actor specifically to avoid it! The only reason I wasn't broke is because I was living in a country where you could buy a steak dinner for two for the price of a loaf of bread back home. I was always just a little bit grubby due to the general crappiness of the shower, and constantly covered in cuts and bruises due to... well, I don't know! For some reason everything that lived and breathed at Santa Martha (and quite a few things that didn't) seemed to want a piece of me. And most of them had gotten one.

Before I knew it I'd spent half a day looking at socks and machetes. The colourful blur of the market was largely ignored around me. Even the mouth-watering smells of strange things a-frying couldn't shake my focus. I'd narrowed my options down to a gargantuan blade almost as long as my arm and cotton socks with Popeye on. It would have made for an interesting package to explain if stopped on the bus. "Why yes officer, they're both gifts for my ten-year-old son..."

I decided to buy the machete. I could already imagine the look Jimmy would give me when I brought it to the *galpón* for him to sharpen – I would doubtless spend the next week listening to him comment on the size of my tool. But at least it was better than the alternative – the only other blades on offer were mini-machetes about ten inches long, probably for use by children in arts and crafts classes. *That* was not something I would easily live down. So my grand haul for the day was a farmyard tool which looked suitable for shaving a woolly mammoth, and one pair of comedy socks.

It wasn't until that afternoon, with a date arranged for the same evening, that I started to get dressed and so realised my error. I'd been so caught up with the question of style that I'd neglected to check the size. The damn socks didn't stretch – they went on over my toes, halfway up my foot and stopped just shy of the heel. Of course they were children's socks. Why else would they have Popeye on them?

Other than that I was looking pretty good. My clothes had been washed, and… that was it. Being clean was such a rare occurrence for me that I was actually counting it as a benefit. I was wearing my best shirt. I was wearing my only shirt! I really had to think about getting another shirt. Though if I changed clothes Lady probably wouldn't recognise me. My hair had finally grown back to a sensible length, so I no longer looked like I had my finger trapped in an electrical socket. I would have checked myself out in the mirror if we'd had one. We didn't, so I didn't. This made shaving a little difficult but I struggled on manfully. It wasn't the first time I'd seen my own blood in the sink and the chances were better than average that it wouldn't be the last. There was still an hour or so before I had to start out down the mountain, so I wandered outside to watch the sunset. It was a beautiful evening.

Then I noticed Johnny walking purposefully towards our house. I smiled and waved. Whatever bombshell he'd come to drop, I was on my way out. Toby could deal with it, and tell me in the morning. But instead of waving back, Johnny called me. "Tony, there's a job for you to do," he said.

Weird. We didn't work on Sundays, much less in the evening. Was some cool new beastie arriving?

"Erm... do you want me to get Toby?" I asked hopefully.

"No, no," came the reply, "we only need you. Don't tell Toby."

What? Interesting! A job that they'd rather I do than Toby! Well, maybe this was something worth doing. A job only I could do, eh? My ego was already kicking in. Toby was king around here, and deservedly so. He worked hard, and did so much more than feed the animals and dig holes. But then so did I. Damn, I worked hard! Maybe it was time for some recognition...

"Come with me," Johnny said, a note of conspiracy in his voice. "You will like this!"

I followed him down the path, filled with excitement. Everyone liked me, after all. Perhaps they'd decided to make me their king! We stopped at the milking shed and Johnny led me inside.

There, in the middle of the concrete floor, lay my prize. On its back with its legs in the air. It was a dead cow.

"Wow," I said to Johnny. "It's... great."

He looked at me and grinned. "Here." He handed me a machete. "You can skin her."

Bucket. I needed a bucket. And not to help in the skinning process.

"Jimmy will show you how." Jimmy was stood off to one side, grinning too. I got the feeling there was some kind of joke here, with a very strong possibility that I was it. There was only one thing to do.

"Yeah, no problem," I said, taking the machete off Johnny.

"Good," he said, and left.

Jimmy came over and clapped me on the shoulder. He was clearly enjoying this way too much. "Let's do it," he said.

What followed was one of the most disgusting things I've ever done in my life. Between us, with me pushing and Jimmy pulling, we broke the cow's legs. Ugh. There is a very definite sound to it that is guaranteed to churn the stomach. The worst thing was that it happened in stages – not one almighty 'CRACK' and it was all over, but with a series of sharp jerks, each one accompanied by just enough of a crack to make me wish I really had asked for that bucket. It went kind of like this:

"Ready?"

"Yeah."

"Pull!"

"Yeah."

"Now! Harder!"

"I'm trying!"

"Tight! Hold tight!"

"I know!"

"Now!"

CRACK!

"Ewwww!!!"

"Again!"

CRACK!

"Ugh. Ugh!"

CRACK!

Crack, Crack, Crack.

CRUNCH!

"Good. Done."

(in English) "I feel sick."

"Okay, next leg..."

Breaking the legs backwards at the knee apparently allows the tendons holding the leg together to be cut. Jimmy attended to this with a few mighty whacks from his machete. The result: four severed lower legs, hooves and all, which he put in a pile for the dogs.

Then it got tricky. After producing a wickedly sharp kitchen knife (Jimmy had an unhealthy obsession with his grinding wheel. I had a sneaking suspicion even the spoons in his house were wickedly sharp), he proceeded to make a long straight slice up the inside of what was left of the first leg, bottom to top. Then he dug his fingers in and peeled back the thick hairy skin.

Now, I was under the impression that the worst was over. Surely once we'd 'opened' the cow, the skin would come off like a Mars bar wrapper, and we could fold it up and go home. No. Not the case. As he peeled back the hide, a thick squelchy layer stayed attached to the cow. This I now know to be the subcutaneous fat. Lovely. With a few words and gestures Jimmy let me know what I had to do. Then he handed me the knife.

It was about this time that I realised I was still wearing my best clothes, and was on my way out for a date. Things may be a little different in Ecuador, but I was fairly sure that Lady would not be impressed by me turning up looking like the victim in a slasher movie. I couldn't do much, but at least I could take off my shirt before I ended up knee deep in cow guts. So I did. I hung my shirt on a rusty nail well out of splatter-range and went to work. Jimmy made no comment on my decision to do my butchery half naked, for which I was very grateful.

So with knife in hand I carefully trimmed the fat layer away from the skin as Jimmy pulled it tight. Slowly, slowly, we removed more and more until we had half a body off. Each leg was dealt with the same way as we came to it, with a vertical slit allowing us to peel the skin off in one piece with the rest of the hide.

Jimmy expertly slit the skin down the belly, and we

switched over to work on the other side. Eventually we had a naked inside of cow, sitting on an inside-out cow-skin rug. And everywhere there was ichor.

It was about to get worse. On the upside, Jimmy produced a bucket from somewhere back in the shed. On the downside he was planning on using it to store all the bits we were about to cut off the cow. He clashed the kitchen knife and machete together by way of sharpening them, in the way I imagine a homicidal axe murderer does before carving his Christmas turkey. Then he squatted next to the body of the cow and started to slice. Mostly my job at this point involved picking up the massive chunks of meat and carrying them to the bucket. I congratulated myself repeatedly on the decision to take my shirt off.

Next he took a few practice swings with the machete (for dramatic emphasis, I was sure) and started smashing his way through the ribs. Halfway through I took over, and the feeling of the blade biting home into bone was just subtly different from chopping into wood. The cow's chest was strong enough to withstand a series of heavy blows, but something about the way it absorbed the impact felt more… organic? Squishy. Sickeningly so – not that I was going to tell that to Jimmy. And then my machete lodged in the dense bone and I had to put my foot on the beast to lever the blade free…

I've always been a proud carnivore, even when working as a volunteer in an animal refuge staffed almost exclusively by vegetarians. I'm of the opinion that man is supposed to eat meat – it's part of our natural diet. Keeping animals chained up in a tiny box for people to poke, that I'm opposed to, but I see no contradiction in caring for animals, and also wanting to fill my belly with some of them. It's nature. But I do believe that if I'm prepared to eat meat, I should be prepared to kill it for this purpose. Hiding from the brutality of killing something for food, yet still being quite happy to eat it when someone else does the dirty work, does strike me as a bit hypocritical. It's only my opinion, and not necessarily the right one, it just makes sense to me. So whilst I don't go around knocking pigs on the head and stealing a quick bite, I figured I should be man enough to cope with this at least once in my life.

This argument was going through my head as I planted my recently cleaned training shoe on the cow's mangled rib cage and wrenched the machete free for the third time.

Once was *definitely* enough.

Finally that bit was over. We shifted operations to the squibbly bits inside the cow, and soon had a separate pile of slimy internal organs next to the bucket. Jimmy was careful to point out the stomachs, and warn me against nicking them with the knife. Apparently this would not only ruin the rest of the meat below, but would also make a horrible smell. Horrible smell? Where the hell did he think he was now, the perfume counter at Selfridges? The whole place stank like someone was chopping up a dead cow. We trimmed out some more meat until the cow looked like a bony canoe. There couldn't be much left now that we could remove. Jimmy seemed to agree. He stood up and wiped the kitchen knife on a rag from his back pocket. He stopped for a breather and eyed the huge pile of meat and sliminess we'd amassed. I looked down at my jeans for any signs of sliminess there. Somehow it seemed I'd escaped the worst of it, though I'd be leaving bloody footprints for a while.

Finished? I thought. Not even close. We'd mercifully left the skin on the head, and after accidentally making eye contact in the first few minutes of the job I'd been trying really hard to avoid looking at it. Not a problem for much longer – a few minute's rest was all Jimmy needed. He walked around what was left of the cow, took careful aim with his machete and hacked the head off in three excessively brutal strokes. More for the dogs.

Well over an hour later I emerged from the milking shed and headed back to the house.

"Still here?" Toby asked as I walked straight past him to the bathroom. "Where've you been then?"

"Trust me," I said, like they do in the movies, "you don't want to know."

But this was the real world, and like anyone else who hears that phrase for real, Toby instantly did want to know. So after scrubbing my hands for a good few minutes, I told him. Poor bugger! It was fairly obvious from the start why they wanted me to do the job as opposed to him, but given his reaction to my report he would have made more mess down there than the cow did. Still, it gave me something to wind him up with. For the next few days all I had to do to make him go green was to make a few innocuous sounds... "Crack... Crack.... CRACK...!"

I really wanted a shower. So I had one. I really wanted to shower in my clothes, but I had nothing else to wear and I couldn't be soggy on a date. There are rules about that sort of thing.

It was getting quite late as I walked quickly down the hill. I was sweating from the exercise, but in my imagination I was still discovering bits of slime I hadn't managed to wash off. That would be a sure hit with Lady. I could just imagine the conversation...

Lady: "Mm, you're sweating. I like a man sweating..."

Me: "No, sorry, that's cow mucus."

My dictionary doesn't even have a Spanish word for mucus. Which is probably a good thing.

Lady was late. I was standing alone in the middle of a shopping centre on the outskirts of Quito, and the temperature inside and out was dropping rapidly. I'd agreed to meet her here after work and was a little late myself due to the surprise butchering party. Every time I smoothed my hands down my jeans I discovered another microscopic fleck of blood. What would I do when she turned up looking stunning, leant in to kiss me and pulled up short to ask why I smelled like something had died of dysentery in my pocket? And as if it couldn't get any worse – I wasn't wearing any socks.

Doubts assailed my mind as the shops began to close around me. Maybe she wasn't coming. Maybe she'd caught sight of me already and left in shock without me even noticing. Maybe I was just paranoid, I thought, stifling a yawn. And very, very tired.

And then there she was! The sight of her rushing towards me, high heels clicking madly on the marble floor, took my breath away. Straight from the office, smartly presented in a black pencil skirt and crisp white blouse, my girlfriend looked stunning. Her long, midnight black hair was piled elaborately on top of her head. And there was me looking like I lived in a cardboard box. But she didn't even notice – she was far too busy apologising to *me*, for being held up at work due to some late deliveries! "Don't worry about it," I told her charitably. I really didn't deserve a woman of this quality.

We watched a film, '*El Día Después de Mañana*', about a global ice age. It was glacially cold outside the cinema, not substantially warmer inside, and we were watching a film about people freezing to death. I thought I was going to be one of them. Even my goose bumps had goose bumps. I lost all feeling in my arms and legs. Only the sensation of Lady's warm body pressed tight up against me kept me from losing the will to live. If only she could warm me overnight! Alas, she had already told me that she had to go home to her children, which meant that I too was going home. By the time the movie finished my whole body was numb and we had no option but to huddle together outside while we waited for a bus.

And waited.

I had a horrible thought – had we missed the last one? Of course we had! She'd arrived so late that we'd had to catch the last showing. It had to be close to midnight. No way public transport would still be operating, even in this bus-crazed country. But Lady still wanted to wait.

Eventually we gave up and flagged a taxi.

We hugged each other tight all the way home. I'd have tried to kiss her, but between shivering and the car bouncing along Quito's uneven highways I'd probably have ended up biting her lips off. Instead we saved our passionate embrace for after we got kicked out at Tambillo town. I pressed myself against her and kissed her for as long as I dared – another few seconds and our lips would have frozen together. Then she was off down the road into town, towards her mother's house on the square.

Had I been back in civilisation, another taxi would have been just what I needed, delivering my shivering self to the warmth of my bed with the minimum of delay. But this was not that place; the volunteer house and everything in it would be the same temperature as the surrounding atmosphere and the only thing warming my bed would be my body heat. Or lack thereof. So I decided to walk. A forty minute hike on a forty-five degree incline was bound to get some blood pumping. There were no street lights of course, but it was a wonderfully clear night. I walked as fast as my trembling legs would carry me, edging past precipices and setting frantic dogs barking every time I skirted a ramshackle residence.

By the time I reached the refuge I was feeling much better. The date had been successful, the night was beautiful... and Johnny was walking down the driveway towards me. The solitary light outside his house threw his shadow into the darkness between us. It was not a happy-looking shadow.

"Tony?" There was caution in his voice.

"*Sí* Johnny. It's me."

He didn't waste any words. "It's not safe for you to walk up the mountain after dark. It's very dangerous – lots of bad people around."

"Hey, it's not a problem," I told him. "I can look after myself quite well." I was considering telling him 'I know Kung Fu!' when I caught the look on his face. I stopped mid smart-arsed response.

"Walking around here in the dark is not clever," Johnny explained. "I thought you might be a burglar. I nearly shot you." It was only then that I noticed the rifle in his hands.

"Please don't do it again. Okay? If you stay late in town, spend the night there, or come up the hill in a taxi. Danielo is on guard too. Next time you might get killed."

I nodded mute acceptance.

Next time, I thought, perhaps I should get a taxi. Three dollars seemed like an unnecessary extravagance until I weighed it against my life. It occurred to me that if I explained this state of affairs to my mother, she wouldn't need much persuading to send me some extra cash to cover taxi fares…

Toby was still awake when I got in, sitting alone at the table wrapped in at least fifteen blankets.

"How was the date mate?" he asked sleepily.

"Developed pneumonia and Johnny nearly shot me," I told him. "So pretty standard really."

Toby didn't even blink. "You get any action?"

"Nope."

"Oh, mate! Your night really sucked!" Evidently this was too big a disaster to be merely shrugged away. He put down the book he'd been scrutinising at point-blank range. It was Spanish vocab. "On the floor by the fridge, mate," he gestured. "Fetch that rum."

Comings and Goings

Toby did love vegetables. Luckily, as he wouldn't eat anything else. He was sick of rice (we were all sick of rice). He hadn't dared eat a lentil since Alice had accidentally poisoned him when they'd snuck away for a weekend at the beach. He didn't like eggs. Basically the guy's options were pretty limited and he was getting skinnier by the day. So it was with great pride and hope for the future that he finally established his vegetable garden in a tiny greenhouse behind the parrot cage. He cleared it and cleaned it, dug the earth and carefully fertilised it. I mean, I never saw him squatting bare-assed over the soil with a handful of bog roll or anything, but I had it on good authority that his garden was well and truly fertilised. Maybe Jimmy told me. He was always full of shit.

Toby had been hoarding seeds from our dinner vegetables almost since I arrived so by now he had enough to kick-start the market economy of a third world nation. He lovingly buried half of his precious stock and returned several times a day to water the ground. He even did one very clever thing. He didn't ask me to look after it.

The girls were delighted when Toby entrusted care of his pet project to them. He gave them very specific instructions and a watering schedule he'd drawn up on a scrap of paper. Because Toby was leaving for England. He'd been living at Santa Martha for close to a year by this point and he was fresh out of money. He was also suffering from borderline malnutrition and probably a fistful of deficiency disorders. Johnny had grudgingly accepted his need to return to England, just for a few weeks, to earn more money. "And bring back a gun," he'd said.

I think he had England a bit confused with somewhere else. At any rate Toby was leaving me in charge of the volunteers. It was a pretty scary prospect as it meant that I would now be the lone conduit through which Johnny poured his wisdom upon us. In Spanish. I was getting much better since I'd been dating Lady, but I was nervous as hell about being the sole point of contact between the boss and his entire workforce. Especially when Toby's parting advice included nuggets like "Don't let Johnny kill that ocelot!" Even though the cat had HIV, she wasn't suffering and neither of us wanted to see her euthanized unnecessarily. Would I be fighting Johnny for her survival? I wasn't going to argue with a shotgun. So it's fair to say that I was relieved and delighted when in the same discussion Toby informed me we were expecting a new, Spanish speaking, volunteer. What he failed to do was to tell me anything else about her. Hence, I was totally unprepared when she swung her smooth legs over the side of the taxi and dropped lithely to the ground. A slender, tanned young girl with tumbling blonde curls and hypnotic blue eyes – I'd never regretted so strongly not having a shower after mucking out the monkey cages.

Gloudina. What could I say? Her arrival on the farm was a sudden revelation of the cosmic beauty of the universe. Was she merely an extension into this dimension of a being so infinitely beautiful as to redefine our paltry human concept of perfection?

Possibly. And she had a great ass.

Gloudina had been working with Leonardo for weeks (which probably explains why we hadn't seen him for so long) and now she had come to Santa Martha to be my wife. She didn't know that yet of course, but I felt it strongly enough for both of us. Or rather, I *wanted* to feel it. Every time she bent over I wanted to feel it. Only time would tell whether she would give me the opportunity. And whilst I was waiting in hope I decided to make Gloudina the official picker-up of anything that I had mistakenly placed on the floor.

Best of all I had the perfect excuse to ask her to marry me. No! I mean ask her to be my assistant. That's right. My complete and total inadequacy for the task I had been appointed to would be both an honest-sounding reason to get close to her and would simultaneously cease to be a problem just because I was close to her. She would hear the commands and I would give them – together we would rule Santa Martha as King and Queen! Naked.

Gloudina's lithe beauty was also good for one more reason. All joking aside, in the last few months Toby had become one of the best friends I'd ever had. We'd spent more time together than most newly wed couples, working, eating and occasionally passing out drunk together. And now, almost without warning, he was leaving. I was really going to miss him.

That night Johnny threw a dinner party to bid farewell to his most trusted aide. I was sad and happy in equal measure. Nancy outdid herself, creating a whole variety of vegetarian cuisine in Toby's honour. Of course, that didn't stop the real men from eating meat.

As morning dawned on the day of Toby's departure, a last minute tragedy came to light. Normally, scratching around in the wire pen in front of the volunteer house we had our very own celebrity. Within days of arriving at the centre I'd spotted her – a chicken that looked exactly like Tina Turner!

The resemblance was uncanny. The fierce eyes. The huge feathery mane. The strut. I could have made a fortune on eBay. She'd narrowly avoided becoming dinner for the jaguar, and had even survived the night time depredations of El Lobo. Toby and I were both very grateful for this; after all she'd become quite a familiar face to us over the months. She added a touch of class to our dirty little world. A certain… Cluck Factor.

I mean, who else has a chicken that looks like Tina Turner?

So when I noticed her gone that morning I sprinted back inside to tell Toby.

"Tina Turner chicken? No!" He was understandably aghast. "How? When?"

"I dunno. She's just —" A nasty thought occurred to me. "You know your good-bye dinner at Johnny's last night? We were all eating those sort of fried strips of…"

"Oh no!" Poor Toby was horrified. "You ATE Tina Turner chicken!"

"I… I guess we did. I had seconds."

"NO!" Came the howl. "How could you?!"

"Ah, Toby, we had no idea. How could we know?"

"But… she's gone… you even said she tasted nice!"

"I know man. Hey, that's the closest I'll get to sinking my teeth into the real thing! She was pretty moist for a tough old bird."

"Mmm."

Then another thought occurred. "Hey Toby, you know what?"

Toby took a few reflective seconds before he responded.

"Mate, if you say she was 'simply the best', so help me I will kick your ass."

Swing Low

What with Toby gone and the other volunteers being entirely female, I felt I was doing the honourable thing by moving into Toby's room. The luxurious double bed had nothing to do with it. But it didn't last long, as within days of Toby's departure we had two more humans to accommodate. Mel and Mark were a proper couple, travelling together and everything, so their need for a private room was greater than mine. Unfortunately. It was hard to bear a grudge though, when they were both so damn friendly! Mark arrived wearing the most ridiculous hat I had ever seen a person wear. I mean, sure there's anorexic supermodels strutting down the catwalk wearing half a grand piano or a live narwhal on their heads, but in real world, actual hat-wearing stakes, this had to be one of the daftest. An enormous, woven straw boater with a wide yellow brim, it shaded his merry eyes, tanned skin and unshaven jaw line. It also hid his hair, or rather his distinct lack of it; Mark was slightly older than the rest of us, and slightly thinning on top. In order to disguise his hair's betrayal, he'd done to it voluntarily what Toby had tricked me into – had it cut so short it looked more like a coffee stain on the top of his head than anything else. To disguise this, he'd bought the hat. Of all his mistakes I held that to be the worst.

His partner in crime, not that I could ever believe her capable of committing a crime, was Mel; a cheerful woman several years his junior, with short auburn hair and a perpetually sunny disposition. Together the two brought some much-needed experience to the group. Firstly, Mark was an ex vet. I don't mean he had fought in 'Nam or anything – just that he used to be an animal doctor. And Mel was… well, she was a woman. We had plenty of *girls* at the moment, for which I was grateful of course, but Mel possessed that cheerful efficiency around the home that kept us all clean and fed, and made the place an altogether more pleasant place to be. I hated to say it, but this was another area in which a lack of Toby had been showing. I'd never really thought about it before, but the more I admired Mel's organisational skills, the more evident the comparison became. Toby had made a damn good woman.

Best of all, Mel was a nurse. I'd been doing stupid things to try and earn recognition from the bosses for so long now it seemed commonplace. Sometimes it even worked. But I'd promised myself that taking over as co-ordinator would mean the end of all that. Now was the time for me to be responsible, to set a good example to the other volunteers and inspire them with strong leadership.

It was exactly this point I was making on a pleasant Saturday afternoon. Currently in between projects, we'd had a fairly slack half-day of it, and were celebrating with banana milkshakes on the porch. I was straddling a milk crate in the way that bosses do, holding forth on my new-found sense of duty, when Mark brought me up short with a wave of his hand.

"I hate to mention it old chap, but, err… the boys seem to be out of their barracks!"

I was utterly confused. Mark gave me a knowing nod and Mel seemed to be studying the floor. Had I missed something? Then Gloudina gave a shriek and twisted around in her hammock to stare off into the distance.

Marie was rather more direct. "Jeezus Tony, yer balls are hanging right out o' yer trousers!"

I yelped. The tough conditions at Santa Martha had been fighting a war of attrition against every item of clothing I owned - and at least as far as my jeans were concerned, they'd won. A pudding-sized threadbare patch on the inside of both thighs had recently disintegrated into a pair of holes. And from one of them, possibly the left, my testicles were dangling free, swinging in the breeze. All I could do was stuff them back in, gingerly, and then make a break for the dorm room. Marie's voice followed me in: "Cover yerself up fer God's sake man, we're about to have lunch!"

Weird and Wonderful

It had been a quiet week since Toby left. I think Johnny, shocked by the abruptness of his leading hand's departure, was still getting used to the idea of me as team spokesman. Perhaps he wasn't yet sure of what I could handle, without Toby backing me up. He certainly wasn't chasing me out the door to go recruiting new volunteers, or beckoning me up to his office to go through all that computer work that seemed to keep Toby so busy whenever a particularly unpleasant task was afoot. We fed the animals and cleaned them out, repaired perches and built new ones, replaced food and water bowls and added little sections of plank roofing over as many cages as possible, to give the inmates a little more protection from the daily rainstorm. The weather seemed more polarised these days; the sun was hotter, the regular rains lasting longer and striking more fiercely. It was also, if it's possible to believe, even colder at night. Just when I thought I'd gotten used to it, the equator turned out to have seasons. I think we were entering the one called 'bad'.

The trickle of new arrivals had also slowed, which was a definite blessing. The sheer number of animals now under our care was daunting to say the least. Squirrel monkeys, spider monkeys and the ever-popular capuchins, coatis – Snotty now had a brace of cell-mates – plus countless parrots large and small, the cats, the bear and the tortoise. The eagles. A rather nervous-looking horse. And something that fell into at least one of those categories, but was otherwise a completely new concept to me. We had a 'jaguarundi'. Can you guess what it is? Well, it had the body of a cat, slightly larger and heavier-set than a domestic variety and so sleekly black that it was almost blue where the sun hit it. But the really peculiar thing about it (which took me several days to spot – at first I thought my eyes were going funny) was that its body was *stretched*, elongated for no reason under God that I could possibly imagine. It was like this: normal cat head; normal cat tail; and in between curved a long, sausage dog-like body that spaced the front and back legs about half again as far apart as they should be. It looked like its back end had gotten stuck in a fence and it had tried altogether too hard to get away. Perhaps we should have named it after some Ancient Egyptian mythological beast, 'Sphinx' or 'Bastet' after the Goddess of cats. But it would never have stuck. Instead I called it Bendy Cat. And it lived up to its name – as observed on several occasions, despite being freakishly longer that any feline of similar size, it could still lick its own balls.

And then came the three-toed sloth. Stupid sloth. It was a crazy-looking beastie, all arms and bristling grey fur; its body was a blob, the kind of shape a six-year-old would draw for a pig, and its face was flattened like a racoon that had run full tilt into a brick wall. A triangular stub of a nose jutted out at an angle beneath a fringe that must have been difficult to see through. In fact, from side-on it looked disturbingly like John Lennon.

But none of this is what made it stupid. It was stupid because it wouldn't *eat*. Now, when I was a kid, I refused my fair share of meals. My mum, bless her heart, was always trying to get us to eat some random healthy shit. As a youngster, there were three things on the menu for me, or none: beans on toast, chips or fish fingers. Healthy enough, I felt. Yet somehow I never actually starved to death. The sloth seemed in very real danger of doing this, and its menu options were even narrower than mine. Sloths are never likely to take over the planet, for two reasons – because they only eat one kind of leaf which only grows in very specific places – and because they are so mind-bogglingly stupid.

So Johnny put him in the first enclosure I'd helped build, where a mouse deer had lived until its release. It had a couple of trees growing in the middle of it and he had high hopes that the fresh greenery might encourage the creature's appetite. Unsurprisingly it didn't.

"Will he be okay in here?" I asked, concerned about the temperature at night.

"Yes," said Johnny, "we can bring him in if it gets too cold."

Fair enough. As we wandered back to the house Mark mentioned that there was no roof on that cage. A good point, I thought, but surely Johnny knew what he was doing.

A slightly more alarming discovery was made a little later. The sloth had abandoned its tree and decided to climb the equally inedible fence instead. It was sitting upside down at the very top of the wire and had that 'Where'd all the leaves go?' sort of expression.

"Won't it be able to escape from there?" Mark asked Johnny, who had also come to check out the situation.

"No," he said. "Because they can only climb up! Not over and down. See? He can't escape." He was presumably basing his argument on the evidence that it hadn't escaped already. Which, in fairness, it hadn't. It still sounded a little dubious to me. But then, what did I know about sloth? I'm more of a lust and gluttony fan myself.

And speaking of gluttony, it was dinner time! Since Mel had joined us, meals had become something worthy of looking forward to. Several weeks back Toby had given up on trying to cook rice, and in a fit of frustration he'd bought an electric rice cooker. Seriously. And he had not been shy of using it. So Mel's practised skill in the kitchen was more beautiful to behold than the swimsuit section of the Miss World competition. When she started dicing chicken it actually brought tears to my eyes. She was now officially in control of the grocery shopping.

So I was relaxing in a hammock, savouring the anticipation of a meal well earned, when Johnny strode up fast, his wrinkled brow reading 'worried'.

"I need your help," he said in a tense voice. "The sloth – he has escaped."

Well shave my llama.

I almost didn't expect that.

"But you said he couldn't climb down the fence!" I pointed out. It sounded less like an emergency and more like the punchline of an old joke. 'Runaway Sloth!' With its stumps for back legs and no neck, it looked like it had been put together backwards by accident and must have a truly abysmal top speed along the ground. I was having visions of running along in slow motion after the casually loping sloth with someone shouting 'He's very slowly getting away!'

"He can't climb down the fence," Johnny said indignantly.

"Then how has he escaped?"

"He climbed up my house."

Ah. That was unexpected.

We gathered Mark from the kitchen and headed out for a look. I couldn't believe it. Slow on the flat it maybe, but this critter had climbed three stories in the time it took us to decide what to have for dinner. He'd scooted around the fence to reach the phone line, slack-wired that to a drain pipe, then one tier after another had scaled the profusion of balconies and window ledges right to the pinnacle of Johnny's house. From the edge of the roof above the top floor balcony he calmly surveyed the scene. I couldn't help but think, if he didn't keep a really strong grip, squashed sloth would be on the menu. Stupid creature.

"We have to stop him," Johnny said.

"Why?" I asked. I sure as hell wasn't climbing up after him.

"Because he's heading for the TV aerial!"

He didn't seem to be headed anywhere to me – just kind of hanging out really. But then I spotted the TV aerial and understood the problem. It was thin, probably not too strong and about twenty feet tall. I guess it has to be when there's a mountain between it and the transmitter.

"If he gets up that we'll never get him down!" Johnny said. And it was true. Though after a few more days without leaves there was a better than average chance he'd fall down of his own accord.

We ran inside and upstairs, and upstairs again, up more stairs than was strictly necessary, to the very top floor. I'd never been here before – it was the boss' private inner sanctum. More accurately it was his bedroom. Brenda, sprawled on the bed reading a magazine, was a bit disturbed as three of us ran past her with gloves and a net.

Out on the balcony we discovered the sloth was making a crawl for it. He was clinging to the roof and inching his way towards the TV mast. I jumped up on the balcony wall, trying hard not to think about the three and a half storey drop beneath my toes, and prepared to grab him.

"Careful!" called Johnny.

This froze me in my tracks. I knew very little of sloths. Muscles rippled beneath the stiff grey fur on its unnaturally long arms. What would it do? Bite? Claw? Wee on me? It looked so harmless, hanging there on the guttering. Carefully I pried its huge hooked claws off the roof. The sloth did nothing.

"It's strong!" Johnny shouted again, followed by "Watch

the back legs!"

I desperately swung the beast away from me in case the claws on those powerful back legs decided to rip into my stomach.

But the sloth couldn't be arsed. It clearly wasn't in the mood to eviscerate anything. With all the formidable strength at its disposal it held on to me.

Brenda was even more disturbed as I carried a large grey sloth, viciously holding on, back through her bedroom.

Back in its old cage the sloth eyed the piles of leaves with disinterest. Perhaps TV aerials are the only other thing sloths eat, and it was secretly thinking 'Damn it! I was *this* close.' We shall never know. At least he didn't seem to hold it against me. Didn't seem to do much at all, except hang there and not eat leaves.

The sloth left as quickly as it had arrived – not under its own power, in other words. It was taken to another centre, one deeper into the mountains that dealt mostly with baby animals. I hoped they would have more luck. As Johnny closed the door of the carrying basket on it, I wagged a finger. "Eat your greens!" I warned, in a passable imitation of my mother. The sloth said nothing, merely gazed calmly back at me. Friggin' hippy.

Cause and Effect

The empty crate provided the perfect excuse. It was full of heavy glass beer bottles that badly needed returning. Actually they'd needed returning over a month ago – by now they had probably been declared MIA. No-one wanted to haul it all the way down to Tambillo, especially since Toby had drunk most of the beers before he left. Even I, who regularly hiked up and down the mountain just to get an empanada, shied away from the immense effort involved.

Until now. Gloudina had mentioned she would like a night out in Quito – and she'd only mentioned it to me. Keeping a party secret from Emer and Marie was like trying smoke a crafty spliff whilst walking through Heathrow Airport. They could just smell it. So I didn't believe I'd pulled it off until we were already halfway down the hill, swinging the crate of beer bottles between us. The perfect crime! Alas, it also meant I'd had to cancel my date with Lady, telling her I was staying home to look after some sick animals. Deceitful, I know. In my defence I'd like to say… absolutely nothing! What could I say? It was blatantly deceitful. I never claimed to be perfect.

The thing is, my trips to Quito with Lady were still fraught with difficulty. We could chat, but we could never fully open our hearts to one another without at least one of us consulting a dictionary. Every so often I longed for an easy night out, a joke-filled party that required no explanation and no pantomime. This was my only chance. And also, there was the very slight possibility that Gloudina was about to make a declaration of undying love, rip off all her clothes and throw herself on top of me. Which would also be nice.

As we reached Tambillo, the potential for disaster waxed strong; we had to cross the square right outside Lady's house to get to the grocery store. Luckily, it was dark by this time, and town would be deserted.

Or not.

People stood in a group on the steps of the church. Lots of them. All chatting merrily away to each other. We rounded the corner and I looked upon my ruin. The square was packed! The whole town had to be here. Everyone was talking loudly and laughing. Kids chased each other around the park in the centre of the square. The chip stand and empanada stand were set up and doing a roaring trade. What the hell was going on?

I noticed the huge wedge of light spilling from the open doors of the church. Of course! It was Saturday evening, and mass must have just finished. No wonder everyone was so happy – they had a whole week before they had to sit through another church service!

Once again God had taken a cosmic crap in my swimming pool. It was just like him to punish my attempted infidelity. After all, I was seriously coveting my neighbour's ass. Still, there was nothing to do but stick to the plan. If Lady was in this crowd she would surely make her presence known to me. Then I'd have some fast talking to do – since whilst laying the groundwork for the grand night out with Gloudina, I might have accidentally given her the impression that I'd broken up with Lady...

The odds were on that I was going to get caught with

my trousers down – and not in a good way. But there was nothing else for it. We plunged into the crowd, down into the park, back up the steps opposite Lady's house and then swung smoothly round the corner into the grocers. Deposited the crate – and legged it. Success! Even if anyone had recognised us, there was no reason to suspect this was anything other than a perfectly innocent chore. Because it was perfectly innocent, damn it. I'd have to do something about that.

On the way out of Tambillo, I celebrated my victory by introducing Gloudina to the delights of an empanada (or two of them!). My addiction to the things was legendary. Over the past two months I must have single-handedly supported this woman's way of life.

"You go for party?" The Empanada Woman asked, with a sly gleam in her eye.

"Me? Never!" I said, and winked.

The party was a fairly standard affair. It involved heavy drinking in my favourite backpackers' hostel, The Centro Del Mundo. They had regular nights (of which this was one) where they thanked their guests by placing a twelve-litre stockpot full of Cuba Libre on the table in the lounge – free drinks all night! When it ran out, assuming there were still people capable of drinking more, everyone chipped in a couple of bucks and for $20 we bought another one!

Suffice to say that whilst there was much merriment and a lot of deep, meaningful conversation, there was never any chance of intimacy. I took Gloudina on a whirlwind tour of the local bars, dancing here and there, even dancing on the bar in one tiny club. We had a great time, and eventually staggered back to the hostel and passed out in separate beds, in separate rooms. Damn it.

We struggled back to the refuge late the next day, taking the time to hike back up the mountain as Gloudina had only ever caught a taxi to the top. We chatted as we went, about life and the future. Gloudina, a South African living in Barcelona, was coming to the realisation that she wanted to devote her life to working with these animals. She was seriously considering not going home. I was having ideas of my own – largely inspired by Toby. He wanted me to help him establish a release centre of our own in the Amazon, to take all the animals from Santa Martha and rehabilitate them. We'd talked about it a lot before he left for England. Part of me was keen on that, but part of me wanted to emulate his life to date; one of the reasons Toby was so confident and self-assured was that he had travelled the world for years, diving, climbing and exploring. If possible, it sounded even more fun than living full-time in the jungle. And throughout it all – the sharing, the soul-searching – I still couldn't figure out whether Gloudina was interested in me. She was harder to read than a Russian–Chinese dictionary.

By the time we arrived back at the refuge our keenness for hiking had borne mixed fruit. As expected we'd accidentally-on-purpose missed a half-day of hard cage cleaning. Unfortunately we'd also missed a quick visit by Leonardo, during which he'd euthanized the ocelot with HIV.

I felt lousy as I made my way to Lady's house that night. Whichever way I looked at it, I'd made some bad decisions recently and they'd had consequences. Messing around in Quito had cost me the chance to save a life; it was my fault, plain and simple. I'd also treated Lady shabbily, putting her off for a night and then sneaking around behind her back. Trotting up the short flight of steps outside her house, I resolved to make it up to her at least, however I could.

Lady answered the door. She gave me a weak kind of a smile and stepped back to let me in. I hugged her tightly for a few seconds before I noticed that it was a very one-sided hug. She didn't seem to be into it. Strange. "Are you okay?" I asked as I released her.

"Yes," she said, and then, "are you going to break up with me?"

WHAT??? This completely blind-sided me. Why would she think that? Was it something I'd said? Something I hadn't said? Something I should have said? With women sometimes it's hard to know.

"Um, no..." I managed. "Why... why do you think that?"

"I don't know," she said. "You didn't want to go out with me..."

"I know, I'm so sorry," I interrupted. "We've all been working really hard. I was so tired..." Even to my own ears it sounded like a lame-assed excuse. Probably because it was.

"And then, you were with that other girl..."

Oh, shit.

"...when you came into town last night."

Triple shit.

"I think you like this girl more than me."

Bollocks!

"What girl?" It was the best I could do. My head was spinning.

"You came into town last night, with another girl from Santa Martha. With blonde hair."

Bugger, bugger, bugger, shit, tits, bollocks. Arse. This was going to take some explaining. I hoped lying in Spanish was easier than telling the truth. "Oh!" I began, "that girl! Yes, she's a volunteer. We all came to town. We needed some medicines for the animals." Good story!

"No," Lady insisted, "there was just you two. I think you went to Quito."

How the hell did she know that? I ran over the

memories in my head. Sure, there had been plenty of people around, but I was sure she wasn't there. I'd been so paranoid I'd developed eyes on all sides of my head.

I abandoned my story because it was crap. "Listen," I tried instead, "that girl is just a friend." True. "She's another volunteer." True. "I don't like her that way!" Which was slightly less true. In fact it was a big fat wriggling lie.

But it worked!

"You don't like her?"

"She's just a friend. I like you."

"Really? You still want me?"

Man, did I feel like an arsehole. "Yes, Lady, of course! I still want you."

All of a sudden she looked so happy my heart skipped a beat. Damn, she was beautiful! I'd almost forgotten. I had the sudden urge to beat myself about the face with a bat, on which the words 'Don't be such a tosser' were inscribed.

My fears began to dissolve as she wrapped her arms around me. I licked my dry lips and the creases on my forehead smoothed. My buttocks unclenched. I began to breathe normally again. It had been a very, very close call.

She gave me a long kiss, and I returned the favour.

And all the while the same thought ran through my mind over and over – I can't *believe* she saw me!

After a while we just stood and looked at each other. Eventually Lady broke the silence. "So. What do you want to do?"

I had no ideas. I was still recovering from shock.

Lady, though, was deep in thought. Suddenly she looked up at me with a new sparkle in her eye. "Why don't we go to a spa?" She suggested.

"A what?" I asked, not having progressed quite that far on my vocabulary. Tools and building materials were now second nature, but leisure activities lay a little beyond my current experience.

Well, I'd figured out 'bed', which had been sufficient so far… She explained in words of one syllable, which didn't necessarily help as they still weren't the names of tools or building materials. Eventually she made me understand. Kind of. "Ah! A spa!" I said it to make her feel better. I still didn't know where we were going, but I didn't really care. I was just relieved we were going.

"Is it near here?" I asked.

"Um… I'm not sure. There might be one in the next town."

Hell, I didn't even know there was a next town!

"I know!" she exclaimed, clearly pleased with herself. "I'll ask my mother. She'll know."

It sounded like a plan. Lady led the way out of the house and onto the road. We crossed the square in the direction of the primary school. Maybe her mother worked there? It occurred to me I'd never actually bothered to ask. She led me towards the road leading back to the highway, past the corner where the Empanada Woman stood.

Actually not past the corner. In fact she stopped right there next to the empanada stand. The Empanada Woman gave me her usual friendly "Hola!" over her cart, then turned her gaze on Lady. "Si?" she enquired.

Lady smiled back at her. "Mum," she said, "do you know if there's a spa near here?"

It took me most of the following taxi ride to comprehend the depth of my stupidity. I must have chatted to Lady's mum a hundred times without ever realising why she was being so friendly to me. Worryingly, I'd stopped to buy an empanada almost every time I'd ever been to Tambillo – even when I'd cancelled dates with Lady to get drunk at the refuge, claiming illness… Oh, the word 'busted' just didn't come close.

Thank the Goddess for Lady. She seemed to be the

tolerant type. She didn't even get mad with the taxi driver the third time he brought us to entirely the wrong place. She just accepted that we would be visiting a hotel instead of a spa, paid and got out. I guess if anyone was used to the complexity of getting what you wanted in this country, it was her. I still hadn't figured out what exactly was involved with a trip to a 'spa', and not having any swimming shorts with me I was happy to leave it that way.

The hotel was more of a guest house, where meals were included in the price and served in a relaxed sitting-cum-dining room with picturesque views over the surrounding countryside. Dinner was set for 7pm, just over two hours away. We took our key, thanked the old proprietor, and I paid the bill in advance, marvelling again at how inexpensive such pleasant lodgings were. It was certainly a small price to buy back my tarnished honour.

Lady locked the door behind us and embraced me. I laughed in sheer relief, that she was still here and happy. Then she kicked off her pointy shoes, crawled onto the bed and crooked her little finger, beckoning me to join her.

We never went for dinner.

Stitched Up.

There were times, in Ecuador, when I wondered what the hell I was doing. Like now for example, as Johnny held the crocodile out for me to take. As crocodiles go, this caiman was a very small one – but still, and my mind kept circling back to this fact, it was A CROCODILE! Was I mad? Was Johnny mad for offering it to me? Or was he finally developing some respect for my hard-won animal-handling skills? Had his faith in me reached such strength that it was now greater than my faith in myself? No. He was clearly mad. I mean, it was a *crocodile* for God's sake!

But there was still a job to do. With no choice left (beyond turning and fleeing, waving my hands above my head and shrieking as I went), I reached out to Johnny and slowly took hold of the beast. I could hardly believe what I was doing. I wrapped one hand around the nose and mouth – very aware of the teeth glistening wetly between my fingers. My other hand curled around the tail, tensed in case the little thing thrashed around and tried to break out of my grip. The ridged scales on its back dug into my palm as I gripped the tail tightly.

"Got him?" Johnny asked?

"*Sí.*"

And he let go. The caiman didn't move a muscle. It just

lay there in my grip, either not wanting to move or not able. Not because of the superhuman effort I was putting into restraining it, but because the fearsome-looking creature was dying. From this angle it was hard not to lose my eyes in the depth of the wound slashed across the creature's neck.

"Sure you got him?" Johnny was concerned after all. Though most likely for the croc.

"*Sí. No problema!*" I hoped he didn't hear the quaver in my voice.

"Okay. I'll be back in a bit."

And he vanished indoors. I stood there, holding my breath and gritting my teeth, willing the injured animal to lie still. I felt a tremor in response, the faintest ghost of a struggle. In one piece this guy would thrash so powerfully I could never have hoped to hold him. As it was, he was nearly cut in half. And I was still nervous. Surely someone was filming my plight for a hidden camera show? Watching and betting on how long I would stand there, clinging to the miniature crocodile, until I broke and ran for help?

But then Johnny was back, calmly tying a strip of cloth around the croc's snout with as much drama as tying his shoe laces. Obviously it was not his first time.

The side door to Johnny's house banged open and Leonardo led Mark out into the yard, straw hat and all. The Ecuadorian vet was lecturing the English one on last minute surgical tips, something which Mark was making a heroic effort to follow. Between them the two carried the few simple items Mark would need for this procedure. A bottle of iodine. A kidney-shaped steel bowl for the implements – and most worrying of all, the implements themselves. I stared in morbid fascination as Mark proceeded to thread the most vicious-looking needle I've ever seen. It was like something an arch-villain would threaten to torture James Bond with – gleaming silver, curved and barbed, with a pointed razor blade on the business end. A 'cutting needle' he named it when he caught my gaze. I could only imagine the mess it would make of his fingers if his grip slipped whilst pushing on it. No anaesthetic for the caiman; it was too far gone already. Quite what reaction it would have when Mark started putting the needle into its flesh was anyone's guess.

The outdoor sink, where we filled the animals' water bowls, was being pressed into service as an operating table. Onto the concrete draining board I lowered the caiman, gingerly, lest he decide not to appreciate it. Needless to say I kept a firm grip on both ends.

Mark looked a little nervous too. Hardly surprising – there can't have been much call for stitching up crocodiles during his career in the UK. Not a very common pet there. He took several deep breaths, and practise-aimed the needle a couple of times. Then he put the needle down and reached for the iodine – for a second I thought he was going to take a quick swig to calm his nerves! No. He doused the wound and probed the edges with his fingertips. It never looked as nasty as it did at that moment, with Mark's fingers all the way inside the torn flesh, lifting and pressing back the different layers of raw meat. I could hardly believe this thing was still alive. The cut, doubtless from a machete, had sliced more than half way through the neck at its deepest point, and the ragged edges of the wound stood testimony to how poorly sharpened the blade had been. A couple of other shallow cuts to either side of the main wound told a story Leonardo could easily read. A farmer had found the caiman in his field, he explained, launching into a graphic re-enactment of the scene. He pointed out an imaginary caiman on the ground in front of him, then stomped with crushing force on its tail. On the table the real caiman had badly ripped and shredded scales on its tail just above where I was holding him. Then with an imaginary machete in hand, Leonardo slashed down once, twice, three times with increasing frustration. "Not good machete," he suggested, pointing out the smaller cuts. Then miming a two-handed grip he made an exaggerated chop groundward – the result of which was the huge gash we were hoping to repair.

The wound cleaned, Mark took up the needle again and pushed the razor-tipped point into the caiman's scales. The caiman didn't even twitch. its innards gleamed a dull, wet grey through the opening in its neck. I had the thought for about the hundredth time: how the hell was this thing still alive?

Mark was having trouble. His first couple of passes with the needle had been difficult, the scaly skin much tougher even than it looked; yet they had been successful and now a few strands of catgut bridged the gap in the creature's flesh. Only now the needle wouldn't go in. Two passes through the croc's tough hide had blunted it, and with all the pressure he could safely put on the needle, Mark still couldn't drive it through again. Leonardo leant over to take a look, then made a suggestion which I caught the gist of. Threading a second of the evil-looking needles, Mark peeled the wound back a little more, and inserted it into the softer flesh just beneath the scales. There was no blood – either crocs don't bleed, or this one had done all the bleeding it could manage. The cutting needle slid much more easily through what Mark described to me as the subcutaneous tissue, and he breathed a small sigh of relief. He passed the needle back and forth faster now, stitching the severed flesh together just below the surface.

Even going much better, it was a nerve-wracking procedure. I could see sweat running down Mark's face, could feel it running down my own. I longed to wipe a drip off my nose, but I knew it would be a good while before I'd have a hand free to do it. A stitch pulled out as the thread followed the needle, and had to be re-sewn slightly deeper. The leading edges started to draw together as the stitching progressed. Mark frequently paused to take up the slack on the thread, shrinking the wound a centimetre at a time. My arms and shoulders ached from the tension, but I was determined not to relax. Though the creature wasn't struggling, Sod's Law would surely come into play the moment my grip faltered. The sun beat down on the concrete yard, so hot on the back of my neck that for a fraction of a second I almost envied Mark his ridiculous straw boater.

Then, with a last couple of stitches, the main task was done. Mark squeezed the edges of the wound together and tugged gently on the thread with his other hand. Slowly the gash pulled closed. The scales overlapped each other and almost nothing could be seen at the surface. Mark stepped back and eyed his handiwork, and allowed himself to breathe again. He wiped his face on his shirt and resettled his hat on his head. I just stayed bent over, elbows resting on the makeshift table and both hands fastened firmly around the patient. It was going to live! I just knew it. No way we could have expended so much stress and effort for nothing.

"Good job old bean," Mark told me generously.

And just like that I realised – we'd done it! Well, more accurately Mark had done it while I held it for him – yet I'd been completely involved, and with the operation over and successful, I felt powerful beyond measure. What could I not do now? Apart from stand up straight, of course, or scratch my nose…

Mark cleaned up the other wounds as best he could, and Leonardo stepped in to demonstrate giving an injection between the scales. Then they followed me as Johnny led us over to our newly-created reptile house.

In the greenhouse where Toby had planted his beloved vegetable garden, there had been a massacre. The infant vegetables had been attacked with *azadóns*, violently disinterred and smashed to bits in the process. The earth had been raked thoroughly, turned over and packed flat again, and a pond efficiently constructed by digging half a plastic barrel into the ground. I was amazed by the speed and brutality of the transformation. The ladies responsible, Mel, Emer and Gloudina, were definitely not to be pissed off when carrying tools. Their ruthless efficiency had created a purpose-built crocodile sanctuary in a couple of hours. A low fence with a latchless gate split the entrance and a small standing area off from the caiman's domain. Even Jimmy was involved, off welding a latch together even as we spoke. Presumably in case the injured croc tried to open the gate and flee. The only thing keeping the place from being perfect was the absence of a great big heat lamp. The girls had already disinfected the whole greenhouse and were busy disposing of the corpses of Toby's vegetables when I arrived with the patient. After a bit of debate we decided to free his nose; I held tight as Johnny untied the rag, then gently settled the croc into his new home... and sprang back with all the reflexes I'd developed in over two months at the centre!

The little guy barely moved. He'd already been through far too much, and his chance of survival rested on.... well, rest. So long as he didn't move too much the stitches should hold, and so long as we got antibiotics into his system any infections should be kept at bay. Leonardo was super-cautious on this point, having inadvertently overdosed our last caiman. Rather than one large injection, instead he'd prescribed several smaller shots, to be administered twice a day. Beyond that it was all down to the croc, and the life-giving energies of the sun.

No-one needed to ask who would be catching the croc twice a day; it was both the advantage and the disadvantage of being the boss. All the things no-one else wanted to do naturally fell to me. I didn't mind though. I was willing the little guy to live with all my heart. I'd never felt so intimately involved in the saving of a life.

Johnny favoured Gloudina and me with a stern look. "Now you must feed him. He needs chicken."

"Is the truck coming today then?" I asked.

"No. Not for a few days. Anyway, he needs fresh meat."

"Oh."

"Go to the chicken enclosure."

"Yeah?"

"Catch one, kill it, and give him that."

WHAT?! I felt the blood drain from my face at the prospect. Johnny must have noticed. "Can you do it?" There was a trace of something in his voice... Humour? Sarcasm? He was enjoying this.

"Yeah, I can do it," I told him. Except I couldn't. I feel guilty for swatting flies. I catch spiders and put them outside. I even own a 'humane' mousetrap. I looked over to Gloudina. Strong, dedicated, female – surely she was tougher than me. "We can do it," I amended.

Johnny walked off chuckling to himself.

I turned to Gloudina. "You kill bulls and things in your country don't you? With big spears?"

"I don't! Not personally! I mean..." she searched for a suitable example, "I don't even kill insects!"

Oh dear. This was going to be difficult.

"Well," I suggested, "we could catch the chicken first, and then worry about it."

We walked slowly towards the chicken run. It was right in front of the volunteers' house, yet we managed to make the walk there last a good five minutes. I was walking slowly in the hope that she'd come to some decision and announce a plan before we arrived. She was doing the same. It didn't help.

Unsurprisingly, the chickens saw us coming. They'd have to be blind not to, us being several hundred times bigger than them. And they ran. Now you might think, being as how they were trapped, that they would have nowhere to run to. This was not the case. Those were some damn fast chickens. They ran left. I ran left. They ran right – I was still going left. By the time I'd skidded to a halt and turned around they were already behind me, and probably having a right old laugh. Little buggers, I thought, when I catch you I really am going to kill you! But luckily for them I couldn't. I did pull off some spectacular sliding tackles though.

"Got one!" Gloudina shouted. She was proudly brandishing a clucking ball of feathers.

"Nice one! Damn, these sons-of-bitches are impossible to catch! Did you jump on it?"

"No, it ran at me and I just sort of picked it up."

"Pah! Well then it deserves to be eaten." I beat the worst of the mud and dust off my jeans and t-shirt and paused to snarl angrily at the rest of the chickens. They didn't seem overly bothered.

We climbed out of the run and stood looking at each other again. Only now it was a three way staring match. I glared at the chicken. It gazed vacantly back.

"Okay," I said to Gloudina. "Kill it."

"You kill it!" she told me. "I caught it! I don't know how to kill a chicken!"

"Um, you... you know, like, strangle it."

"Eww!"

"Well you can't tickle it to death!"

"I can't strangle it, I'm holding it!"

Good point, and one to be quickly exploited. I made a quick grab and took over the heavy responsibility of holding the beast. "Okay, I've got it. Now strangle it."

Gloudina stared doubtfully at the chicken. "I can't! It just looked right at me!"

"Well I'm holding it!" I complained.

Gloudina flexed her fingers momentarily. "No, I can't do

it."

The chicken merely dangled and surveyed the area, serenely unaware that its life hung in the balance.

The idea occurred to both of us at exactly the same moment.

"MARK!"

Together we made our way back to the monkey cages, where the other volunteers were now doling out oaty, fruity goodness by the ladleful. Mark, having paused only long enough to inhale a cheese sandwich, was already back out and helping with the feed. Gloudina jogged towards him as I shuffled along behind with my hands wrapped around a now slightly perturbed chicken.

"What's up?" Mark was cheerful as always. With good reason today, as he'd already saved one life. And I was about to ask him to end another. In my heart I knew that he had the hands of a killer. Of chickens.

"We have to, err, you know, for the caiman," Gloudina drew a finger across her throat for emphasis. "But we can't do it. Neither of us has ever killed a chicken."

"I've slapped a few for looking at my girlfriend though," I quipped. The joke fell on deaf ears. Or, possibly, on ears that didn't find it funny.

Mark looked at the chicken squirming in my hands, then at me. "It's years since I've done anything like this," he said, coming in for a closer look. "I don't know if I can still remember." He looked me full in the face. "Usually, what I'd do..." And with inhuman speed his hands shot forward mid-sentence, twisting the chicken's neck completely around about fifteen times like they were opening a bottle of Coke. It was over before I even registered what was happening. The chicken thrashed in my grip. In shock and horror I looked at Mark, then at Gloudina, then back to Mark.

Mark was grinning at me. "No problem!" he said.

"I thought you were... Thought you were... Going to tell

me when..." my mind hadn't fully caught up yet.

"It's easier like that. Didn't want to worry you."

"Ur... thanks Mark..." I managed.

Gloudina recovered quickly and clapped me on the shoulder. "Let's go then!"

The chicken convulsed again. I let out a pitiful moan. "It's still moving!"

"Yeah, it'll do that for a bit," Mark said as he steered me by the elbow along the path to the caiman's greenhouse. "Careful! You'll get blood on you."

I looked down and saw blood pissing out of the chicken's torn neck.

"I ripped the neck a little bit," Mark confessed.

My stomach turned over. The chicken gave a last pathetic shudder and was still. My hands were warm, and my fingers were wet.

"You're okay, aren't you?" Mark asked in sincere concern.

"Yeah, yeah. Fine."

"Good man! Same again tomorrow eh?" And he turned and wandered back to the feeding.

I felt violated. And not in a good way.

The caiman didn't seem at all impressed with his dinner. I lobbed it at him from a safe distance, but he didn't even flinch. The drama ebbed out of the situation. We clearly weren't about to witness a mindless feeding frenzy. All of a sudden I felt tired. And filthy.

"Maybe you should wash your hands," Gloudina suggested. She sniffed the air. "And take a shower." Her eyes travelled down to the fresh blood stains spreading across my jeans. "Maybe take a shower in all your clothes."

And maybe you should join me in the shower, I was inspired to say. Yet somehow, standing there dripping entrails, it just didn't seem like the right time.

Snap!

The end of another week loomed large. We were all booting
up for work when a couple of taxis pulled up, crammed with
school kids. They'd arrived as they usually did – a complete
surprise to everyone but themselves, and Johnny, who
clearly thought that the imminent arrival of a school outing
at his centre was 'need to know' information. We lowly
volunteers did not need to know. Despite the fact that we
were the ones who would have to control this rampaging
horde of sugar-fuelled mayhem.

I was over the moon when Gloudina volunteered to lead
the tour. I'd led a couple of them when there'd only been
Toby and me to do it, fielding rapid-fire questions from a
hundred directions whilst constantly hooking stray limbs
and poking fingers away from cages full of hungry
monkeys. They were not amongst my fondest memories.

As I trawled the cleaning rake around the top cages I
noted her progress past the parrots and monkeys, and was
expecting her to lead the kids down the steps to the crap-
encrusted main road and off to visit Osita. Instead she
turned aside and took the narrow path towards the
greenhouse where the caiman now lived amongst the ruins
of Toby's garden.

Those kids shouldn't be in there, I thought with a mental

growl. It's not like they were in any danger – I was more worried for the caiman actually – but something just told me that we should keep this area off-limits. For one thing, the caiman was hardly in a condition to receive visitors. I jogged over and caught the group up just as the last of them squeezed into the greenhouse. I shoved my way in, and through the pack to the gate. I opened it and stepped through, which act alone brought everyone's attention on to me.

"We need to take them out of here," I told Gloudina in English. She nodded her agreement.

I addressed the group. "You cannot stay in here," I said, trying to sound authoritative.

None of the kids seemed particularly impressed.

"See the caiman?" I looked around the group, making eye contact where I could. "*El es muy peligroso!*" (he is very dangerous!)

Which, of course was a lie, but it had the desired effect. With a few gasps and nervous glances the children retreated ever so slightly from the fence. I crouched down at this point, to take a quick look at my charge. He seemed unchanged. I looked back at the kids and opened my mouth to impart more reptile-based wisdom. As I did this, I gestured behind me at the motionless croc.

And in the blink of an eye he surged up from the water, lashed his snout around and sank his teeth into my arm.

I screamed like a girl. More from the shock than the pain, of course. The children also screamed like girls (which most of them were), and fled the greenhouse en masse. The croc, having made his point, released me straight away, and was once again motionless in his pond.

I stood up, shaking, in shock and disbelief. It had happened so fast! That thing moved like lightning. I took a few seconds to breathe. Gloudina ducked her head back in through the doorway. She'd kept her cool completely, and had gone after the kids to stop them running wild. Now she had a moment to check on me. "Are you okay?" she asked.

I kept my arm behind my back, clutched in my other hand. I could feel blood trickling through my fingers. "Yeah, I'm fine. Bit surprised though!" All I could think of was not to make a scene. Much as I wanted her sympathy, I didn't want her to see my face when I finally looked at the injury. "He didn't really get me," I lied.

"Woah, that was scary!" she said, and shot me a worried look. "Sure you're okay?"

I managed a nod, and a feeble smile.

Gloudina shook her head and went back out to the waiting children. I heard my name featured a couple of times in her rapid Spanish explanation, then she lead the group away down the path, and down the steep steps to the road. Soon they'd be too busy dodging poo to worry about me. I allowed myself a few more calming breaths and stepped slowly, very, very slowly, away from the caiman's pond. He never moved a muscle. Once through the gate, but still in the greenhouse and so fairly well hidden from the rest of the area, I risked a quick look at the injury. It had bled a lot. But the blood flow was slow, and not quite as dramatic as I'd imagined. Standing there with it tucked out of sight behind my back I'd gone through every variation of extreme croc damage my mind could summon up. I was expecting terrible gashes and blood sheeting my whole arm. Thankfully, small croc means small teeth and in fairness this was a very small croc. I could tell there were a few punctures, and enough blood to soak my hand, and that was it. It didn't even hurt! That's when I realised I was in actual shock. As opposed to just mildly ticked off. I tucked my arm behind my back again and headed to the volunteer house for a closer look.

I'd only been there for a few minutes, sitting at the kitchen table and prodding myself, when Mel arrived.

"Oh dear, what happened then?" She slipped instantly into concerned mother mode as soon as she crossed the threshold. "Gloudina said you got... Oh, blooming heck!" Mel, bless her, wasn't big on swearing.

I was hunched over, fixated on my arm and probably still a bit white. "It's not too bad," I told her, hoping it was the truth. "It doesn't even hurt."

"You're probably in shock," she pointed out. Full points to Mel. She held my arm gingerly, bending over it and muttering under her breath; "Couple of stitches in the big ones... must have missed the major blood vessels... maybe sutures..."

"I'll be okay though, right?"

"We'll see. Go wash it."

"Aw, but I wanted to show everyone while it still looks gruesome!"

"Oh, you silly... Get it washed!"

My moment of glory was over so quickly. I went to the bathroom and tried to cram my forearm under the tap. There was no chance it would fit, so I cupped handfuls of water and spilled them down my arm. I wiped the blood, old and new, away from a series of quite small, yet quite deep, punctures. They ran in a very satisfying pair of parallel lines up to my elbow. I went back to show Mel, taking a handful of bog-roll with me to mop up the fresh leakage.

She frowned over the injury, twisting my arm back and forth and studying it with a practised eye. When she concluded her examination with a despairing sigh, I braced myself for the kind of lecture which, having a nurse for a mother, I'd become well used to. Instead Mel's serious facade broke all at once. "You're going to have some lovely scars there!"

"Yeah!" I grinned back. "When I get asked 'What happened there?' I'll be like, 'Oh, got bitten by a crocodile...' Ha! My parents will go mental!"

It wasn't long before the story got around, and everyone came to watch Mel patch me up. The best thing of course was that the caiman had moved at all. He was alive! Well okay, the best thing was how cool my scars would look when they healed, but right after that came the fact that the caiman was alive. I was really, genuinely, happy. For about two hours.

"So," Mark asked after he'd finished examining my injury, "are you still going to catch him after?"

The ground dropped away from under me. It was now afternoon. The four o'clock feed was finished. And Mark had come to fetch me for my favourite part of the day – when I, and I alone, got to handle the caiman, to catch it and hold it while he injected it with antibiotics.

I'd caught the thing twice a day, every day, since it had arrived, but 'caught' was a bit of a misnomer. The first time since the operation, as I approached the pond, I'd been scared. The fact that the beast had been largely immobile the whole time we'd had care of him meant nothing – he'd been dying, and I was surrounded by vets and bosses. Here I was on my own, at least as far as the catching was concerned. I'd felt brave when I'd been awarded the job, and I knew no-one else wanted to do it. Actually summoning up the balls to do it was a little different. I'd taken a good few deep breaths, put on and taken off the thick gloves a couple of times, all to buy myself time while I decided how best not to lose a limb. In the end I'd just held my breath and grabbed. No problem. He'd seemed to strain a bit in my grip, but that could have been my imagination. It was certainly nothing I couldn't handle.

But things were a little different now. Mark led the way to the greenhouse. I walked slowly, and chatted to him, whilst inside I felt like I was walking to an execution. Mine. We entered the greenhouse and Mark held the gate open for me as I stepped through into the enclosure. He busied himself with his syringes and bottles while I looked at the instrument of my death.

I was terrified.

I walked carefully over to the pond and stood there, looking down. I half expected him to go for my ankles in a blur of green scales and teeth. He didn't. Mark announced he was ready. He also seemed a little apprehensive, but not dramatically so. Mark knew his stuff, and must have seen plenty of nasty situations in twenty-odd years of vetting. He was also an exceptionally smart and brave individual.

I was feeling neither of those qualities as I contemplated the task ahead of me. I managed to kneel down in my usual position – well, perhaps just slightly further away than normal. My mind kept dredging up helpful snippets of information, like the fact that kneeling further away would make the whole process more difficult, and therefore more likely to result in the loss of a hand. It was also reminding me of just how fast the croc had been. Faster than me, I'd bet money on it. In fact I was betting my fingers on it.

Since that first time I hadn't worried about missing the catch. But what if, said my mind, what if you're so nervous now that you flinch at the last second and miss completely? Then you'll be in the shit!

Ever noticed how utterly, perversely and inescapably negative your own mind can be at times like this? Maybe it's just me. I'd have given anything for an internal monologue that ran 'hey, no problems, this guy's asleep anyway! And your hand wouldn't fit in his mouth even if you were so slow that you gave him half a chance!' But no. It said 'you are going to die. You may only lose some fingers, but once he gets his teeth into your wrist? They don't have helicopter ambulances here. You'll bleed to death before they get you to the bottom of the mountain'. It was the pain I was most afraid of though. Shock can be a wonderful thing, but I don't think it works if you're expecting it. This time I was waiting, and when the bite came...

"Come on!" I said out loud. To myself. I'd been crouched over the pond for a couple of minutes while all this ran through my head. This whole trip had been about conquering my fears from start to finish, and so far I was doing well. Every time something crazy needed doing, my colossal mouth was there to volunteer my services before I had the chance to think too much about it. The one positive side of having a cakehole like the Rift Valley is that life is never dull. And yet this was something else entirely.

"Come on," I told myself again. Mark looked at me in honest sympathy. He was letting me take my time.

"Just grab," became my mantra. "Just grab! Easy. No problems!" I looked back at Mark. "Just give me a minute," I apologised.

"Don't worry. Take your time."

"Right. I'll do it now. You ready?"

He nodded.

"Okay, I'll do it now."

I did nothing.

"Well, this time. Now I'll do it." I took a deep breath. Then another. "Right, now!"

I started to reach, then stopped abruptly.

"Holy shit," I said to Mark, "I am so fucking scared!"

Mark smiled and said nothing.

"Okay... I'll do it now. Just grab! Here we go."

A few more breaths. The croc eyed me with evil intent.

"Oh crap," I muttered, and grabbed.

Four feet of lethal reptile, scaled, clawed and largely composed of teeth – did absolutely nothing. With one hand around the nose full of fangs and one gripping the powerful tail, I lifted the caiman out of its pond and held it up triumphantly! "YES!" I couldn't resist an exultant shout. I had conquered the beast! Or more accurately had conquered my fear of it. Again. The creature itself became once again a rather small, seriously ill thing, and something to be pitied. Mark came forward and administered the jab, and I returned the caiman to the water. It gave a little wriggle as I released it, and I stepped calmly back. 'That water's too cold,' was my first thought. Poor little critter.

As we left the cage I felt a weight lift from me. I looked back and realised just how scared I'd really been. Truly, honestly, the most scared I'd been in my whole time in the animal refuge. I'd had time to think about it, to worry at the situation like Machita at my socks – the ten minutes between being reminded of the duty, and arriving in the greenhouse to do it, had been the longest of my life. But I'd managed it. Eventually. This was definitely a story to tell Lady! Which suddenly reminded me of the next item on my agenda – phone Lady. Might as well do it while I was feeling invulnerable!

"And by tomorrow morning," Mark pointed out, "you'll have forgotten all about it. It'll be easy again!"

Tomorrow morning. And that afternoon. And the next morning. It was a good job I enjoyed overcoming my fears, came the chilling thought. I was going to get a lot more practice.

Take Two

Unbelievable. Johnny had decided he wanted a new tortoise enclosure building for Meldrew. What was so ridiculous about this idea, was that we had already built one – but in the wrong place. It had always been the wrong place; right at the bottom of the valley, where the dirt was iron-hard. Days of digging, tearing enough stone to build a small house out of every hole with blistered and bleeding hands under a withering hail of abuse from my least favourite person in the whole world. I had a flashback of Layla, her face like a slapped arse, as she stood watching my efforts in disgust.

At the time I'd foreseen only one other problem with the location – well, aside from having to carry a half-ton bale of wire mesh down a hillside covered in spiky bitch plants to build it – and that was how the hell were we supposed to get the tortoise down there? Johnny had waved this away, as one well used to ignoring the petty concerns of simple-minded foreigners.

Now, after a bit more time thinking about it, he'd come to the same conclusion. There were only three methods by which Meldrew could ever take up residence at the bottom of the valley; crane, helicopter or act of God. We had neither vehicle and as we have already established, God hates me.

However, complaining about hard work to an

Ecuadorian is never likely to result in an easier life. In this case venting my frustrations at Jimmy merely reminded him that sitting somewhere in the bottom of the valley was a half-ton bale of wire mesh, which would need to be carried back up the hill to the site of the new enclosure. By me.

Johnny's latest discovery was a swamp. He reasoned that, with a little creative landscaping, it could be turned into a dry enclosure with a stream and so would give the tortoise his own supply of fresh water. Lovely idea! On the downside, it did involve several days of dredging the ickiest, slippery grey mud from the bog by the hundreds of spades-full. We were knee-deep in the shit and it smelled like a sewage works. I had a brief moment of panic – what if it was a sewage works? I was under no illusion that our toilets led into a nice concrete sewer running all the way down the mountain. And, predictably, my left welly was leaking.

"Ah well. Shit happens!" was Mark's cheerful response when I voiced my fears.

I was making a trench to divert some of the water – in theory at least. Each sucking spadeful grudgingly gave way with a slurp and a blast of sulphurous stench. Then the hole filled with water and the mud oozed back in to reclaim its burrow. It was like painting with invisible ink only much, much fouler. Oh, and it involved more swearing. My boots had developed a tendency not to follow my feet out of the swamp, which had two possible outcomes. Going forwards it resulted in plunging a naked foot deep into the sickly stuff, as my socks had long since given up any pretence of staying on. Getting stuck whilst going backwards gave me chance to demonstrate my finest windmill impression, before measuring my length arse-first in the bog. I'd never been happier to see that shower, even if I did spend most of the evening relighting it.

Excavating an entire swamp by hand might seem like a

ridiculously strenuous task – until you compare it to lifting a giant Galapagos tortoise by hand. It was like trying to lift a small scaly planet. Except that it could bite.

"Ow! Ya bastid!" said Steve. That was the sound of his initiation as the newest member of our team. Steve had arrived from England in the morning and had already lost blood on his first day of work. In fact he'd come frighteningly close to losing a finger. Steve was already showing promise.

Thinking of England made me miss two people; Toby, who was still over there and probably having a considerably better time than I was, and Gloudina whom I hoped to kidnap one day and take back with me. If Toby had have been here, I thought, he'd have found a better way than this. Gloudina was spending the day in Quito, working at Leonardo's surgery. If she'd been here... well, at least I'd have been able to look down her shirt as we all bent over.

Six men each gripped an edge of shell. Being further up the Santa Martha hierarchy naturally earned you a place further away from that beak; I was safe enough, along with Jimmy, Johnny and Danielo. Mark and Steve were less lucky. Ten-second lift; it was all we could manage, ten hellish seconds of gritted teeth and burning muscles. Followed by two minutes recovery time and we'd moved about three feet closer to the road. And repeat. For three hours. I still don't know how we pulled it off. Johnny's truck sure wasn't keen on the passenger, complaining loudly when a monumental effort finally slid him up into the back. Mel tried to feed him a banana as we walked along next to the slowly-moving vehicle. A stray memory clicked – a crate full of small tortoises crapping like fury for eight hours solid all the way to the jungle. "Uh, Mel, I wouldn't give him too much of that," I warned. If this guy emptied his bowels in the back of the truck he'd probably fill it.

To get down to the new enclosure we'd been forced to

carve steep steps into the slope. They ran through a narrow gap between trees and thick bramble bushes. The gap was almost exactly one giant tortoise wide, which meant that for the trip down the stairs only four people could get at him to lift him; two at the back and two at the front. I took a back corner.

Jimmy and Danielo edged backwards down the steps until the tortoise was level with their waists. We all took the strain and lifted. With gritted teeth we moved Meldrew just over the edge. He tipped dangerously downwards. It was only then, far past the point of no return, that both Johnny and me realised there was no way on this earth we could hold him back with our tenuous grip on the edge of his shell. There was a desperate cry of "*Cuidado!*" from Johnny, and Meldrew slipped from our fingers.

Jimmy and Danielo both possessed reflexes conditioned by a life of constant danger. Or else they were bloody lucky. They'd seen the flaw in our plan at exactly the same time as we had, and with no other choice had reacted accordingly.

The tortoise careened downhill, picking up speed like a gigantic green skateboard.

On my left Jimmy now writhed in the middle of a bush full of spiky bitch plants. To my right Danielo had thrown himself head first into the swamp.

Neither of them looked particularly happy.

Meldrew had carved a path through the steps, which in his wake had become a ramp. He ended up lodged against a fence post at a crazy angle with all his limbs drawn into his shell. It must have been one hell of a ride.

And that was that. Meldrew emerged and was fed, Johnny pronounced himself satisfied and we all turned and hiked back up the slope. As we were leaving Mark pointed out a long black smear running down the centre of my t-shirt from neck to navel. He himself was suspiciously clean. What had I done that he hadn't? Aha! Taken a back corner.

Shit, it seemed, had happened after all.

Hole

In between working, which often knocked off at 2:30pm, and the second daily feed at 4pm, we liked to take a bit of time for ourselves. It wasn't worth getting showered and changed just to have some monkey climb all over you with hands and feet caked in his dinner, so this spare time was the perfect time to relax and regroup, especially after a physically demanding day. It was also the most pleasant time to be outside, a sort of ideal equilibrium between the harshest heat of the day and the icy chill of night.

I was reclining in a hammock with my little dog on my belly. I had one hand behind my head and the other draped across Machita's ribs. I could feel her breathing through a growing layer of puppy fat, and was gazing out at one of my favourite views. The hillside fell gently away from the front of the house, then plunged down steeply towards the valley floor, itself out of sight a few hundred metres below. Everything glowed a brilliant green in the strong sunshine, the whole view was the very image of Eden. I loved these gorgeous, lazy days. And there seemed to be an endless supply of them. In my mood of contentment, I didn't mind at all being disturbed by a fraught-looking Brenda, approaching from the direction of the animal enclosures.

She didn't wave, which was unusual. She just came to

the gate and beckoned me over. I gently scooped my sleeping dog up and deposited her on the ground.

"*Hola!*" I smiled at Brenda. She didn't smile back.

"I'm sorry," she said, "the caiman is dead."

What? "No, no," I explained, "he doesn't move much. He doesn't move at all. He's always like that."

"Come and see," she told me. "I am sure he is dead."

I followed her to the open ground in the middle of all the cages. We'd taken to leaving the croc sitting out in the sun during the day, in the hope that the direct rays would warm his blood and boost his healing. He was there, sitting motionless exactly where I'd left him that morning. I'd gone down to feed Osita after that, and hadn't been around this area at all since then.

I got right up close, within easy striking distance. Nothing happened. My heart was beating rapidly, stress and fear for both myself and the reptile. Closer I edged until I could lay a trembling finger tip on the tough pointed scales of his back. Still nothing. I was knelt down beside him, bending right over, praying that he was both alive and in a forgiving mood. My hand moved off and hovered in the air above his head for a few seconds – then I dipped down to touch his snout. It was stone cold. There was no breath. The caiman was dead.

The tension left my body and I sprawled sideways onto the grass. The relief at not being attacked welled up, a short rush of adrenaline, and was gone in less time than it takes to tell. Behind it, it left a strange emptiness, a weariness, a sinking feeling in my stomach that had begun on the walk over. All that work. All that time. So much... emotion invested. I felt... gutted. Robbed. Snatched away when we were so close, so very fucking close... All gone now. Nothing prepared me for the shock – not even the tragic yet inevitable death of the ocelot only days before. The cat's time had come, sooner perhaps than I'd have ordained, but this was... different. I'd been cheated. We all had been. I couldn't imagine any of the others being so unreasonable, but there it was. I'd bled for that creature, faced terror to help treat it, I'd felt bound to it almost. And now it was dead.

I picked myself up off the floor, stood staring disconsolately at the spot where just a few hours ago my bare hands had placed a living, breathing crocodile. I kept thinking I should cry, that I was certainly expecting to. The death was affecting me as no previous one had. But I didn't cry.

"We should bury him," Brenda spoke softly behind me. I turned to see Mel and Mark, Gloudina and Emer standing nearby. Everyone wore a sad expression. But they were all looking at me. They knew, I thought, they knew how close I felt... It all seemed stupid now. "I'll bury him," I said.

Wordlessly, Brenda fetched a shovel and passed it over. Moving robotically back to the patch of grass I raised the shovel and drove it into the ground. For a second it occurred to me that the others probably thought I was overreacting, but when I looked over my shoulder they'd all drifted off, giving me the space they could tell I needed. Sometimes it was like that, living so close to people through so many intense experiences, you could just tell what they needed without asking. So they carried on with their day and I dug a grave. It wasn't very deep; the ground, tough enough to dislodge with the *excavadora*, yielded slowly and grudgingly to the shovel. But it was deep enough by the time I was finished, and quite neat for my first.

I placed the caiman in the hole, and only then realised that alone of all the creatures I'd formed an attachment to, I'd never given him a name. I dropped the first shovel full of loose earth back over the hard, scaly body and it looked so out of place there. And then the tears came.

I finished the burial, eyes and nose streaming, shoulders shuddering, breath coming in ragged gasps. I was hot now, not empty but burning with effort and anger. I wanted to lash out at anything, hit something just for the satisfaction of feeling it. There was nothing nearby that I could risk damaging, so I took the shovel, made a few steps towards the empty field in front of our house and launched the thing with a cry. And that done, there was nothing else to do. I just sat, alone on the grass next to the slight bump of bare earth, and let the tears flow.

Mark was in the lounge as I passed through, headed for my bunk. "Sorry Tony," he said, one hand going automatically to my shoulder. "Sometimes it's just like that."

No-one else said anything to me that day.

The Perils of Boar-dom

The programme of new enclosure building was still barrelling along full force. It seemed like there wasn't a tiny corner of land anywhere that Johnny didn't want a cage putting on. Jimmy would lead us on a procession around the land, tools on shoulders like the Seven Dwarves off to work singing "Hi-ho!" Eventually he'd arrive at a certain spot and explain that today we'd be building a cage for an aardvark/starfish/fruit bat/plesiosaur*.

(*NB. We didn't actually have any plesiosaurs at Santa Martha, as they became extinct in the Cretaceous period, about 65 million years ago. However, some of our tools did date from this period.)

None of us bothered to use gloves any more – our hands were much tougher now, or else we were. What I would have previously considered a 'slice' from a ragged metal edge was now a 'scratch', no matter how much it bled. We were becoming very proficient at this unique form of construction, and small enclosures were often the work of one day.

Johnny had taken to visiting the volunteer house of an evening, giving us a few clues on what to expect over the coming days. I think this informal arrangement had taken the place of Toby's regular morning visits to Johnny's house, which I had secretly dreaded having to make. Thankfully my tactic of simply not bothering had paid off in spades, and now instead of having to 'discuss' details of the day's work in Spanish with *'El Jefe'* (the boss) we just waited on the porch for Jimmy to collect us. Johnny's little visits on the other hand were perfect for me to practice my language skills. He always spoke slowly, as was his way, looking around at all of us. I found it easy to sit concentrating on his voice and working out suitable responses, as with a table full of volunteers to absorb his focus I didn't feel so pressured. Although this system did render my official status as co-ordinator somewhat redundant, the others evidently decided to spare my feelings and let me at least act like the boss. It didn't matter one bit to me – though I felt honoured and immeasurably proud to have been asked to be volunteer co-ordinator in Toby's absence, I was under no illusions about who was in charge. And I was also kind of glossing over the fact that, at the precise time Toby had departed, there was literally no-one else. I had no reason to believe that that had influenced Johnny's decision in any way.

Along with explaining some financial issues the farm was facing and sharing his vision for the glorious future of Santa Martha, Johnny would occasionally let slip the identity of some creature or other soon to be added to our stable.

So it took Jimmy only minimal pantomiming to inform us that the enclosure we were currently constructing was to house a wild pig. Actually I already knew the word for 'pig'. *'Puerca'*, sounding not too dissimilar to 'porker' was fairly easy to guess. I was sure most of the others knew too. We just all found it far too entertaining to watch Jimmy, pointed fingers held against his cheeks as tusks, pawing the ground and rooting through some imaginary bush. I could hear the repressed laughter in Mel's voice as she feigned sudden understanding: "Oh, it's a giraffe!"

"No," said Steve, "One o'them chipmunk type things,

with them little teeth!"

"Um, *un anaconda*, Jimmy?" I offered.

The pig, or more accurately the wild boar, was every bit as friendly as his not-wild relatives were vicious. I'd loathed, detested and feared feeding Johnny's pigs since the very first time; whenever I approached with a bucket of kitchen scraps they would go wild, mobbing the door I had to get through in order to feed them. I knew they would tear through my flesh with the same mindless ferocity they attacked their food with, if they ever got the chance. If I slipped over in their sty there was a good chance I wouldn't be getting up again. They were massive, savage and in the grip of a constant feeding frenzy – and quite honestly they scared the living shit out of me.

So the contrast with the boar was truly remarkable. And relieving, since once the fence was built and the little fellow in residence, we had to feed him every morning.

"He eats vegetables," Johnny had sagely informed me when I enquired, "and fruit."

So the same as everything else then.

Routines being as they are it usually fell to either Mark or myself to feed 'Shortly' the boar. I never minded, except for one very peculiar habit. I mentioned it to Mark one time as we approached the enclosure.

"Watch what he does," I told a bemused Mark. "Seriously! It's really weird!"

With that I swung myself over the low, stout fence, cradling an armful of apples and potatoes. Immediately the boar waddled over and began to nuzzle my knees. I kept my legs firmly together. I could tell from the smirk that Mark knew what was coming.

"Now look," I said. I allowed a slight gap to appear between my legs. Instantly the boar was in it, shoving through with all his worth. He worked his powerful head and forequarters between my legs with much wiggling and jiggling of the rest of him.

Mark was already cracking up at the sight, and called to Mel to come look.

Safely wedged between my knees the boar was finally able to achieve his aim. Quivering all over he began to toss his head back, like a horse shooing a fly, over and over again. And each time at the apex of its arc, his snout slapped me squarely in the bollocks.

Mel came hurrying over to find her boyfriend doubled over with laughter, tears streaming down his face, as the pig redoubled his efforts. Each flick seemed increasingly energetic and my balls were starting to protest the rough treatment. I'd let the behaviour continue far longer than normal for demonstration purposes, and was already starting to regret it. By now the pig's front legs were leaving the ground with momentum as he continued to reverse-head-butt me in the knackers.

When I tried to lift a leg to step away it only made my package a better target, and the pig moved with me so that when I put the leg down again I was still straddling him. Both Mel and Mark were now in hysterics as I took an unlucky hit that drove the breath from my lungs. I lunged for the fence and fell across it to safety. I lay on the ground curled into a foetal position for a few seconds, belatedly protecting my jewels. Mel and Mark were far too far gone to be of any help.

I slowly stood and stretched, gingerly patting my crotch. No obvious damage. That had all gotten a little out of hand.

When Mark could breath again he offered me his considered medical opinion.

"Oh Tony," he gasped, "I think he likes you!"

"It's a good job you weren't wearing your other work jeans," he added as we made our way back past the parrot cage.

"You know, the, um, crotchless ones. I mean, his hair can be quite prickly."

"Not to mention if he thought it was feeding time!" Mel commented.

It was a bit uncomfortable, the others discussing my genital exposure so casually.

"I'm gonna throw those trousers out," I decided.

"Oh! Thank God for that!" Mel was positively jubilant. "You should tell Emer and Marie. They'll be over the moon to know! I think they've been getting quite disturbed about it."

I caught my breath at the depth of the conspiracy. They'd been talking about my balls behind my back! Or more accurately, about my balls in plain sight... Had Gloudina been included in these clandestine conversations? God I hoped not. I loved those jeans. But since Machita had faithfully dissected most of my underwear I'd been going commando quite a lot. Maybe too much... I was suddenly eager to change the topic of conversation.

"Weird what that pig does though, isn't it? You ever seen that before?"

Mark was happy to oblige. "Ah yes, you see, he has a scent gland on the back of his neck, and he's rubbing it on you. He rubs it on me sometimes, too, only not so... enthusiastically!"

"Oh. Why me then?"

Mel had a theory. "Maybe you're giving off some kind of irresistible pig pheromone? Do pigs normally go crazy around you?"

I considered how to answer this for a few seconds.

"No." It wasn't, strictly speaking, the truth.

"I don't know then. Maybe it's your deodorant..."

"I don't wear deodorant!" I protested.

They exchanged a knowing look before Mark replied for the both of them.

"Ah. Well then. Maybe that's it."

And they stepped smugly into the house together, a perfectly matched pair of cheeky, cheeky bastards.

You Can't Handle The Tooth!

There are some things that just don't mix; like Toby and globules of decomposing chicken mucus for example, or me and electricity. The morning after my twenty-fourth birthday I discovered another pair of mutually antagonistic elements: the whine of a dentist's drill and the epic hangover caused by drinking half a vat of free *Cuba libre*. Result: loss of one's breakfast in Johnny's sink.

It had been yet another week of fond farewells. Gloudina had left in the evening, slipping out of my life as effortlessly as she'd slipped in. I hoped to see her again, as she was staying on in Quito to work at Leonardo's surgery. But fate, never my biggest fan, conspired against me. I'd laid my eyes on her lithe, tanned form for the last time. Mel and Mark, thank the Goddess, stayed with me. I don't think I could have coped without them. Emer left quietly the day before her sister, planning to meet up for one final night out (which conveniently corresponded with my birthday, the legacy of which I was just experiencing).

That left just one person. Marie's departure was very nearly as hectic as Marie's arrival. There was a great deal of mess and there was a great deal of noise. Plenty of cheerful swearing, punctuated by bouts of less cheerful swearing. And then, like a friendly (but still rather violent) tornado, she swept off down the mountain. The hole she left was considerably bigger than she was – largely due to the fact that she'd been storing every item she owned on the floor around her bed like a gigantic moat of underwear and hairdryers, curlers, books and dresses. The efficiency of her organisation had been staggering; items not needed were simply added to the pile at its lowest point. Finding anything from a toothbrush upwards had required extensive excavation, usually accompanied by a running commentary in her lilting Irish brogue. It was like having our own private comedy act, showing several times a day, and never funnier than twenty minutes after she was supposed to have left for work (which was usually about the time she tried to discover that toothbrush).

The farewell party had been epic. I'd staggered back from Quito resolving to die messily in my bunk, only to discover that Johnny had picked today to recruit one of the most feared individuals in the known world; *el dentista* had come to Santa Martha.

Now I'm all for a bit of karma, so even in my weakened state I had to appreciate the irony; the dentist, bless him, was terrified. His eyes were wide and he couldn't take them off the inert form of the jaguar, lying on her side on Johnny's dining table. I'd arrived just in time to help anaesthetise the immense cat, and cradling her head in my lap in the back of Johnny's truck had been made even more surreal by the fact that I was still wearing my shiny shoes and my last going-out shirt. Both were now liberally coated in drool. Yet standing there at the head of the table while the dentist fumbled with his tools was a crowning moment of weirdness. It looked like any moment he would brandish a carving knife and start serving up big-cat-of-the-day.

Leonardo and Mark had pried open the jaguar's fearsome jaws, looping string around each before tying them off to the table legs. As if she hadn't seemed threatening enough already, she now seemed frozen mid-snarl, her impressive fangs bared beneath staring, hate-filled eyes. Whatever the dentist had done to end up in this predicament, I never found out. The poor bloke looked like he was about to shit himself. I sincerely hoped the jaw strings were securely knotted. I had a feeling that when released they'd snap shut like a steel trap. Anything inside at that point probably wasn't coming out again.

One of the jaguar's fangs had sheared off, leaving a truncated stump with a blackened end. The dentist rather reluctantly took up a miniature electric drill with a disc attachment, span the disc a few times, mouthed a brief prayer and reached into the Jaguar's maw.

It was then, as the grinder sang and the tooth enamel screeched, that my breakfast decided it wanted out. The sickening squeal of metal blade on bone was biting into my brain. I squeezed sideways through the crowd, backwards through the door and made it as far as the kitchen sink before I heaved, heaved again and spewed semi-digested blueberry pancakes all over the plughole.

Nancy was standing two feet away, half an onion forgotten on her chopping board as she wrinkled her nose in disgust. Luckily for her she hadn't been washing potatoes.

"*El dentista?*" she asked.

Johnny found me in the kitchen, cleaning up my mess. The way he clapped me on the shoulder, in that 'don't worry, it can only get better' way, I could tell that things were about to get worse.

"Let's go catch that spider monkey!" he said.

Absolute bastard, I thought. He wasn't at all blind to my condition. He was just enjoying it too much.

The spider monkey in question had a gigantic overbite. One of four current residents, he'd been rescued from yet another illegal circus and was long overdue for some dental work. But that didn't mean he was going to come quietly. Now, most monkeys are smart little critters. Not so, spider monkeys. They are smart *big* critters. Unfortunately the rest of his group knew exactly who we were after, and they weren't keen on making it easy. They had the drop on us from the start. We started out with nets, but they soon took those off us. Our last batch of spider monkeys had been so affectionate we'd had to pry ourselves loose from their hugs or risk wearing a live monkey for hours at a time. But we'd left them at Amazoonico months ago, and their replacements weren't nearly as tractable.

All of a sudden, Overbite made a break for it.

"MONKEY!" I shouted as he swung out of the door and onto the path. The chase was on.

He skipped off down the path with incredible speed dodging round the corner and heading for freedom as though he'd thought of nothing but this moment for years. I bolted after him, grabbing the edge of a cage to help swing me round the corner. The monkey was a good way ahead of me, and far more manoeuvrable. But I was faster on the straight. I accelerated down the narrow corridor between enclosures, and was closing the distance between us when he reached the steps down to the main road through the farm. This was my chance – if he paused, if he found the stairs confusing, I'd be on him. But no. Being a monkey, he didn't have much use for stairs. He just jumped.

He made the ten foot leap to the ground with ease, landed on all fours, and scurried off down the road. Pounding along behind him I had less than a second to make the choice. If I slowed to negotiate the stairs even part of the way down, it would all be over. Once he reached the trees by the first bend in the road he'd be gone for good.

Time was up. I reached the top of the steps at a dead run and launched myself over the edge.

In the seconds I was airborne my entire life flashed

before my eyes. I seemed to have spent a disproportionate amount of it chasing monkeys.

Somehow I landed on my feet, with bone jarring force. I was only a step behind the monkey – my leap had taken me considerably further than his – but my body was moving too fast for my legs. I managed to push off with my feet at the same moment I started to fall headlong on the ground. The result: I bounced forwards another metre, sailing high above the form of the fleeing monkey, then crashed to earth and flattened the fucker.

The impact knocked the stuffing out of me. It temporarily turned the monkey two-dimensional. Pain shot through me. I felt like I'd fallen ten feet onto a small primate. For the monkey it must have been like being beaten around the head with a banana tree. For a split second neither of us could move.

He recovered quicker than I did. Amazingly he wriggled out from under me and leapt towards freedom, just as I, still lying prone, reached out with both arms and caught him.

And when I say caught, that is exactly what I mean. I had both hands around him at the same time. In no way did that constitute restraint.

In far less time than it takes to tell, the monkey writhed around in my grasp and sank his fangs into my hand.

"ARGH!"

The monkey switched his attention to my other hand and bit down harder.

"Arrrr!" I shrieked. I let go with the recently bitten hand, but I had no other options – I had to grab him again or lose him. He was flailing wildly with all four limbs, scratching the shit out of every bit of me he could reach. As I tried to grab his neck he bit me again, puncturing the thick leather glove easily and scoring my vulnerable flesh. He bit down again and again, faster than I could even register the damage.

I lay on my belly, flat out on the floor, both arms outstretched in front of me and both hands wrapped around a furry blur of teeth and rage. There was sod all I could do – without my hands free I couldn't get to my feet, and without standing up I had no way of controlling the monster. So I lay there and swore at the fucker as he bit me over and over. If you asked anyone else, they'd probably say I was doing a fair bit of screaming and howling too. There came a moment of clarity amidst the agony, when I realised that I had succeeded where the others had failed; the monkey currently taking chunks out of me at high speed was exactly the one we'd been hoping to catch. We'd scheduled him for dentistry on account of his massively overdeveloped overbite... Of course this made me much happier about becoming his chew toy.

Eventually I got my feet under me. Capturing his head was easy at that point. "Now try and bite me ya bastard!" I bawled. Slowly the pain of my various injuries began to make itself known. My knees and legs were skinned from high velocity impact with the ground. There was a monkey-shaped section in the middle of me that was relatively undamaged – everything else was beat to buggery. Every bite was throbbing and most of them were oozing blood. I figured I'd been bitten about twenty times, with the nastiest set of incisors I'd ever seen on a creature this size. I was still shaking from the shock. I turned the thrashing monkey's head around so I could stare him in the face. He screeched and hissed and flailed. I had to resist a sudden urge to drop kick the lanky git into the milking shed.

"You-are-so-fucking-lucky!" I growled at him. "Why don't I see if the vet will cut your balls off while you're asleep, eh?" Desire for revenge coursed through my blood. An unscheduled castration was never going to happen. But Leonardo would understand. Surely he'd let me shave a rude word into him?

Just for once I wished someone else would be the Monkey Man. It was a singularly painful occupation.

Disaster!

A few days later we inherited an even more fractious creature – a brand new ocelot with crisp black markings and fierce eyes. She was another recent rescue from the backyards of the rich and famous, but obviously hadn't been incarcerated long enough to break her spirit. You can take the cat out of the jungle easily enough, but sometimes the jungle doesn't come quietly. Waking up from a hefty ketamine trip to find herself in yet another strange environment, the cat had made a few vocal complaints as we went about our morning rounds. Now she was growling continually under her breath, a rumbling, threatening sound like a gigantic motorbike idling at the lights. Every so often it exploded into an ear-splitting roar, of the kind you usually only hear once – in the split second before being torn apart.

Feeding her was nerve-wracking. Because she was an unknown quantity, and now mindful of the dangers of feline HIV amongst other diseases, Johnny had chosen to keep her separate for the time being. I agreed totally. The thought of letting her loose into the existing ocelot enclosure, only to watch her tear through the semi-tame residents in a fury, was too horrible to contemplate.

We'd been building a grand new ocelot enclosure on and off for weeks now, with no danger of it approaching completion. And now there were only four of us. I was desperately worried that I'd have to leave before the thing was finished – a disaster on two fronts, since I'd convinced myself that my quality control was the only thing stopping Jimmy from building it out of gaffer tape. Until the new pad was ready, our latest arrival would be staying in a rather small cage designed to house monkeys. The cage was comfy enough, with a dirt floor and a few logs scattered around for interest, but the distance from the door to the back wall was not great. So it was with trepidation, to say the least, that we few hardy souls made a ring around the door as Steve opened it to fling the cat's dinner inside. The job was over in seconds, the catch fumbled back into place, and the ocelot was glaring at us from behind her favourite log, her growl unrelenting.

We left her to it.

It was later that afternoon when the real difficulty presented itself. The ocelot, given a day to herself to explore, had chosen to settle in the middle of the cage while she took brunch. Once there she must have decided the spot was more comfortable than the hollow behind her log and so she stayed. So when we approached with our rakes and shovels to clean out her space, she was already in it.

There was no way around it – we had to at least attempt to remove the remains of her meal before they began to decompose. But this was a dramatically more involved operation than Steve had performed earlier, when the door had been open only long enough to fling a dead bird inside. The small, square portal was at ground level, on the right hand side of the cage front. Access was in one way only: head first on hands and knees. Well, assuming I didn't want to go in backwards. It would put the cat, with her decidedly dubious temperament, within a metre and a half of my unprotected face. She had formidable claws and teeth that would mess me up as easily as she had dismembered that chicken. And my only defence would be a flying head-butt. I mentally added a full set of American Football armour to my ideal work outfit.

First off, I gave the broom handle a go, probing the nearest corners successfully from outside the cage door. But the chicken corpse was in no-man's-land between the two of us. I'd have to have at least my head and shoulders in the cage to get the angle and leverage right. Whilst waving a big stick practically under her nose. No matter how I looked at it, I could only see pain in my future.

When Mark volunteered I felt guilty and cowardly in equal measure, but more relieved than I dared let on. Mark was the logical choice after all; his control over animals was almost hypnotic, his confidence unfailing, and his testicles carved of the same stuff they make aeroplane black boxes out of.

"I wonder if my travel insurance covers acts of abject insanity?" he quipped. He crouched in front of the cage door, open all this while with seemingly no interest in it from the cat. Slowly, calmly, he crawled inside and stretched out a hand for the debris.

There was just the slightest warning twitch from the ocelot. An instant later it pounced.

Mark came flying back out of the cage like a jack-in-a-box released. His yell drew a shocked echo from all of us. Almost instantly the cage door was slammed shut and fastened as Mark sat stunned on the dirt.

In his hand was a dead chicken. Or most of one. Drawing on reflexes neither of us had known he possessed, he'd sprung out of the way at exactly the right moment.

His hat on the other hand, had not.

The ocelot, so lithe and deadly, had made her kill. Mark looked horrified as the cat shredded the wide straw brim and started to gnaw on the remains.

"That was my favourite hat!" was all he could say.

"You're okay though?" I asked him, rather more concerned for his well-being.

"Oh yeah, I'm fine," he confirmed. "But... that was my favourite hat!"

A few tactless souls amongst the observers were already starting to see the funny side. I was one of them.

"We might be able to get it back?" I offered.

"How? She's eaten it! I don't fancy your chances of getting anything off her." Mark climbed to his feet, dusted himself off and gazed forlornly into the cage.

"It's made of straw," I pointed out.

"So? I know you weren't too keen on it, but I really liked that hat!"

By now I couldn't help myself.

"Yeah, but she can't digest straw. She's gotta take a shit sometime!"

Mark muttered something under his breath as he stomped off towards the house.

"What was that?"

"You're a cruel man," Mel chastised me.

"Not true!" I protested. "Honestly, I think a trip through an ocelot's digestive tract was exactly what that hat needed. It might even improve the colour!"

And Then There Were Three...

The first few weeks of on-off work on the new ocelot enclosure had produced an extremely long fence that was about as stable as my mental condition, which is to say not very. As the project progressed we'd been forced to shore up the entire hillside, after days of arriving in the morning to find all our fence posts had slipped halfway down the slope. We'd removed so many trees as potential escape routes that the soil was losing the will to resist gravity. Terraces and stepped foundations stopped it escaping into the valley below, but used up most of the available materials we'd earmarked to build the place. So, predictably, we'd augmented our less-than-formidable defences with crap recovered from demolishing the cage of the euthanized ocelot – a bunch of soggy, splitting boards and chicken wire that would be hard-pushed to restrain chickens. At last Johnny had come good with another load of the green plastic-coated fencing mesh, and we'd happily reinforced the entire structure. Jimmy had welded together a monster door that looked fit for a WWII concentration camp and we'd back-filled, and back-filled, and back-filled... endless days of forcing our solid steel homemade wheelbarrow uphill through the stump-cluttered remains of the undergrowth, bringing load after load of earth from the landslides that had plagued our initial excavations, all the way back to the top of the enclosure where we needed it to bury the foundations. It had been tough, tiring, and (inevitably) bloody. Would it hold? None of us would have bet much money on it. But then I showed up daily at the jaguar enclosure expecting to see a jaguar-shaped hole in the fence and so far I'd been disappointed. Though on the upside I'd also avoided being killed and eaten by the beast for my part in her incarceration. So there was an air of triumph on the day Jimmy announced himself satisfied. I would be happy enough if I never saw that wheelbarrow again.

The next morning there was a flash in the sky and a deafening sonic BOOM! And Toby stood in the driveway, his cape fluttering in the breeze. Strong and tall like the heroes of old (though somewhat skinnier), he strode through the entrance way and cast his luggage upon the ground. Twice halfway around the world he had flown, and yet seemed unchanged by the ordeal. He glowed with health and vitality, which could mean only one thing – whilst in England he had consumed the entire fruit and vegetable harvest of a medium-sized country. And probably got laid afterwards.

"Alright mate! How's things?"

"Ah, Toby, I'm so glad you're back," I told him. "Things are great!"

And they were.

I introduced Mel and Mark to him, though it seemed a bit pointless; as ships that pass in the night, they were. Mel and Mark were leaving that same day. It was often this way at Santa Martha; the timings of comings and goings coincided, causing a day of bittersweet emotions that never failed to surprise me with their potency. Though I hesitate to use the phrase (and certainly beg their forgiveness for doing so), Mel and Mark had been like parents to me during their stay. Not that they were dramatically much older than me, more that their combination of calm, rational experience and generous, caring spirit had given me strength and comfort to draw upon throughout the daily hardships that made life here so overwhelming. Losing them to their callously prearranged travel plans would have seemed a doubly harsh blow were it not for the Return of the Tobi.

Still smartly attired in un-ripped jeans and a shirt with more sleeves than food stains, Toby stepped back outside to announce his arrival to Johnny. His hair gleamed bronze in the midmorning sun – at least until he jammed his tatty pink baseball cap over it. I'd introduced him to Steve as well, which had seemed almost as pointless; Steve would be leaving himself in three days.

As would I.

It was something I was trying very hard not to think about.

As Mel and Mark hauled their luggage out of the 'master' bedroom, Toby dumped his in it. The changeover from one ruling regime to another was all but complete. Back in the lounge I ceremonially handed over the baton of leadership. He didn't seem particularly impressed by the gravity of the occasion – or by the fact that I'd actually made a baton of leadership. But then, Toby was a natural. I had an almost unhealthy amount of love for him.

"Johnny was pleased to see you, I bet." I was sitting on the spare single bed in Toby's room, watching him unpack.

"Yeah. The first thing he said was 'Did you bring the gun? I'd almost forgotten how Johnny is!"

"Ha! So what did you tell him?"

Toby shrugged. "I told him yes."

"Really? But… why, man?"

"'Cause here it is." He pulled a wide package onto the

bed and tore a long strip off the brown paper wrapping. Revealed underneath was the trigger section of the picture on the box. "Wanna see before I take it over to him?"

I was awed and unnerved in equal measure. "Toby?" I felt compelled to ask. "Who the fuck are you?"

Mark was fascinated by the weapon. Laid out in a custom foam case that would have presidential bodyguards the world over checking their insurance was paid up, the sections of the rifle gleamed menacingly. A separate case held small (empty) compressed gas canisters, and a cocoon of bubble wrap protected a selection of slim, hollow darts.

"You'll fill them with ketamine then?" Mark sounded excited. Poor bloke, he was being teased, to see such a tool arrive only to know that he'd be long gone before we used it.

"Leonardo will have to figure all that out," Toby admitted. He lowered the lid and snapped the case latches shut. "I had enough trouble figuring out how to get this through without worrying about transporting Class A narcotics!"

"I've seen them used in zoos of course, but never actually fired one. Never had the need to." Now Mark sounded wistful.

Mel had a last word of advice for me before carting her bags out to the waiting taxi. "Don't go shooting yourself in the foot! Ketamine isn't nearly as fun as some people think!"

I'd seen enough of its effect on monkeys. "Hell no! Though I wouldn't want to be in the area if Jimmy was firing it. Thank God it doesn't have a 'fully automatic' mode!"

And then, with hugs all round and enough forced laughter to mask the real emotions, the two were gone from the centre, and gone from my world. Well, temporarily at least. I had a feeling I'd be seeing them again at some point.

Of the three of us left, only Toby was in genuine high spirits. "It's so good to be back!" he exclaimed. He cast a satisfied glance around his beloved refuge and we headed back inside.

"It'll be quiet for a while," I warned him.

"Sweet!" he replied. "So, Steve, you play chess?"

An Ocelot Odyssey

My penultimate day at the centre promised to be as exciting as any I'd had. Having busted a gut (not to mention fingernails, fingers, feet and toes, and a fair proportion of what lay in between) to get the new ocelot enclosure finished before I left, we were now rewarded with the glorious opportunity of transferring the animals to their new home. It was another beautiful morning on the farm, very nearly my last, and I was feeling positively poetic.

Toby had been wandering around the refuge, casting a critical eye over our handiwork of the last few weeks. Mostly, he seemed impressed. In the comparatively short time he'd been gone, close to a dozen new cages had sprung up – at least one of them ending his hopes of a kitchen garden in the process – and almost all of them were stuffed to the gills with screaming, cheeping, howling, snorting life. It must have looked to him like we'd been putting fertility drugs in the breakfast mash.

When it came time to inspect our latest achievement I could hardly bear to admit to building it.

"Nice door," Toby commented, giving the outsized latch bolt a wiggle.

"It's the strongest bit," I admitted. "And when we were back filling the buried section I dropped a full wheelbarrow on my hand!" I held up the back of my hand, where a wide band of angry pink skin was growing back. "And you know, that was more than a week ago and I haven't been injured since!" I was justifiably proud of this, since it was not often I could make such a claim. It seemed fitting that I should end my amazing experience on such a high note. Santa Martha was a tough world, more so than I had ever expected, but I had conquered it nonetheless.

"Don't jinx it," Toby warned me, pointing at the sun. "The day is yet young!"

Johnny's plan for the move was, as usual, an essay in subtlety. Catch the cats. Tranquillise them. Drive them to the new enclosure in the back of his truck. It glossed over some of the minor details, like how we were supposed to find six perfectly camouflaged, super-stealthy hunting cats in close to an acre of dense tropical foliage. And how we were supposed to avoid being eaten by them in the process.

Okay, I'll admit that that was a slight exaggeration. The cats ranged in size from not substantially bigger than a large house cat, to that of a decent-sized family dog. They weren't going to be swallowing us whole or anything. But they were dangerous enough that volunteers weren't normally encouraged to go inside without good reason. This time though, we were armed – by which I mean, Leonardo and Johnny were armed. Jimmy of course had a machete in his hand, but then Jimmy probably watched TV with a machete in his hand. It was more of a comforter than a tool, and disturbingly appropriate for it. For the rest of us, defence against a mauling was limited to a thick pair of welding gloves.

I didn't care. This was one of the moments it was all about for me; we were going to discover the secretive heart of the ocelot lair, to get right up close to these beautiful, elusive animals. And shoot them.

I'd only been inside the enclosure for a handful of heartbeats when a rustle in the undergrowth announced our first visitor. Out came the friendly ocelot, recognisable less by the bright white spots above her eyes than by the way she stalked straight up to me, purring like a Harley Davidson, and started nuzzling against my legs.

"Ahhh!" I bent down to pet her just as the dart slammed into her side with enough force to make her stagger sideways.

"Jimmy! Fuck!" I yelled in shock.

"See? It works now." He handed the assembled dart gun back to Johnny.

What with the gun's instructions being in English, there had been some difficulty in assembling it in the long grass outside the enclosure. Toby's explanation had been studded with words like '*pneumático*' and the occasional cry of 'Shit! Anyone see where that torsion spring went?' For some unfathomable reason I wasn't allowed anywhere near the thing.

By my feet the tame ocelot was already struggling to stay standing. I wanted to reach out to her, to apologise. She took a couple more woozy steps and collapsed on her side.

"Ha! Easy!" Jimmy cawed.

I felt a sudden urge to tranquillise him. It was a bloody good job no-one had trusted me with a gun.

The next couple of cats were much harder to spot, and once spotted proved much harder targets. We retrieved a few darts from assorted trees and shrubs, none of which seemed much sleepier for their trouble.

We floundered up and down the enclosure, climbing, falling and crawling more than walking. We saw nothing. Still, our noisy, complaining presence in the more remote environs of the enclosure was scaring the cats closer to the guns.

One by one the cats were caught. We carried them out of

the enclosure, straining beneath the weight. They were so much heavier than they looked, especially after two hours of watching them effortlessly dodge dart after dart with breathtaking swiftness. It came to the point where the cats sleeping peacefully in the truck outnumbered the ones we were still stalking (or being stalked by). Toby and Johnny were watching over the sleepers anxiously while the rest of us searched frantically for the last two still at large. There was a shout from Jimmy – he'd scored another hit, and further up the paddock another ocelot was down.

But before we could struggle up the sheer slope the cat had gotten up, shaken itself and loped off into the undergrowth.

"*Puta!*" Jimmy was incensed. "*Segundo vez! Puta madre!*"

Apparently this was the cat's second dose and it was still up and running.

"The alpha male," Leonardo surmised from where he stood scanning the paddock.

"How much can he take?" I asked.

"Difficult to tell," he said. "The smaller ones, one dart is plenty, but with ketamine… sometimes, the animals, they can fight it. Sometimes they still wake up after a massive dose. It's just not reliable. But, it's what we have."

This was not the best news I could have heard. "What about the other cats then? The ones in the truck? When will they wake up?"

"Yes, we will have to go soon. Take the first ones before they wake up, then come back for the others."

While we'd been chatting another cat had collapsed. It had been darted earlier, and like the alpha male was proving particularly resilient to the ketamine. When Steve closed in the cat was already sound asleep, having spent its last strength fighting the drug. Two darts were protruding from different sides of the inert form. Jimmy came up to help manoeuvre the cat out of the gate.

"We'll go now," Leonardo decided. "Help Jimmy. Try to find the big one. We'll be back soon."

And off they sped, a truck full of sleeping cats and hyper-tense humans. The road was rugged to say the least, and I winced in sympathy as the truck hit a bump. If the ketamine started to wear off on the first customers, the back of that truck was not going to be a fun place to be.

So that left one cat, and two of us. And one of us was Jimmy. I felt distinctly outnumbered. Nevertheless, fortune favours the brave. What it does to idiots I'm not sure, so I wanted to be as far from Jimmy as possible when he found out. I set out again to scout the now familiar territory around the top of the enclosure. Since most of the cats had been darted around there, it seemed likely that it contained a den of sorts. Which was pretty lucky; if they'd chosen to build a den at the bottom of the enclosure we'd have been hauling their shaggy asses up the mountainside until tomorrow morning.

A warning growl stopped me in my tracks. It was close. I scanned the dense undergrowth at eye level, spinning slowly on the spot. Stupid! Unless the cat was stood on his hind legs, balancing on tiptoe on top of a box, he wasn't going to be at eye level. I swung back around checking lower, and there, not two metres from my feet, was our errant moggie. He was lying down in the middle of a bush; body flat but head up and staring right at me. Magnificent! It was the only word to describe the sight of such a creature at such close range. He had a dart in his side, and was obviously feeling the effects. This then would be the most dangerous time to be around him – he was probably scared out of his mind, hallucinating crazily, yet still alert enough to tear me a new arsehole. I did nothing. Over the next few minutes the cat's eyes began to lose focus. He rested his head on the ground for progressively longer periods of time, blinking heavily, panting and twitching. Around the time he lay down for the last time Jimmy crunched through the bushes to join me.

"He's sleeping now?" he asked.

"Not very much! I think still very dangerous."

Jimmy snorted his opinion of that and strode over to the inert form. Prodded it none too gently with the toe of his boot. He grinned back at me. "Yeah, very dangerous!"

I gave it up. After three months I had finally realised that there was no way to win with Jimmy. Maybe because after all was said and done, he was the genuine article. Immensely strong. Apparently fearless. Intensely annoying. He had the ego of several ancient Greek heroes all rolled into the body of one weather-beaten dwarf. But you always knew where you stood with Jimmy. I'd impressed him enough times to take any rancour out of his taunts. He would never view me as an equal, but then neither would I him – he could kick my ass in a machete fight (with both arms tied behind his back and a bag over his head) but he'd never be much for scrabble. It was awfully hypocritical of me to complain about his inflated sense of superiority, and I'd certainly had my share of jokes at his expense. A bizarre thought was occurring to me. I was going to miss Jimmy. Now that really was a surprise.

The cat was fast asleep. Jimmy rolled him over to retrieve not one but two other darts from the flank he'd been lying on, making three darts in total. That much ketamine would turn Chuck Norris into a drooling vegetable.

All we had to do now was wait. We moved him out of the enclosure between us, then Jimmy headed back in to fetch his weapons. I stood by the cat and watched him pant in his sleep, eyes wide open and unblinking. Man it was creepy!

The others were taking their sweet time. It felt like I'd been waiting forever for the truck to return, probably because I was so nervous that the cat might wake up. I had no idea whether or not Leonardo and co. had gotten the other cats across the farm in time. He'd certainly seemed concerned when they set off. How long could this stuff be relied upon to keep a cat like Shere Kahn here sleeping like a kitten? *Three* darts it had taken to put him down. If he came to before the others got back... I really didn't want to be responsible for letting a semi-comatose cat get away from me. Not on my last shift.

So gently, ever so gently, I rolled his head into my arms. I slid my arms around his body and rested his head on my shoulder. Then holding him tightly against me I stood up. He wasn't that heavy after all! At least, that's what I resolved to tell the others. I grunted at Jimmy, who had watched my efforts without comment. Obviously he wanted to stay with the guns.

And staggering slightly, I set off down the path towards the new enclosure. With every step the cat became heavier and I recognised a serious flaw in my plan. If I didn't make it all the way, the returning truck would find me standing halfway down the road for no apparent reason with the poor cat lying in the dirt at my feet. Then I'd just look like a dickhead.

Which perhaps would serve me right. I tightened my grip and accelerated.

It must have presented a strange image; as the truck full of people rounded a bend in the track they caught sight of me, shuffling at full-tilt towards them, with an enormous jungle cat draped over me like an exotic shawl. My knees were sagging under the weight of the beast and I staggered the last few steps to where the truck skidded to a halt. Toby was there instantly, and another three or four sets of hands plunged in from all sides, all grabbing hold of a leg, an ear, or a handful of fur. The ocelot suddenly became weightless in my arms, then rose above me into the truck. I scrambled up after it and sank down gratefully with my back against the cab.

Then they dropped the cat back onto me, which I wasn't expecting. They'd all assumed that I was crawling into place ready to take the critter back off them to hold onto for the journey. I on the other hand had figured that my part in this struggle was finally over, and so I was distinctly unprepared for being flattened under half a tonne of still life. As the wind rushed out of me I made a sound not unlike a moose approaching orgasm.

"Jeez-us! You alright mate?" Toby's concern was touching, if belated. I didn't have enough air in my lungs to answer him, so I concentrated on trying to breath past the cat on my stomach.

"Let's go!" he shouted in earnest.

Everyone else piled back into the truck, the engine gunned, and we sped away, bouncing down the track at breakneck speed.

"Woah!" I gasped, "Slower!" I waved at Toby for emphasis, but he was already thinking along the same lines. He slapped the car roof and bawled *"Lento, lento!"*

The car slowed, which was a mercy as every good bump saw the chunky cat propelled fractionally skywards, only to slam back down onto me an instant later. My arse was being driven through the floor of the truck – sooner or later one or the other had to give.

Then we hit a pothole. Sprawled across me, the ocelot felt the ferocious impact and twitched in his sleep. His paws flexed and his eyes slid into focus for a second before he was lost to the drugs again.

"Shit! Toby! He's waking up!" I wheezed.

"LENTO!" Toby all but screamed, and the car speed dropped another notch. I managed to haul myself back into a seated position, cradling the cat across my knees. Its head now rested on my chest, which made it all the more

alarming the next time its eyes moved. For a heartbeat it was looking right at me, and I swear I could feel its malice. Its teeth, inch-long daggers, were less than a handspan from my throat.

"Guys, he's really waking up…" There was genuine fear in my voice.

"It's okay," hissed Toby, "we're here."

People scrambled out of the truck as I scooted forwards. Leonardo was already there with a huge wire cage, fumbling with the door as I cradled the ocelot to my chest, shifted to a crouch, and jumped down from the tailgate.

The impact of my heels on the solid ground sent a shock wave through my body.

It also woke the ocelot.

All of a sudden instead of holding a hugely heavy slab of inert fur-clad flesh I was grappling with a tiger. Not a big tiger, and not actually a tiger as it happens, but it was the similarities rather than the differences that flashed through my mind as the thing came alive in my arms.

In a second it was thrashing around, arching its powerful body, raking claws down everything in reach.

The only thing in reach was me. I howled in pain as it ripped at my arms and my chest, and all I could think to do was to hold the beast tighter. I squeezed it against me with a strength borne of desperation, pinning us chest to chest with his legs splayed out all around me. He was still very dazed and couldn't see well enough to bite so I was spared an unplanned tracheotomy.

Leonardo already had half of the beast inside the cage, and Toby was capturing errant limbs. I gritted my teeth, tensed my arms and pushed. I fell away backwards and the cat fell into the cage. Leonardo snapped the door shut smartly and it was over.

The ocelot snarled and writhed in his cage for a few seconds, then retreated to the back and snarled. Slowly,

slowly, the growling faded to a soft rumbling broken by the occasional snort and violent twitch which shook the cage. He had succumbed to the ketamine once again.

I simply lay on the ground behind the truck, feeling the terror ebb away, trying not to analyse my injuries. Lines of fire carved diagonally across both sides of my chest. I could already feel the blood welling, trickling warm and wet down my ribs. Sweet Jesus, it hurt.

The cage was still. The beast was sleeping. The others turned their attention to where my sprawled form lay motionless in the dirt. Toby offered a hand to help me up.

"Man, that was close!" he exclaimed. "He didn't scratch you did he?"

The End.

Osita was a bugger. You think you've made friends with a bear – you build her a house, talk to her nice, feed her your sandwiches – and then as soon as your back's turned she pulls the plug out of her pond and eats it.

This was the situation that greeted me as I stood in front of Osita's enclosure on the morning of my last day. Less than a week ago I'd spent hours filling the pond with nice clean water, fending her off the whole time and trying to persuade her not to chew on the hose. It was a long, boring job, and I must have done it about a hundred times.

I felt betrayed.

"Why?" I admonished her as she approached the fence. "Why did you have to eat your Goddamn plug? If you're lonely just tell me! I promise I'll sit and talk to you. But please, stop eating your bloody plug."

Osita looked suitably chastised. She poked her nose at me through the fence in that irresistible way.

"Okay," I said, "I forgive you. Here's breakfast."

I braced myself for a struggle with the disintegrating padlock, but it seems I'd finally acquired the knack and it sprang open straight away. I unfastened the chain, drew back the bolt and opened the gate for what I suddenly realised was almost certainly the last time.

I had to stop for a moment as sadness overwhelmed me. In the long, cold evenings I looked forward to going home, to warmth and family, to sprawling on a sofa while my injuries healed and watching TV with my folks. But it was on the feeds in the mornings, with tendrils of mist still curling through the fields, the sun just warming up overhead, and the cacophony of animal calls celebrating the arrival of breakfast, that I realised how much this place had come to mean to me. And how much I was going to miss it.

Never more so than on that heartbreakingly perfect morning.

I even cried as I closed the gate on Osita, and watched her charge for the bowl of fruit and begin to shred it. She loved the apples. She even looked up at me for a second, in what my depressingly romantic soul dared to call gratitude. Then she returned to the serious business of flinging her food around the cage.

That was the end of the feed. Before long the refuge would be filled to capacity, distributing the food would take hours and be interspersed with escape attempts and inconvenient displays of affection. But I would be no part of it. Volunteers would come and volunteers would go, most of them being thrashed at chess by Toby in the process, and the heart of Santa Martha would beat on. But from thousands of miles away, on the other side of the world, I wouldn't be able to hear it.

With nothing more to do but pack, and maybe a few tearful good-byes to say, I was at a bit of a loss. After a meagre breakfast, noticeably lacking Mel's traditional offerings of pancakes and thick porridge, Steve and I started to trawl though our stuff, choosing what to keep and what to leave. It felt good to sacrifice jumpers and jeans to the cause. Covered in ten kinds of shit, most of my clothes wouldn't make it past customs let alone be allowed on the plane. It also felt like I was leaving a part of myself behind, keeping a link alive to prepare for my eventual return. I couldn't face the thought of not coming back.

Every few minutes I lapsed into daydreams, discovering a blood-stained belt that set off a memory of cow dissection or a shredded sock that put me in mind of Machita. Toby had already assured me that he'd keep the little dog out of trouble, though he hadn't explained how. Maybe while he was in England he'd also attained omniscience.

Every item I touched reminded me of some unbelievable story or embarrassing accident. Those memories set off others in turn. It was about this time I realised that living and working at Santa Martha had been the single most important experience of my life. I was going to miss this place more than I'd ever missed anything.

Packing turned out to be a very short process. I made a pile of good stuff and left it on a shelf in the dormitory. I made a pile for the bin and binned it. I drew in all the strings, straps, tapes and webbing on my rucksack to compensate for its lack of contents. I laid out my last 'good' clothes to change into before I left, at which point everything I was wearing now would probably crawl through the lounge, out the front door, across the porch and into the bin on its own.

I had no phone. I had no socks. I did have the skin of one small cow sticking randomly out the top of my bag, a last minute gift from Johnny that I hadn't known how to refuse. Who in the entire world (including Ecuador) would ever need the carefully cured, hairy hide of half a calf? The mind boggles.

I wandered outside to check there was nothing I'd forgotten. Holey wellies. The most comfortable hammocks in the world. My little dog! She came chasing around my feet, yipping furiously. She was blissfully unaware that I was about to abandon her to the fickle fortunes of life on the farm. Poor beast, she was very nearly as stupid as she was cute, and she was cute right to the verge of utterly adorable. I growled at her and chased her around the porch for a bit, until she found a plastic bag floating around and let that chase her.

A lone item of my underwear was still draped over the wall. I'd consistently forgotten about these pants every day for at least two weeks. They'd been on the line for a week before that, soaked with rain every morning, dry by midday, ignored all afternoon and frozen solid each night. They'd been a barometer of my last few weeks at the centre and they weren't in the best condition for it. Mouldy and torn, stained by leaves and exposure to the elements... well, they'd been a little stained to begin with.

Then an idea struck me. A plastic bag, pair of good cloth underpants... and an opportunity to pay a last visit to a close friend. I ran down the path to the side of the milking shed and switched on the water pump for the hose.

I would plug that bear's pond if it was the last thing I did.

"I was looking for you," Toby mentioned as I strode happily back through the gate to our house. "I've got them photos you wanted." He handed me a CD ROM full of memories.

"Great! Thanks man, I was hoping you'd get round to it. My folks will go nuts when they see some of these!"

"Yeah, there's some of mine, and there's Mel and Mark's photos on there too. All the best ones. So..." He glanced around. I could tell he was groping for something to say. Of all the good-byes this was going to be by far the hardest. Toby had been my mentor and my best friend. He'd led me full-tilt into every mad, terrifying experience I'd had – then left me in the middle of most of them and fucked off to Quito. I couldn't imagine my life without Santa Martha, and I couldn't imagine Santa Martha without Toby. I couldn't even begin to thank him and start saying my farewells.

Instead I decided to relate my latest piece of genius to him.

"I filled Osita's pond. I couldn't believe the bloody thing was empty again. But I made a new plug *again*, and I think it's holding!"

"Sweet. What did you use?" Toby asked.

"Well, I got some plastic bags and all that, and you know that pair of minging pants I was going to throw away?"

A look of horror crossed Toby's face. "Oh mate, you didn't..."

"Yeah, I used them! Thought I'd leave my mark on the place, you know."

"You fucker! When she pulls them out I'm gonna have to find them and pick them up!"

"Oh yeah! Sorry man, I hadn't thought of that," I lied. "They weren't too badly stained you know. And they got washed every time it rained – for, like, the last three weeks..."

"If that bear eats your stinking pants and gets really ill, and dies of arse-poisoning, it'll be your fault," he informed me.

"I tell you what," I offered, "if that bear eats my pants I'm gonna go home and write a book about all of this. And I'll call it That Bear Ate My Pants!"

And I did.

Epilogue

My last night in Quito had passed in a whirlwind of rum-drinking and hands restraining me every time I attempted to approach the dance floor. Quito, I was reliably informed, had yet to recover from the last time I'd been let loose. Apparently my birthday party had gotten a bit out of control. I'd ended up dancing on the bar in one of our favourite clubs, stark bollock naked. Alice had been there, as had some of her students – one of whom, she told me, had been unable to eat a sausage ever since.

Fate had shown a cruel side in allowing me to become able to have full conversations with Lady just before I had to leave. As a consequence I'd grown closer than ever to her. I'd even made the mistake of allowing her to plan a 'surprise' for me. Visions of some deliciously sordid sexual activity had evaporated as she'd eagerly dragged me out of bed at crazy o'clock in the morning and led me off into the maze-like side streets of downtown Quito.

The surprise was a culinary treat to which she had wanted to expose me for a long time, and thus far I'd been fortunate enough to avoid. '*Ceviche*' was a dish of inedible raw seafood chunks in a disgusting spicy brown sauce. It looked like someone had overdosed on sushi, then developed chronic diarrhoea when only my plate lay between them and the toilet. And you know what? That's exactly how it tasted too.

Oh yes, *ceviche* was a surprise all right. It was also a bloody expensive one that she had insisted on paying for. Which left me in the awkward position of having to choose – either refuse to eat on the grounds that the plate in front of me contained nothing I considered edible, thereby upsetting Lady, or force the stuff down, projectile vomit for ten minutes then pass out in a puddle of sick and die of botulism, which wouldn't make me popular with the restaurant owner.

I chose to split the difference. I ate some, then bolted to the loo and spewed my ring, before returning to inform Lady that it was interesting, and that I'd now had quite enough thank-you very much. The taste, however, stayed with me.

WHY?? Why don't women understand? How hard can it possibly be? What do we want for a 'surprise'? SEX! Even if we've just had sex... then it'll be that much more of a surprise! And much less hassle than an early morning crusade through grim, grey streets to sit in a dingy cafe choking down half the cast of Finding Nemo covered in shit!

I survived, though the event remains fixed in my memory as one of my least pleasant experiences in Ecuador.

I said a passionate good-bye to Lady at the airport, and told her fervently not to wait for me, on the grounds that it was likely to be a very long time before I had the chance to return. ("I unnerstan," she responded in English, "I wait for you!" "No, no," I explained, "I said *don't* wait for me." She favoured me with a smile that broke my heart. "I unnerstan! I love you too! I wait for YOO!!")

Comedy and tragedy entwined – the moment was too much for me and I cried like a ten-year-old girl. I hadn't dared embarrass myself in front of Johnny or Jimmy and somehow I'd maintained some semblance of composure even when a suitably firm handshake had marked the end of my adventures with Toby. (I'd shed a few tears once out of sight around a bend in the driveway of course, and I have it on reliable authority that Toby did the same – not that either of us will ever admit it. Being men.)

Lady, I think, appreciated the display of emotion more, and reciprocated in kind. We clung desperately together; I sobbed into her hair and she sobbed into my chest. We parted a soggy mess, keeping fingertip contact even when we were too far apart to see each other through the tears.

The rapidly closing airport doors very nearly deprived me of a hand. Rubbing my wrist and cursing under my breath I followed a somewhat embarrassed Steve into the check-in hall. He was kind enough to stay silent and allow me my moment of reflection. Lady was gone from my life, perhaps forever – there's more than just half a planet of cold water separating England from Ecuador after all. Life back home would be very different. The whole mindset that I'd developed over months of living in this simple, beautiful place would be no match for the frantic pace of Real Life. It was likely to be a rude awakening, and I was dreading it. Money and timekeeping, worrying what people thought of me and the need to maintain an 'image' – all these concepts, happily forgotten due to their comparative irrelevance to a scruffy volunteer living on a farm halfway up a mountain – would come crashing back around me with shocking speed. I could fly out of Quito with a handful of dollars to my name and jeans that were more holes than fabric, but in London I'd be hungry and thirsty and cold. And I'd look like a tramp.

Maybe if I sat outside the airport for long enough I'd make enough cash for a coffee. That made me smile. But always my thoughts turned to Lady. So radiant, so excitable… absolutely gorgeous, and completely beyond my reach. Maybe she always had been.

The airport was a Mecca for seekers of crap kitsch. And they must exist, these people, or how else would the shop owners be able to eat? How many 'Pilsner' baseball caps and strings of authentic wooden beads (made in China) would they each have to sell to feed their families? Well, not too many since the prices in the airport were even more ridiculous than the products themselves, but that still leaves a bare minimum of crap which must be purchased by some complete tool to ensure the continued existence of said crap (and those that pedal it). Who does it? Was there just the one lunatic, pushing a supermarket trolley full of poorly-carved wooden parrots, whilst doubtless wearing a bright woollen poncho and carrying half a dozen carpets? Whoever it was, they had a lot to answer for.

"You getting any souvenirs?" asked Steve.

I fixed him with a glare.

I was in a philosophical mood as I climbed from the featureless concrete airfield into the waiting plane. Technology! Metal staircase! After all my exploits at Santa Martha I half expected the ground crew to prop a knackered ladder against an ailing donkey and offer me a leg-up.

The lights of London awaited me, cold, hard, impersonal. England was inexorable in its approach. My old life was waiting to swallow me up, spit out the new bits and chew me back into my previous shape. Behind me the wildness of the volcanic mountains faded into the distance. There was a tearing sensation as the plane roared out over the ocean – it seems that without noticing it I'd inadvertently left part of my soul behind. Ecuador had come and gone. But it had not left me unchanged. I resolved that when real life started to swamp me I would be ready. Before I sank back into the morass of consumerism, of thoughts dominated by wanting and buying and working and paying, before the life I had lived previously managed to sink its claws into me, I would do... what? Anything! I didn't really want to go back at all. I mean, what was there to do for me at home after Santa Martha? Sit behind a desk? Buy a new phone to organise my life by, some smart black trousers and a few crisp white shirts to iron?

I'd lived without a phone for longer than I'd have thought possible. I didn't need the most expensive branded designer clothes any more – I was wearing my favourite $10 jeans from Machachi market on the flight home as they were the only thing I had left that my balls didn't hang out of. That was something I'd achieved in the last three months; shameless promotion of crotchless work wear! Strategically Vented Trousers I could call them. They were bound to catch on.

What else? Well, I could cut a tree in half with a single blow from a machete, and drink a litre of battery acid without flinching. Useful skills if I considered going into investment banking.

I'd become much more mature. Ha! No I hadn't. But I tried the idea on for size until I realised that coming up with a suitable 'mature face' probably wasn't sufficient grounds for proof.

I was physically much stronger. Still skinny but with muscles now, and I was a whole lot tougher. I'd been bitten, clawed and mauled by more species of life than most people can name. Blinded, electrocuted and very nearly shot. I had no fear of seeing my own blood any more.

That was it – I had no fear! Well, I was worried that Machita's life expectancy had just dropped dramatically, and I was a little concerned when I saw the pilot kicking the tyres of the plane – but I wasn't scared. Not of people and not of any situation I could imagine (short of having to introduce myself to a Miss World contestant). I suddenly recognised the confidence within me, as compared to my abject terror upon arrival. I felt powerful – I could go anywhere, do anything! I was, if not bulletproof, then certainly jaguar-proof! How many people could say that? "I am one tough *puta madre*," I told myself.

Wait a minute – SPANISH! My progress had been slow at first, then slightly slower, until eventually it seemed to stop altogether. For the last month I hadn't even bothered to keep track of it. And yet... I checked my short-term memory. Yes! I'd been speaking Spanish in the taxi all the way to the airport! In fact I'd even checked my short-term memory in Spanish. At last, I had discovered a quantifiable achievement.

I'd made friends too. Some good ones, like Steve sitting next to me (squinting at the carving on his wooden parrot) and Ashley. Some great ones like Toby and Alice, both of whom I was resolved to stay close to. I was also leaving behind, for the first time in my life, a potential True Love. Would I ever see Lady again? Hell it would be worth the price of a return ticket just for that!

The idea grew inside me for a few moments. I'd always said I'd be back one day, to see how things were doing and help Toby with his plans for a new release centre. But I was only half serious. It had been tough, sometimes very much so, to work at Santa Martha and I wasn't sure I wanted to go through it all again. I'd left some vague hints and promises, but had carefully avoided being pinned down on when, if ever, I would return. And now? I flicked through the mental list I'd been making. Hard-won qualities one and all, yet I'd go through it all again in a heartbeat to keep them. Especially this new-found sense of surety, of confidence. The new me would kick the old me's ass if he tried to chicken out of doing anything. In fact the new me would kick the old me's ass just for the hell of it! I *was* a man now. It wasn't something I felt the need to boast about or prove, it was just something I knew. And I also knew, had known since the thought first occurred to me, that I would be back.

"As soon as I get home, I buy my next ticket away again," Toby had told me, "it's the only way I can stay sane."

A genuine piece of advice, and given before it was needed! That was a rarity indeed. It was Toby's parting gift to me. I would do as he suggested. Maybe I'd have to get a job, for a bit. There was a good chance I'd have to buy a new phone too. How else would I organise my life? I would save as much as I could, as fast as I could. Research my options and plan the next adventure. Toby would help me if I sent him an email; he'd already done almost everything I wanted to do.

Where had Toby been? Australia. Thailand! He'd studied diving there. I'd always wanted to dive. He'd been very good at it until a boat ran him over. I was reasonably sure my reflexes were faster than his. How fast can a boat really go anyway? Maybe I'd find out. There was a whole world out there waiting to be explored. Beautiful women waiting to be... uh... explored. Oceans and beaches and temples and jungle. And plenty of animals. Maybe there's a refuge in Thailand, I thought to myself and smiled at the prospect. I would have to look into it. I could tour the world, diving, working with animals and having crazy adventures! And someday soon I would return to Santa Martha, of this I was sure. After all, I'd left my little dog there.

THE END.

Hi folks! Tony here...

Thank-you so much for buying and reading my book! I hope you enjoyed it. If you have any questions, or feedback (or want to punch me in the face just for writing it), I'd love to hear from you. I believe that the best way to grow as an author is by listening to my readers, so don't be shy!

You can find me on Twitter:
@TonyJamesSlater
Or catch me on Facebook:
www.facebook.com/TonyJamesSlater
Or if you get the urge, you can always email me:
TonyJamesSlater@hotmail.com

Also, please consider leaving a review on Amazon. It only has to be a line or two, and it's the best way you can help me out (beyond convincing everyone in your Aunt Mabel's spinning class to buy a copy!). Word of mouth is vital in this game. I love getting reviews – I really appreciate the effort, and I read every single one!
Just go to Amazon.co.uk or Amazon.com and search for:
'That Bear Ate My Pants!'
– I *promise* you there's only one book called that!

About the Author

Tony James Slater is a very, very strange man. He believes himself to be indestructible, despite considerable evidence to the contrary. He is often to be found making strange faces whilst pretending to be attacked by inanimate objects. And sometimes – not always, but often enough to be of concern – his testicles hang out of the holes in his trousers.

It is for this reason (amongst others) that he chooses to spend his life far from mainstream civilization, tackling ridiculous challenges and subjecting himself to constant danger. He gets hurt quite a lot.

To see pictures of the animals, read Tony's blog, or complain about his shameless self promotion, please visit:
www.TonyJamesSlater.com
But BE WARNED! Some of the writing is in red.

Tony's second book, about what happened to him after he got back from Ecuador (which may or my not be called 'It's Not My Monkey!') should be available from Amazon in December 2012. If it's not, blame Canada – or possibly climate change – or the fact that Tony can only type with two fingers at once. Rest assured, he's working it…

Volunteering

If 'That Bear Ate My Pants!' inspired you to do a bit of volunteering, take a look at an amazing book called:
'700 Places To Volunteer Before You Die'.
It's available from Amazon, and it's the most comprehensive listing of volunteer opportunities anywhere in the world. Projects are listed by country, subject and cost, and it features a 'how to' guide that will answer all your questions about getting involved.

Although I'm far from an expert on volunteering, I'm happy to chat about the pros and cons, and can point you towards loads of information and resources about it. Just drop me an email, tweet or Facebook message.

You have now read all the words. There are no more words. None. You can stop reading now. And be happy! Tony loves you too.

HOOKSETT PUBLIC LIBRARY
HOOKSETT, NH 03106
603.485.6092
http://hooksettlibrary.org

35590287R00234

Made in the USA
Middletown, DE
09 October 2016